BRITISH MEDICAL BULLETIN
VOLUME 57   2001

Depression

Scientific Editors

Malcolm H Lader

Philip J Cowen

Series Editors
L K Borysiewicz PhD FRCP
M J Walport PhD FRCP

OXFORD
UNIVERSITY PRESS

PUBLISHED FOR THE BRITISH COUNCIL BY
OXFORD UNIVERSITY PRESS

OXFORD UNIVERSITY PRESS
Great Clarendon Street, Oxford OX2 6DP, UK

British Library Cataloguing in Publication Data
A catalogue record for this book is available from the British Library
ISBN 0–19–922487–0
ISSN 0007–1420

Subscription information *British Medical Bulletin* is published quarterly on behalf of The British Council. Subscription rates for 2001 are £160/$275 for four volumes, each of one issue. Prices include distribution and is distributed by surface mail within Europe, by air freight and second class post within the USA*, and by various methods of air-speeded delivery to all other countries. Subscription orders, single issue orders and enquiries for 2001 should be sent to:

Oxford University Press, Great Clarendon Street, Oxford OX2 6DP, UK (Tel +44 (0)1865 267907; Fax +44(0)1865 267485; E-mail: jnl.orders@oup.co.uk

*Periodicals postage paid at Rahway, NJ. US Postmaster: Send address changes to *British Medical Bulletin*, c/o Mercury Airfreight International Ltd, 365 Blair Road, Avenel, NJ 07001, USA.

Back numbers of titles published 1996–2000 (see inside back cover) are available from The Royal Society of Medicine Press Limited, 1 Wimpole St, London W1G 0AE, UK. (Tel. +44 (0)20 7290 2921; Fax +44 (0)20 7290 2929); www.rsm.ac.uk/pub/bmb/htm).

Pre-1996 back numbers: Contact Jill Kettley, Subscriptions Manager, Harcourt Brace, Foots Cray, Sidcup, Kent DA14 5HP (Tel +44 (0)20 8308 5700; Fax +44 (0)20 8309 0807).

This journal is indexed, abstracted and/or published online in the following media: Adonis, Biosis, BRS Colleague (full text), Chemical Abstracts, Colleague (Online), Current Contents/ Clinical Medicine, Current Contents/Life Sciences, Elsevier BIOBASE/Current Awareness in Biological Sciences, EMBASE/Excerpta Medica, Index Medicus/Medline, Medical Documentation Service, Reference Update, Research Alert, Science Citation Index, Scisearch, SIIC-Database Argentina, UMI (Microfilms)

Editorial services and typesetting by BA & GM Haddock, Ford, Midlothian, Scotland Printed in Great Britain by Bell & Bain Ltd, Glasgow, Scotland.

BRITISH MEDICAL BULLETIN · Volume 57 2001

Depression

Scientific Editors: Malcolm H Lader and Philip J Cowen

http://www.bmb.oupjournals.org

Acknowledgements

The planning committee for this issue of the *British Medical Bulletin* was chaired by Malcolm Lader and also included Philip Cowen, Michael Barkham, Tirril Harris and Glyn Lewis.

The British Council and Oxford University Press are most grateful to them for their help and advice and particularly for the valuable work of the Scientific Editors in completing this issue.

Preface

Depression is an all-too-common disorder that can affect anyone.
Indeed, the chance of developing a depressive illness is estimated to be 1
in 5 for women and 1 in 10 for men making it a particularly common
affliction of mankind. The World Health Organization estimates that
within 20 years, recurrent depressive disorder will be the second most
serious cause of morbidity in the world.

The term depression can apply to a transient mood, a sustained change
in affect, a symptom, a syndrome, or a psychiatric illness. It can be an
understandable reaction to adverse circumstances or loss and, therefore,
within the ambit of normality. However, if it is excessive in severity or
persistence, lacks precipitating circumstances or contains elements of
psychosis, *i.e.* loss of contact with reality, then it is abnormal, morbid
and is regarded as a psychiatric disorder. Such depression can be
secondary to a physical illness such as influenza or carcinoma, to
another psychiatric condition such as schizophrenia or to substance
misuse, or to drug therapy such as antihypertensive agents or steroids.
Its relationship to other symptoms and disorders is quite complex, that
to anxiety in particular.

In all branches of medicine, particularly primary care, depression is
encountered frequently as an illness with a wide and often confusing
range of symptoms. Some of the symptoms are primarily physical and
some psychological, but a range of distressing complaints is frequent.
This can give rise to much secondary morbidity such as impairment of
work capacity. Social functioning is also diminished and the patient's
family may suffer as well, particularly if the disorder is prolonged.
Typically, the patient will describe the sensation of being depressed as
beyond normal experience, with an ineffably painful quality.

In this issue of the *British Medical Bulletin*, we have taken a wide
overview of the subject of depression but have also concentrated on
areas in which there is lively current debate and/or research. We have
commissioned review chapters from a range of psychiatrists, psychologists, and others so that we cover, for example, recent concepts in the
neurobiology of depression through to the equally important sociological and cultural aspects. We have concentrated to some extent on the
therapy of depressive conditions with chapters on cognitive behavioural
therapy, interpersonal therapy and counselling and even self-help on the
Internet. The need for longer-term management therapy is stressed
because it has become increasingly apparent that depression is a chronic
or relapsing condition carrying often a life-time burden of illness.
Depression can often puzzle the caring professions and this may lead to
some stigmatisation of depressed individuals. The treatment of

depression lies primarily in the context of general practice with referral to psychiatrists for those with more severe and long-term difficulties. Both psychological and pharmacological treatments remain the mainstay of management, together with care and sympathy from family, friends, and professional advisers.

We hope that this issue of *British Medical Bulletin* will provide a wide variety of professionals with an insight into current thinking into depressive disorders, as a spectrum of conditions which need to be understood and managed on both the neurobiological and psychosocial levels. We hope that such an approach will encourage a holistic understanding of this common and serious condition.

Malcolm Lader
Philip Cowen

Classification, disability and the public health agenda

Glyn Lewis and **Ricardo Araya**

Department of Psychological Medicine, University of Wales College of Medicine, Cardiff, UK

Depression is a common and disabling illness. For some time the disability has been relatively neglected by those interested in public health. Public health priorities have largely been determined by statistics on mortality. The World Health Organization has argued for some time that public health should be concerned with 'adding life to years' as well as 'adding years to life'. This article will argue that depression should be a key priority for public health research.

Classification

The classification and measurement of depression has attracted interest and controversy for many years. The great emphasis that has been given to measurement in psychiatry has often been a distraction, but accurate measurement and clarity about diagnostic issues is an essential prerequisite of any scientific process. Before discussing some of the more recent consensus about classification in depression, it is worth mentioning the general principles behind classification and measurement.

Classification has a purpose and is intended to help doctors with their work[1]. There are three main functions: (i) communication; (ii) guiding treatment or prognosis; and (iii) informing research. Classifications have to be useful to survive in clinical practice, and will persist if they are used, even if they find little favour in the scientific journals. If these functions of classification are to be 'effectively' fulfilled, psychiatric diagnoses need to be reliable. Though the reliability of diagnosis tends to be largely a concern of the research community, we should not forget that clinicians also need to be able to make diagnoses with sufficient reliability in order to communicate with each other, their patients and to apply the results of research studies to their clinical work. In parallel with the discussion of reliability is that concerning the 'validity' of diagnostic categories. This expression is best thought of as utility in the absence of 'gold standard' measures. If diagnoses aid communication, treatment decisions and prognostic predictions then they are useful and in that sense 'valid'.

Correspondence to:
Professor Glyn Lewis,
Department of
Psychological Medicine,
Monmouth House,
University of Wales
College of Medicine,
Heath Park,
Cardiff CF14 4XN, UK

There is now an international consensus over the diagnostic categories of depression and it is reassuring that both the major diagnostic manuals, DSM-IV and ICD-10, have the same diagnostic criteria for unipolar depression. Of particular note is that the criteria for major depressive disorder can be met even if a person complains of loss of interest rather than low mood. The criteria also allow for hypersomnia and increased appetite as well as the more conventional syndrome in which there is less sleep and poor appetite. Our current classification retains the opportunity to code the somatic syndrome of depression: early morning wakening, weight loss, diurnal variation, retardation or agitation and loss of libido.

There has been a trend to give less emphasis to the somatic syndrome of depression over recent years. In the past, these 'biological' symptoms were thought to reflect an illness more endogenous and less linked to adverse events in the environment in contrast to neurotic depression. Biological symptoms were also thought to indicate likely response to antidepressant medication. However, both of these statements have been challenged. There is evidence that life events are as common before depression with somatic symptoms as before depression without somatic symptoms[2]. The link between a depressive episode and environmental adversity seems more important for the first episode of depression and subsequent episodes seem less linked to adverse events[3]. The antidepressants have also been successfully used in depressed patients without the somatic syndrome[4].

The change in the perceived utility of the somatic syndrome has led to more emphasis on thinking of depression along a continuum of severity[5,6]. This is in tune with a long tradition within medical epidemiology that argues that almost all medical conditions in the community are most accurately viewed along a continuum[7]. For clinicians, categories are useful in order to guide decision making, but in the real world most illnesses including depression do not exist in simple categories but along continua. Kendell's classic study illustrated the continuum between the neurotic and endogenous forms of depression[8]. Likewise, community surveys illustrate that the key symptoms of depression are common in the community and exist across the whole range of severity[9].

Most patients with depression are treated in primary care or its equivalent[10,11], and it is important to be aware that in primary care the whole range of depressive syndromes will be seen. Primary care physicians will see a large number of people in a 'grey' area where treatment decisions are difficult to make. One of the major challenges of research in this area is to help primary care physicians rapidly assess the severity of depression and link this with decisions about pharmacological and psychological treatment. There is increasing concern within primary care that patients with very mild depressive symptoms or problems of living are being medicalised and treated with anti-depressants. Making the diagnosis of depression is at the heart of this controversy and in the context of primary care regarding depression along a continuum of severity seems particularly important.

Co-morbidity

The overlap between the symptoms of anxiety, depression and other neurotic symptoms are legendary. This area has been given the new name of co-morbidity. The advent of operationalised criteria has highlighted the overlap between symptoms and syndromes when a categorical approach is taken towards diagnosis. A National Co-morbidity Survey has been carried out in the US[12]. An alternative and probably simpler view is that depression and anxiety are two correlated dimensions[13], though some might argue for a single dimension[14–16]. One can certainly argue that a single dimension does describe neurotic symptoms in the community, even if a more complex classification is also of value.

The primary concern for clinicians and patients must be how classification and diagnosis is related to treatment. At present, anti-depressants and psychotherapy, including cognitive behavioural therapy are the main options for both depressive and anxiety disorders and there is little guidance on which patients will benefit from which approach[17–21]. These diagnostic issues will only be resolved by future research to investigate whether treatment response or outcome differs systematically according to clinical characteristics.

Methods of measurement

There are a wide range of standardised methods for assessing depressive disorders with a confusing range of acronyms. It is useful to classify the methods into four different types: (i) rating scales; (ii) semi-structured interviews; (iii) fully structured interviews; and (iv) self-administered questionnaires.

Rating scales such as the Hamilton Rating Scales for Depression (HAMD)[22] do not provide any guidance on the questions to be used though they provide (some) more guidance on how to code symptoms when present. They can, therefore, only be administered by trained clinicians. Though poorly standardised, the HAMD has become one of the most widely used assessments particularly in pharmaceutical trials. One suspects that its use will be superseded by more standardised methods of assessment. Semi-standardised interviews, such as the Schedules for Clinical Assessment in Neuropsychiatry (SCAN)[23], allow the interviewer some discretion in the use of questions but provide much more guidance about the conduct of the interviewer and a glossary of terms. This kind of methodology is probably essential for some of the most severe depressions seen in hospitals, for example those accompanied by delusions. However, for the more common, less severe depressions, more structured assessments have been developed.

In the UK, the revised clinical interview schedule (CIS-R)[24] has become widely used, including in the OPCS Psychiatric Morbidity Survey carried out in 1993, a household survey on 10,000 individuals representative of the UK population[25,26]. The CIS-R is a fully structured assessment, suitable for trained social survey interviewers and does not require any expert knowledge on the part of the interviewers. As such, it can also be administered using personal computers in which the subjects self-complete the questionnaire[27]. The CIS-R elicits responses to 14 areas of symptoms including depression, anxiety, sleep and fatigue. It can be used to generate a total score, analogous to the single continuum approach, as well as diagnostic categories according to ICD-10. The World Health Organization has encouraged the development of the Composite International Diagnostic Interview (CIDI), a fully-structured interview based upon a US interview[28]. The CIDI exists in a variety of versions (CIDI)[29] and adopts a similar approach to the CIS-R though it takes longer to administer and is based upon diagnostic criteria rather than structured around symptoms.

Self-administered questionnaires such as the General Health Questionnaire (GHQ)[30] and Beck Depression Inventory (BDI)[31] have also been widely used. The GHQ asks general questions about symptoms and functioning though the BDI is more focused on the key symptoms of depression. The BDI has been frequently used as an outcome measure in studies of depression.

There are still some doubts about the 'validity' of the fully structured interviews such as the CIS-R and CIDI. A recent UK study found very low levels of agreement between the CIS-R, CIDI and the SCAN though the severity of depression for the SCAN and CISR showed better agreement[32,33]. Unfortunately, we still know little about the reliability of the SCAN assessment when used in the community though we know that clinical judgement alone is fairly unreliable. Most researchers now accept that fully structured interviews are the only feasible methodology for large scale community studies that often involve up to 200 interviewers. These assessments ensure that all subjects in a study are asked the same questions and this should reduce interobserver variability and ensure comparison with other studies.

These standardised methods are rarely used in clinical practice though many who use Beck's version of cognitive therapy[34] tend to assess progress using the BDI. It is important though that clinically relevant research keeps in touch with clinical practice and leads to results with practical implications. The research community is carrying out research that will hopefully benefit patients. If the criteria used in research are wildly different from those used by clinicians, the value of the research will be seriously undermined.

Disability and depression

Several studies have shown a close association between depression and disability in both western and non-industrialised countries[35,36]. The association persists after statistical adjustment for the presence of physical illness and across time. Wells et al[37] studied more than 11,000 patients with different chronic diseases to find that the level of disability among patients with depressive symptoms, whether or not meeting diagnostic criteria for depression, was comparable or greater than that associated with the most frequent physical chronic diseases such as diabetes and hypertension.

Common mental disorders have also been linked to important indirect costs due to either diminished productivity or absence from work. Broadhead et al[35] found that people with depression had a 4.8 times higher risk than people without symptoms of having had sickness leave. More recently, an American study found that for every 100 workers, 6 days of work are lost for sickness leave and 31 days are lost for diminished productivity every month due to poor mental health[38].

These statistics will come as no surprise to clinicians used to treating those with depression or others familiar with the syndrome. Depression is often an exceptionally disabling condition, leading to difficulties in working and carrying out household tasks. Unlike many physical conditions, it can also lead to a profound deterioration of relationships with friends, family and work colleagues that can provide particular difficulties.

Despite the empirical and clinical evidence for a substantial population disability associated with depression, it has proved difficult to establish depression as a public health priority. Public health statistics have relied exclusively upon mortality rates to determine priorities and so conditions that lead to morbidity rather than mortality have been relatively neglected. The World Bank attempted to change this agenda by adopting a methodology that calculated the Disability Adjusted Life Years or DALYs lost to various diseases. This approach was designed to enable morbidity and mortality to be compared and, therefore, allow a rational setting of public health priorities.

Disability Adjusted Life Years: the DALY

The novelty of this method was to try to adjust for the level of disability when calculating years lost as a result of ill health. If someone dies prematurely, then each year lost counts as one whole DALY. If someone has an illness, such as depression, then each year affected by illness will count as a proportion of a DALY. The controversial and difficult aspect of this method is in estimating what proportion should be used when calculating DALYs for non-fatal conditions. The higher the proportion, the more disabling the condition. Most criticism of the method has focused on the fact that two of the most important components of this indicator, the degree of disability produced by each specific disease and the relative value of each year of life achieved, are determined by a panel of 'experts' through an ill-defined and rather unsystematic process. Anecdotal accounts of 'horse trading' in relation to these estimates have also undermined confidence in the precise estimates that have been calculated. However, attempts are being made to base these estimates on a firmer empirical footing. A further limitation concerns the quality of the data on prevalence. The quality of much of the epidemiological information that has been used to estimate the burden of diseases around the world is of questionable reliability, particularly in relation to non-industrialised countries where few large scale surveys on representative samples have been carried out.

Despite these limitations, the World Bank Report and associated publications[39-41] have provided the first estimates that have allowed comparison between depression, other psychiatric disorders and physical illness leading to death. The report estimated that neuropsychiatric disorders led to 8% of the global burden of disease (GBD) measured in DALYs lost to illness (Table 1). For adults aged 15–44 years, psychiatric disorders are estimated to account for 12% of the GBD; if 'self-inflicted, unintentional injuries' are added, the proportion reaches 15.1% for women and 16.1% for men. In fact, mental disorders are projected to increase to 15% of the global disease burden and major depression is expected to become second only to ischaemic heart disease in terms of disease burden by the year 2020 (Table 2)[41].

Table 2 Global burden of disease (GBD) measured in disability adjusted life years (DALYs) lost in illness[39-41]

Illness	% of DALYs lost
Mental health problems	8.1
Maternal/perinatal	9.5
Respiratory	9
Cancer	5.8
Heart disease	4.4
Cerebrovascular disease	3.2
Malaria	2.6
Other communicable diseases	5.3
Other non-communicable diseases	18
Behaviour-related illnesses	34

Table 2 The global burden of disease in 2020

	% DALYs lost to illness
Ischaemic heart disease	5.9
Unipolar depression	5.7
Road traffic accidents	5.0
Cerebrovascular disease	4.4%

Psychiatric disorder has received little priority in the non-industrialised world. Demographic transition and improved measures to combat infectious disease are leading to a change in the pattern of disease in many poor countries[42]. In Chile, for example, life expectancy is now over 70 years and, along with many other areas of the world, the burden of disease is largely produced by non-communicable diseases familiar to those in the West. These changes will contribute to the growing importance of depression and other psychiatric disorders in world health.

These figures, with all their caveats, have profound implications for public health and epidemiological research. Depression in particular, is as big a potential public health issue as ischaemic heart disease (IHD). For IHD, the major risk factors of high cholesterol, smoking and hypertension are well known and preventive strategies are proposed in relation to all these factors. In contrast, little is known about the aetiology of depression and, in particular, there is little evidence for strategies that would lead to primary prevention of depression.

Severity and disability

For clinicians, the more severely affected individuals will always retain clinical priority. As a result, most secondary mental health services, at least in the UK, have a policy to target those with severe mental illness and most cases of depression are, therefore, treated within primary care. The same argument holds for those with depression of varying degrees of severity. Clinical priority, within primary and secondary care will give priority to those with the more severe illnesses who are more disabled by their illness. This priority changes when a public health perspective is taken. In a population, it is the aggregate disability that is important. There are many more people with mild illness than severe illness. As a result, the aggregate burden of disability associated with depression of mild severity may be greater than the disability associated with the smaller number of people with the more severe depressions. Broadhead *et al*[35] have illustrated this phenomenon using data from the Epidemiological

Table 3 Relationship between major depression, subthreshold affective disorders and disability days

	Major depression	Minor depression (with mood disorder)	Minor depression (without mood disorder)
Sample size	49	178	696
Mean disability days (SD)	11.0 (29.0)	6.1 (21.4)	4.0 (16.3)
Excess disability days	474	712	1356

From Broadhead et al[35].

Catchment Area Study in the US (Table 3). The population burden of disability is greater for those who fall below the DSM-III threshold than for those who meet the criteria for major depression. The more depressed individuals are more disabled, but there are fewer of them.

This phenomenon is frequently seen in epidemiology as illustrated by Rose[43,44]. For example, most cerebrovascular disease occurs in those with average blood pressure even though individuals with high blood pressure are at greater individual risk. This observation has important implications for preventive strategies. Rose argued that reducing the mean diastolic blood pressure by 1 mmHg would save as many deaths from cerebrovascular disease as all the hypertension clinics then in the UK. The most effective way of preventing cerebrovascular disease is, therefore, to change the population mean blood pressure rather than trying to target those with the highest blood pressure. Individuals with hypertension need to have treatment because of their high individual level of risk. In most circumstances, though, targeting those at high individual risk will have little impact upon the burden of disease in the population.

It is likely that population-based approaches designed to reduce the prevalence of depression will be needed. Depressed individuals need treatment for their symptoms and associated disability, but this will do nothing to reduce the burden of disease attributable to depressive symptoms that fall below the usual criteria for defining major depression. Research to establish risk factors for depression is required which in turn will inform preventive strategies targeted at the whole population.

Life events

The concept of life events has been an important one in the epidemiology of depression[45]. In the UK, Brown's approach towards the measurement of life events has been particularly influential[46,47]. Research on life events has provided good evidence that environmental stresses increase the risk of developing depression[45]. However, the life events methodology has not led to practical preventive strategies based upon a population approach.

The most commonly used method to measure life events in the UK has been the Life Events and Difficulties Schedule (LEDS). It provides a composite measure of life event plus context (i.e. the circumstances of that individual rated by a panel). Brown and colleagues have persuasively argued that the association between life events and depression is much stronger when such ratings of context have been taken into account[46]. Indeed, one interpretation of the life events literature is that it demonstrates the importance of the psychosocial context in the aetiology of depression. Life events on their own are not that important. Low socio-economic status is clearly one important element of context that influences LEDS ratings and is effectively incorporated in the analysis by combining it within the life event measure.

The emphasis on life events has often been misinterpreted in the literature. For example, policy makers have often erroneously regarded the life events literature as supporting the idea that depression is caused by 'acts of God' and, therefore, nothing can be done to prevent them[48]. This conclusion has led to an emphasis on providing social support to those who might experience life events in the hope that this will reduce the possible impact of an adverse occurrence. Providing support to those at high risk may be beneficial for those individuals at high risk. However, from a public health perspective, this kind of approach is unlikely to lead to a large population impact on the prevalence of depression.

Socio-economic status and depression

What kind of research will help to establish risk factors for depression, that will lead on to practical preventive strategies? At present, the area of socio-economic inequalities might be a promising avenue for future research.

Most of the literature concerning socio-economic status has investigated associations with the common mental disorders of depression and anxiety. However, the associations are probably similar with depression when considered alone[49]. The current literature on socio-economic status and common mental disorder is quite confusing. In part this is because socio-economic status has been measured in a variety of different ways. In the UK, there is now good evidence that the main association is between low standard of living and the prevalence of common mental disorder. This is independent of registrar general social class and educational attainment. For example, Lewis *et al*[49] in the OPCS Psychiatric Morbidity Survey found an independent effect of owning a car and owning rather than renting a home on the prevalence of common mental disorder assessed using the CIS-R.

Such cross sectional data cannot address two important issues. First, is there an association between socio-economic status and duration of disorder rather than incidence. Data from the BHPS suggest that socio-economic measures appear to delay recovery rather than increase incidence[50]. There is also a possibility that those with poor mental health have a reduced capacity to earn more. This is usually called social selection. Unsurprisingly, there is some evidence for social selection[51-53], but it does not appear to be able to explain the whole socio-economic gradient. There is evidence from the US that low income is associated with incidence[54].

All the data referred to above have been collected in industrialised countries. There is now data emerging from non-industrialised countries where similar analyses have been undertaken in which the various measurable aspects of socio-economic status have been studied. For example, Ludermir and Lewis[55] in a community survey in a poor area of Recife, Brazil found that years in education were independently associated with prevalence of common mental disorder. Araya et al[56], in a larger community study in Santiago, have described a similar finding. At present, it is not clear why these Latin American countries should have found different results from studies carried out in the UK. There is certainly more variation in the level of education in non-industrialised countries. Perhaps, education is a more important determinant of life opportunity in the industrialised world? In a non-industrialised country, education might reflect the socio-economic status of the person's own upbringing more accurately than in western countries.

It is likely that low socio-economic status is an important determinant of rates of depression in the community. If this evidence is confirmed and strengthened, it might provide a route to preventive policies directed at the whole population. Future research will need to put more emphasis on longitudinal studies and begin to work out the possible mechanisms that link poverty, education and depression.

Depression and public health

Depression is a major public health problem. Very soon it will lead to almost as much disability as ischaemic heart disease, but, in contrast, very little is know about the risk factors for depression that could inform preventive approaches. Epidemiological research is needed in order to establish risk factors for depression. Most people expect that the risk factors will involve matters such as socio-economic status as well as family upbringing and the influence of these on personality. If this is true, preventive policies will need to influence some fundamental aspects of government social and economic policy. Income distribution, the care of young children and policies with relevance to the family may all have an impact on the rates of depression. If we are to influence this debate, we will need robust evidence from well designed and conducted studies to convince politicians and their advisers. From the perspective of public health, depression must, therefore, be a major priority for research.

References

1   Kendell RE. *The Role of Diagnosis in Psychiatry*, 1st edn. Oxford: Blackwell, 1975
2   Brown GW, Bhrolchain NIM, Harris TO. Psychotic and neurotic depression. Part 3. Aetiological and background factors. *J Affect Disord* 1979; 1: 195–211
3   Lewinsohn PM, Allen NB, Seeley JR, Gotlib IH. First onset versus recurrence of depression: differential processes of psychosocial risk. *J Abnorm Psychol* 1999; 108: 483–9
4   Geddes JR, Butler R, Warner J. Depressive disorders. In: Godlee F. (ed) *Clinical Evidence*, 3rd edn. London: BMJ, 2000; 434–8
5   Lewinsohn PM, Solomon A, Seeley JR, Zeiss A. Clinical implications of 'subthreshold' depressive symptoms. *J Abnorm Psychol* 2000; 109: 345–51
6   Paykel ES, Priest RG. Recognition and management of depression in general practice: consensus statement. *BMJ* 1992; 305: 1198–202
7   Rose G A, Barker DJP. What is a case? Dichotomy or continuum? *BMJ* 1978; ii: 873–4
8   Kendell RE. *The Classification of Depressive Illness. Maudsley Monographs 18*, 1st edn, Oxford: Oxford University Press, 1968
9   Jenkins R, Lewis G, Bebbington P *et al*. The National Psychiatric Morbidity Surveys of Great Britain: initial findings from the Household Survey. *Psychol Med* 1997; 27: 775–90
10 Regier DA, Goldberg ID, Taube CA. The *de facto* United States mental health services system. *Arch Gen Psychiatry* 1978; 35: 685–93
11 Shepherd MS, Cooper B, Brown AC, Kalton G. *Psychiatric Disorders in General Practice*. Oxford: Oxford University Press, 1966
12 Kessler RC, McGonagle KA, Zhao S *et al*. Lifetime and 12-month prevalence of DSM-III-R psychiatric disorders in the United States. *Arch Gen Psychiatry* 1994; 51: 8–19
13 Goldberg D, Huxley P. *Common Mental Disorders: a Biopsychosocial Approach*. London: Routledge, 1992
14 Jacob KS, Everitt B, Patel V, Weich S, Araya R, Lewis G. The comparison of latent trait variable models of non-psychotic psychiatric morbidity in four culturally diverse populations. *Psychol Med* 1998; 28: 145–52
15 Lewis G. Observer bias and the assessment of anxiety and depression. *Social Psychiatry Psychiatr Epidemiol* 1991; 26: 265–72
16 Tyrer PJ. The division of neurosis: a failed classification. *J R Soc Med* 1990; 83: 614–6
17 Depression Guideline Panel. *Depression in Primary Care: Volume 2. Treatment of major depression. Clinical Practice Guideline Number 5*. Rockville, MD: US Dept of Health and Human Services, 1993
18 Effective Health Care. The treatment of depression in primary care. *Effect Health Care Bull* 1993; 5
19 Joyce PR, Paykel ES. Predictors of drug response in depression. *Arch Gen Psychiatry* 1989; 46: 89–99
20 Lader MH. Guidelines for the management of patients with generalised anxiety. *Psychiatr Bull* 1992; 16: 560–6
21 Marks I, Dar R. Fear reduction by psychotherapies. Recent findings, future directions. *Br J Psychiatry* 2000; 176: 507–11
22 Hamilton M. A rating scale for depression. *J Neurol Neurosurg Psychiatry* 1960; 23: 56–62

23 Wing JK, Babor T, Brugha T *et al.* SCAN: Schedules for Clinical Assessment in Neuropsychiatry. *Arch Gen Psychiatry* 1990; **47**: 589–93

24 Lewis G, Pelosi AJ, Araya R, Dunn G. Measuring psychiatric disorder in the community: a standardised assessment for use by lay interviewers. *Psychol Med* 1992; **22**: 465–86

25 Jenkins R, Bebbington P, Brugha T *et al.* The National Psychiatric Morbidity Surveys of Great Britain: strategy and methods. *Psychol Med* 1997; **27**: 765–74

26 Meltzer H, Gill B, Petticrew M, Hinds K. *OPCS Surveys of Psychiatric Morbidity. Report 1. The prevalence of psychiatric morbidity among adults aged 16-64 living in private households in Great Britain.* London: HMSO, 1995

27 Lewis G. Assessing psychiatric disorder with a human interviewer or a computer. *J Epidemiol Community Health* 1994; **48**: 207–10

28 Robins LN, Helzer JE, Croughan J, Ratcliff KS. National Institute of Mental Health Diagnostic Interview Schedule; its history, characteristics and validity. *Arch Gen Psychiatry* 1981; **38**: 381–9

29 Robins LN, Wing JK, Wittchen H-U *et al.* The Composite International Diagnostic Interview. An epidemiologic instrument for use in conjunction with different diagnostic systems and in different cultures. *Arch Gen Psychiatry* 1988; **45**: 1069–77

30 Goldberg DP, Williams P. *The User's Guide to the General Health Questionnaire*, 1st edn. Windsor: NFER-NELSON, 1988

31 Beck AT, Ward CH, Mendelsohn M, Mock J, Erbaugh J. An inventory for measuring depression. *Arch Gen Psychiatry* 1961; **4**: 561–71

32 Brugha T, Bebbington P, Jenkins R *et al. Cross-validation of the lay diagnostic instruments used in the Great Britain National Survey of Psychiatric Morbidity with instruments used in the National Surveys abroad.* London: Department of Health, 1997

33 Brugha T, Bebbington P, Jenkins R *et al.* Cross-validation of a general population survey diagnostic interview: a comparison of CIS-R with SCAN ICD-1- diagnostic categories. *Psychol Med* 1999; **29**: 1029–42

34 Beck AT, Rush AJ, Shaw BF, Emery G. *Cognitive Therapy of Depression.* New York: Wiley, 1979

35 Broadhead WE, Blazer D, George L, Tse C. Depression, disability days and days lost from work. *JAMA* 1990; **264**: 2524–8

36 Ormel J, von Korff M, Ustun B, Pini B, Korten A, Oldehinkel T. Common mental disorders and disability across cultures: results from the WHO collaborative study on psychological problems in general health care. *JAMA* 1994; **272**: 1741–8

37 Wells KB, Stewart A, Hays RD *et al.* The functioning and well-being of depressed patients: results from the medical outcomes study. *JAMA* 1989; 262: 914–9

38 Kessler C, Frank R. The impact of psychiatric disorders on work loss days. *Psychol Med* 1997; **27**: 861–73

39 Murray CJ, Lopez AD. Global mortality, disability, and the contribution of risk factors: Global Burden of Disease Study. *Lancet* 1997; **349**: 1436–42

40 Murray CJ, Lopez AD. Regional patterns of disability-free life expectancy and disability-adjusted life expectancy: global Burden of Disease Study. *Lancet* 1997; **349**: 1347–52

41 Murray CJ, Lopez AD. Alternative projections of mortality and disability by cause 1990–2020: Global Burden of Disease Study. *Lancet* 1997; **349**: 1498–504

42 Feachem R, Kjellstrom T, Murray C. (eds) *The Health of Adults in the Developing World.* Washington, DC: World Bank, 1992

43 Rose G. The mental health of populations. In: Williams P, Wilkinson G, Rawnsley K. (eds) *The Scope of Epidemiological Psychiatry.* London: Routledge, 1989; 155–71

44 Rose G. *The Strategy of Preventive Medicine.* Oxford: Oxford University Press, 1992

45 Paykel ES, Cooper Z. Life events and social stress. In: Paykel ES. (ed) *Handbook of Affective Disorders*, 2nd edn. Edinburgh: Churchill Livingstone, 1991; 183–97

46 Brown GW, Harris TO. *Social Origins of Depression.* London: Tavistock, 1978

47 Brown GW, Harris TO. (eds) *Life Events and Illness.* New York: Guilford, 1989

48 Jenkins R. Depression and anxiety: an overview of preventive strategies. In: Jenkins R, Newton J, Young R. (eds) *The Prevention of Depression and Anxiety: the Role of the Primary Care Team.* London: HMSO, 1992; 11–21

49 Lewis G, Bebbington P, Brugha T *et al.* Socioeconomic status, standard of living and neurotic disorder. *Lancet* 1998; **352**: 605–9
50 Weich S, Lewis G. Poverty, unemployment and the common mental disorders: a population based cohort study. *BMJ* 1998; **317**: 115–9
51 Dahl E. Social inequalities in ill-health: the significance of occupational status, education and income – results from a Norwegian survey. *Sociol Health Illness.* 1994; **16**: 644–67
52 Timms DWG. Social mobility and mental health in a Swedish cohort. *Social Psychiatry Psychiatr Epidemiol* 1996; **31**: 38–48
53 West P. Rethinking the health selection explanation for health inequalities. *Social Sci Med* 1991; **32**: 373–84
54 Bruce ML, Takeuchi DT, Leaf PJ. Poverty and psychiatric status. Longitudinal evidence from the New Haven Epidemiologic Catchment Area Study. *Arch Gen Psychiatry* 1991; **48**: 470–4
55 Ludermir A, Lewis G. Links between social class and common mental disorders in northeast Brazil, *Social Psychiatry Psychiatr Epidemiol* 2001;**36**: 101–7
56 Araya R, Rojas G, Fritsch R, Acuna J, Lewis G. Santiago Mental Disorders Survey: prevalence and risk factors. *Br J Psychiatry* 2001; **178**: 228–33

Recent developments in understanding the psychosocial aspects of depression

Tirril Harris

Socio-Medical Research Centre, Academic Department of Psychiatry, St Thomas' Hospital, London, UK

Recent advances in the psychosocial understanding of depression have elaborated an already complex aetiological model. Yet each new strand seems to echo, and forge links with, themes uncovered earlier, making it easier to see what is common about the 'final common pathway' to onset. For example, although recent stressors have for some time been recognised predictors of onset, new insights about the origins of these stressors have overlapped with other new work on depression and childhood adversity to identify a group who 'produce' their own severe life events in response to early negative experience. And recent studies have traced the well-known gender difference in depressive prevalence to differences both in gender role involvement with the provoking life events and in styles of support-seeking/support-giving. What emerges is the powerlessness, loss and humiliation characterising the final pathway. Both naturalistic studies and controlled trials suggest that psychosocial situations reflecting the opposite emotional meaning, that is new hope, characterise a similar pathway to remission. Conclusions speculate whether awareness of this pathway might enhance purely pharmacological treatment.

Correspondence to:
Dr Tirril Harris,
Socio-Medical Research
Centre, Academic
Department of Psychiatry,
St Thomas' Hospital,
Lambeth Palace Road,
London SE1 7EH, UK

For some years now, lip service has been paid to a tripartite 'bio-psychosocial' model of human development and disease, but the full-scale integration of perspectives implied by such homage is still slow to come about in practice: research, and thus understanding, is still by and large boundaried by the academic departments through which funding is administered. The topic of depression is no exception: even within the 'social' part of the triad, epidemiological and sociological research workers do not always attempt a shared vision and, while respectful of each others' contributions, authors of pharmacological and psychological papers rarely bother to include each other's predictors as control variables in models of depressive onset or remission. The last decade has, however, seen more of a rapprochement between those investigating the disorder *via* the impact of the social outer world and those mapping its relation to the psychic inner world, with the epithet 'psychosocial' increasingly correctly describing such work. This convergence has perhaps occurred more frequently in the context of intervention projects attempting to promote recovery where theory is inevitably forced to reshape itself in relation to the buffets incurred in trying to change the world. But it is more appropriate to begin with an account of recent advances in the aetiological theories on which these interventions were based, even though space limitations mean it is impossible to do justice to the wealth of recent evidence.

Differential prevalence and current environmental precipitation or adversity

An integral part of the multidisciplinary perspective on the aetiology of depression was a view that there existed a final common pathway[1]. For some years there has been an acknowledgement that this pathway was likely to involve the triad of cognitions described by Beck[2] – the self as worthless, the world as pointless and the future as hopeless – cognitions which overlap to some degree with what some psychiatric schedules label depressive symptoms. That self-depreciation and social withdrawal were seen as integral to the disorder created a climate where the prodromal roles of low self-esteem and lack of social support became accepted during the 1980s. It is against this background that the following recent developments in the social strands of the multi-disciplinary model should be viewed.

Social class differences: the role of severe life events

Other chapters have focused on cultural differences in rates of depression so these will not be discussed here. Suffice it to say that demographic differences in rates of depression noted in the 1970s, such as higher rates in the lower social status groups, continue to be reported[3,4].

However, often there is no further examination of variables which could explain such demographic differences (see comments in Van Os[5]), only a brief reference to (unmeasured) poverty or lack of education. However, work in the 1970s had already pinpointed severe life events and ongoing difficulties as the key determinants of class[6] and urban–rural[7,8] differences, so it is fitting to turn to these next.

Life events and meaning

Humiliation/entrapment (H/E) and depressive onset
Reworking qualitative data on individuals' experiences of stress has brought new insights. First the severe events[6] or events with negative impact[9] identified as preceding depressive onset have been examined in more detail and categorised according to their emotional meaning in order to note any 'match' with prior vulnerabilities: whereas attention used to

be specially given to events involving loss, either of person, object or of cherished idea, later refinement identified experiences of humiliation or entrapment as particularly prominent before depressive onset among the losses of cherished idea[10]. Those losses which did not involve humiliation – for example redundancy and temporary unemployment as a result of a large firm going bankrupt, a loss for which the interviewee would, therefore, not be held to blame – were followed by a much lower rate of depressive onset (13% as compared with 31%). The 'match' between the shamefulness of such events and the shame felt by people with low self esteem, whose vulnerability to depression was already acknowledged, encouraged a perspective akin to that of Gilbert's insights about shame and depression[11] and to evolutionary theory[12] with its challenging notions that depression has proved a condition of great functional benefit for the survival of the human species.

Fresh start experiences and remission from depression

Even more thought-provoking was the investigation of the 'meaning' of those fresh start experiences which, more often than not, preceded depressive remission[13-16]. Although all these data were collected retrospectively, the time order between these and remission, and the high proportion of such events which were independent of the subject's agency, lent plausibility to this being the effect of the environment on pathology. It seemed fresh starts were the mirror image of those producing the generalised hopelessness of Beck's depressive cognitive triad[2]. They either involved events like starting a new job after months unemployed, starting a course after years as a housewife, establishing a regular relationship with a new boy friend/girl friend after many months single, or the reduction of a severe difficulty, usually with interpersonal relationships, housing or finance. They seemed to embody the promise of new hope against a background of deprivation. It was notable that even for women who continued to experience difficulties of a depressogenic severity in one life domain such as marriage, a fresh start in another life domain – starting an access course – often seemed to tip the balance and set them on course for remission.

Event production

One recent important elaboration of the psychosocial model of depression has been the quest for the origins of the severe life events that had emerged as so crucial before onset[17]. For this it became important to distinguish events brought about by the persons themselves (variously 'contingent', 'controllable' or 'dependent' events) from those coming, as it were, from outside ('independent' or 'uncontrollable' events)[18]. Unsurprisingly, one set of sources was identified as environmental with not only social class position and inner-city residence as critical influences, but also certain past experiences (see below): people in some environments seemed to have mounted a conveyor belt to continued adversity from which they could only exit with extraordinary effort. Of other more internal sources considered, depression itself was a prime candidate, either previous[19,20] or current[21]. High neuroticism scores were also found to be highly predictive[22-24] along with extraversion[25]. One longitudinal study was able to predict adult severe events by teenage behaviour problems measured on the Rutter B scale[26]. A similar predictor was current dramatic (cluster B) personality disorder which nearly doubled the rate of humiliation/entrapment (H/E) events, and quadrupled the rate of contingent H/E events[27]. Studies with twin pairs also found that the 'controllable' events were the ones particularly due to genetic influence[28], or, in the terminology of another genetic study, 'personal' as opposed to 'network' events[24]. Personality traits such as impulsiveness, frustration tolerance and risk taking were suggested as the possible genetically influenced origins of these events. It was rare for studies to pursue the possible origins of such traits in yet earlier experiences of events (see below on childhood adversity)[27].

Social capital

One new way of looking at demographic differences which seems to span this divide between an individual's events/difficulties and the more epidemiological features of a locality is to incorporate the notion of social capital, a concept rapidly gaining credence in the public health field as New Labour has invited Putnam[29] to give seminars in Downing Street. Defined[30] as 'consisting of features of social organisation – such as trust between citizens, norms of reciprocity and group membership – that facilitate collective action', it is conceivable as a factor (low levels of which could act to provoke depression independently of actual personal experiences): living in an area with many burglaries/assaults might prove depressogenic even in the absence of actual experience of these by the subject or his immediate neighbours (only the latter would count as on-going difficulties/events)[31]. Initial investigations in relation to mental health are still being analysed – although one study reports that the 'social milieu' can be protective against depression[32]. This promises to be an area of interesting data in the next few years.

Endogenous depression

Before leaving the topic of environmental provocation of depression, it is perhaps important to mention the classic debate concerning depressive subtype. According to mid-20th century orthodoxy, syndromes involving the more vegetative symptoms such as early waking, morning worsening and lack of reactivity were 'endogenous' in the sense of lacking environmental provocation. Standardisation of life event measures had produced data that caused a radical reconsideration of this perspective[6,33] with one team even changing sides when their second data set challenged the orthodox view supported by their first[34,35]. Yet, despite the new consensus, there was still a sense that depressions without this type of provocation did often show the specified symptom pattern. New light was thrown on the puzzling inconsistency of previous results by the reports in two data sets of different rates of provocation between first and subsequent melancholic episodes, with experience of at least one severe event for first melancholic episodes as high as for all with neurotic depression[36,37]. It was suggested that the lower percentages for later melancholic episodes resembled Post's work on the role of sensitisation, or scarring, after a first episode, particularly for bipolar disorder[38].

Differential prevalence and past adversity

The 1990s placed childhood sexual abuse in the forefront of attention as a source of adult mental health problems. But it was important to heed, but not outdo, earlier scepticism concerning the frequency of such abuse which some attributed to retrospectively distorted accounts of childhood[39]. Moreover the psychiatric literature on the long-term effects of adverse childhood experiences was already riven with contradictions, even for experiences such as parental death or divorce that could be independently corroborated by civil certificates. Towards the end of the 1980s, some consensus emerged over the conflicting findings concerning the impact of childhood parental loss on adult depression: parental death seemed less depressogenic than parental divorce[40], but the key predictor of later depression was less the loss than the on-going deprivation of adequate care which often accompanied such loss and was found to play a similar role even in families without such loss[41-43]. Later refinement of an interview measure of such neglect also focused on the depressogenic impact of physical and sexual abuse, identifying a raised rate of depression among those with such 'childhood adversity' using the Childhood Experience of Care and Abuse or CECA[44-47], particularly in samples of the homeless[48,49]. Other research teams focusing on such abuse, even without also investigating neglect, also came up with increased rates[50-53]. CECA-defined childhood adversity was also found to predict chronicity of depression both in a patient[54] and a community sample[55]. Despite the retrospective nature of the CECA, a series of sister pairs provided evidence of high corroboration of their sister's account of any abuse or neglect experienced as a child[56,57]. A study of mothers and their teenage daughters revealed a strong association between repeated abuse/neglect among the daughters and early inadequate parenting during the mothers' childhoods[58], highlighting the process of intergenerational transmission of vulnerability to depression heralded by Rutter and Madge[59].

Parallel work on the effects of maternal depression on children's emotional and cognitive development seemed to be echoing this theme: it seemed that a rearing style involving neglect or abuse was often a corollary of a mother's depression[60] (see Murray & Cooper[61] for key references). A number of alternative models have been elaborated to explain these aetiological pathways: most involve long-term damage to self-esteem or to attachment style (and thus to the ability to access emotional support) as a result of the early toxic relationships with key care-givers, the two factors mentioned above in connection with the final common pathway to depressive onset[62,63]. It is in the context of interventions with postnatally depressed mothers that these models can best be evaluated.

Differential prevalence and gender

The flood of evidence linking depression with childhood adversity suggested the possibility that this might be able to account for one of the best established associations between the disorder and sociodemographic factors – the 2-fold greater prevalence among women. Could this be due to a greater tendency for girls to suffer childhood abuse? Pathare and Craig investigated this possibility in a series of 83 brother–sister pairs[47]: the expected gender differences in depression, both current and life-time, were found but childhood experience could not be held accountable, as although rates of **sexual** abuse were higher among the sisters, overall rates including neglect and physical abuse were not so different. Sisters were asked to corroborate their brothers' experiences and there was little evidence of systematic under-reporting by men. What was striking, however, was the tendency among the brothers for childhood adversity to be associated only with externalising disorders such as substance abuse, whereas among the sisters it was with depression, conventionally seen as an internalising disorder. A similar picture emerged in a sample of 96 young men[64], brothers of the young women mentioned earlier as examined alongside their mothers[58].

A more promising avenue for the exploration of gender differential rates came from a study of couples selected for experience of a shared severe life event in order to compare the ways in which women would respond differently from men[65]. Similarity of experience was maximised by excluding couples where the event was severe for one but not for the other (for example the death of one spouse's sibling would only be severe for the other in unusual circumstances). Among those with severe events involving work or marriage, rates of depression were much the same, but among the 47 couples with events concerning children, reproduction or housing, the expected higher female rate was found, and it was possible to relate this to women's higher rate of 'commitment" and 'involvement' in such domains. For 13 of these 47 crises, 'role salience' was rated considerably less given the relatively greater involvement of the male partner in the home, and here there was no difference in rate of depressive onset. In this series, gender differences in social support were also interesting[66]: while a supportive marriage was protective for both, women expressed greater **need** for support within marriage, and were also more likely to seek support from close relationships outside marriage. Receiving support from outside marriage, which was protective for women, was associated with higher depression among men. The authors speculate that this may be due to men feeling more demeaned by confiding their emotions and so postponing support seeking until they are under more emotional pressure to do so, that is, perhaps, until depressive disorder has already begun.

One final comment: these findings concerning the types of provoking events that account for gender differences in depression must have a bearing on recent reports of single mothers as even more prone to depression than other mothers, through their higher rates of H/E events and their lower levels of self-esteem and social support[67]. An empirical investigation of maternal depression and factors associated with it in child and family care social work highlighted the high proportion both of depression and of lone mothers (either divorced or always single) among this client group, along with a higher number of problems with parenting and behavioural difficulties with children[68]. Despite this high frequency, social workers were very poor at identifying depression and their interventions did not differ in any marked respect compared to families without depressed mothers.

Differential prevalence and social support with adversity

Confirmation of the key protective role of social support has continued[69], whether examined in terms of the positive provision of a confidant[62] or the absence of negative input such as marital difficulties[54,55] or 'critical comments' (references cited in Leff et al[71])[70], although there has been one failure to replicate this latter[72]. As with the growth of interest in **origins**, not merely impact, of events, there has been a corresponding development of interest in the origins of poor support. Here too, personality, if not actually PD, has begun to be explored as the source of support deficits, and again Attachment Theory has been co-opted, with its subclassification of different personal styles of failed intimacy, the fearful or the dismissive who avoid seeking support compared with the enmeshed and ambivalent who may alienate potential confidants[73].

Psychosocial interventions for depression

The rise of evidence-based medicine has brought a wave of specialist treatment trials in the last decade, many of which are reviewed in other papers in this issue. Although from the inter-disciplinary point of view, there is an impressive number of comparisons of antidepressants with psychological treatments such as cognitive-behavioural therapy (CBT) and interpersonal therapy (IPT), any more social aspects of these psychological interventions are ignored in the write-ups (see critique in Parry[74]). Comparisons of CBT with couple therapy (cited in Leff *et al*[71]) have been exceptions here, probably because, with the marital/partner relationship being the focus of couple therapy, changes in its quality would inevitably also need to be monitored in the CBT comparison group. However, other psychosocial factors (for example conflict with in-laws) were not so monitored. Another exception is the series of trials of problem-solving[75] in primary care[76,77]. But the potential impact of the problem solving upon the relevant social predictors is unclear from the analyses: just how many problems did the patients face at intake and how many were actually reduced or eliminated before recovery, and could such a disappearance be justifiably attributed to the treatment or was it independent? It could be argued that such an estimate of the psychosocial context is long overdue for all treatments, not just for those like problem solving which target such factors. Andrews[78] has drawn attention to what he calls the 'bane of depression outcome research', the combination of high spontaneous recovery (at least for episodes of 2 months or less) and placebo response, which mean that high recovery rates within RCT control groups often obscure the interpretation of the effects of the targeted treatments. Introducing some of the psychosocial measures detailed earlier could perhaps illuminate the mechanism of spontaneous recovery (perhaps *via* fresh start experiences) and the process of the placebo response (perhaps some form of social support). Certainly incorporating such measures could serve to monitor the oft repeated finding that the effect size of drug and psychological treatments is not dissimilar and that combinations of drug and psychological do not add over and above one treatment alone. Does each act through a different initial route towards a final common pathway to remission[1] which if reached through one path cannot further facilitate the attainment of recovery through another?

Certainly notions concerning the preventive role of social support have been the prime inspiration of the various social, as opposed to psychological therapy, interventions reported. Translated into more communitarian life-span versions, they have also underpinned a number of recent government initiatives in the Health Action Zones, such as Sure Start, which targets children under 4 years and their mothers living in disadvantaged areas as an investment in the mental health of its future citizens. It aims to use health visitors to promote support and positive parenting groups to halt the intergenerational spiral whereby maternal depression promotes child disturbance which in turn exacerbates maternal depression. Many such schemes are too recent for serious evaluation here, but evaluations of similar interventions deserve attention not only for their contribution to understanding depression but also for their promise in defeating it.

One RCT with a chronically depressed elderly group in London suggested that regular visits from a community nurse providing emotional support had contributed substantially to remission[79]. Another RCT in an adjacent London borough with 86 chronically depressed women, using volunteer befrienders given minimal supervision by social-worker counsellors, found an effect of similar size (65% versus 39%)[80]. The latter study specifically measured the degree of support offered throughout the period by the volunteers, from the perspective of both befriendee and befriender, for which there was high agreement. This was indeed identified as a mediating factor[81], but absence of any new severe stressor and presence of fresh-start events during follow-up, as well as baseline attachment style, were also needed to model remission[82].

Another set of interventions with postnatally depressed mothers, explicitly targeted at different components of the correlations between maternal and infant moods, behaviours and interactions, came up with the surprising finding that all interventions, whether focused on the depression or the mother–child interaction, were equally effective at relieving depression but equally ineffective in influencing mother–child interaction or infant behaviour[61]. This 'Cambridge Treatment Trial' included two groups identical to an earlier trial that had identified 8 weekly non-directive counselling sessions by health visitors as a significant improvement over routine primary care (69% *versus* 38% remission), but added two extra intervention groups involving 42 with CBT and 48 with a form of dynamic psychotherapy in which an understanding of the mother's representation of her infant and her relationship with him was promoted by exploring aspects of the mother's own early attachment history. A later intervention by all health visitors working in the Cambridge National Health Service sector with a 6 half-day training in basic counselling skills and basic cognitive-behavioural strategies essentially replicated the Cambridge controlled trial[83]. Murray and Cooper[61] comment that 'a common feature of all the treatments was that they provided women with an opportunity to discuss their problems managing their infants and it is conceivable that this opportunity enabled therapeutic change of this dimension'. However, it is important to mention here one negative result for depression in Canada, a comparison of 8 social support group therapy sessions with a no-intervention group, although there was some evidence of an effect on mother–infant interaction[84].

Another set of interventions, focused on children in contexts liable to promote childhood depression or behavioural problems, such as bereavement (24 intervention families and 31 controls) or parental separation (34 and 36), also provided theoretical insights[85]. For the first, the intervention consisted of a family grief workshop followed by a highly structured 12-session adviser programme targeted on each of four putative mediators defined by the aetiological model, parental warmth, parental demoralisation, promoting stable positive events and coping with negative stress events. This programme led to parental ratings of decreased depression problems and conduct disorder in the older children, and increased warmth in relationships with their children, satisfaction with social support and maintenance of family discussion of grief-related issues. The second programme (parental separation) involved 10 weekly group and 2 individual sessions. It indicated the following changes in the five targeted mediators: higher quality mother-child relationships, and discipline, and fewer negative divorce events for programme participants than for controls, along with better mental health outcomes, although the latter were more notable by mothers' than by children's reports. (Mothers were only rated on a scale of demoralisation whereas children were assessed for depression and conduct disorder.) Analyses revealed that improvements in the mother–child relationship partially mediated the effects on mental health outcomes.

Biopsychosocial investigations

It would be misleading to end without paying due tribute to work which has made the effort to incorporate the biological part of the tripartite model in the range of its variables. Such work falls into two broad groups – that concerned with genetic factors and that relating biological measures such as hormone levels to depression in combination with the key psychosocial predictors.

Genetic models

Unfortunately, space precludes the lengthy exposition owed to the work of Kendler and his colleagues who have used the Virginia Twin register to incorporate genetic analyses along with a full range of psychosocial measures, including independent and dependent events[86,87]. His recent examination of monozygotic twin pairs discordant for major depression[88] confirms his previous reports that both genetic and environmental effects are involved in major depression, giving additional insights, for example distinguishing the largely genetically mediated role of neuroticism from the environmentally mediated role of low self-esteem. This work, seemingly inspired by a 'genetic' perspective, has also confirmed the recent elaborations of the life-span psychosocial model, the link between childhood and current adversity along with the roles of self-esteem and social support[86].

Integrating hormone measures

Strickland and colleagues used a range of Brown's psychosocial measures along with a range of biological measures to predict onset one year later[89]. Results were essentially negative. Goodyer and colleagues collected data among adolescents on cortisol and the key psychosocial predictors identified by their team[90], and more recently Herbert encouraged Harris and Brown to combine his team's measures of cortisol with their psychosocial instruments[91]. The results of investigating depressive onset among adult women specially selected for psychosocial vulnerability and followed up after 12 months provided an encouraging parallel to the adolescents followed up by Goodyer and colleagues[90]. High baseline levels of cortisol at 8 am, although unrelated to any of the psychosocial measures, did independently predict subsequent onset.

Concluding comments

This resumé has covered a wide range of pathways to depression which have emerged repeatedly in recent research on the psychosocial aetiology of affective disorder. What stands out is the complex interweaving of social and psychological strands throughout the developmental history: how the severe humiliation entrapment events which precede onset issue not only from an inclement environment but are sometimes produced by the subjects themselves; that the lack of any supportive relationship which might protect against onset issues not always from the hostile networks into which life has currently thrust them but sometimes from their own attachment styles which have led them to avoid intimacy or to alienate potentially supportive figures by their needs for enmeshment. Moreover, such behavioural styles involving event-production or attachment tendencies in adulthood can repeatedly be traced to early adverse interpersonal experiences involving neglect and abuse in childhood, with their acknowledged impact on subsequent personality. Such a developmental perspective has echoes of psychodynamic explanatory models, particularly since the amendments introduced by Attachment Theory have rendered these more amenable to empirical test. Certainly the time is ripe for a rapprochement between psychodynamic psychotherapists and evidence-based practice, medical or other, with depressed patients. There is much to learn, but also much to unlearn, on both sides, especially an appreciation of the impact of social context for the mechanisms by which other biological or psychological factors exert their influence upon depression.

Key points for clinical practice

- An understanding of a depressed person's on-going problems, particularly interpersonal difficulties, can afford clinicians the opportunity to promote fresh start experiences, such as reconciliations, which have emerged as so important for remission

- An understanding of patients' childhood experiences may alert clinicians to those needing help to avoid producing more humiliating events for themselves in the current period

- Fresh-start experiences in one domain, for example a housewife embarking on a part-time training, can often prove therapeutic despite continuation of severe difficulties in another domain, such as a poor marriage

- Confirmation of the positive role of social support, not only as protection against depressive onset but also as promoting recovery, suggests clinicians should routinely assess patients' support networks and encourage their utilisation and development

- The psychosocial role of the consultation itself, both as listening support and as potential fresh-start, should not be underestimated: if during consultation, attention is paid to the social context of a depressive episode, including any adversity in childhood, this supportive role will be preserved and adherence to prescribed medication may thus be increased

References

1   Akiskal HS, McKinney Jr WT. Depressive disorders: towards a unified hypothesis. *Science* 1973; **182**: 20–9

2   Beck AT. *Depression: Clinical, Experimental and Theoretical Aspects*. London: Staples, 1967

3   Eaton WW, Harrison G. Epidemiology, social deprivation and community psychiatry. *Curr Opin Psychiatry* 2000; **13**: 185–7

4   Andrade L. Surveys of morbidity and psychiatric comorbidity. *Curr Opin Psychiatry* 2000; **13**: 201–7

5   Van Os J. Social influences on risk for disorder and natural history. *Curr Opin Psychiatry* 2000; **13**: 209–13

6   Brown GW, Harris TO. *Social Origins of Depression: A Study of Psychiatric Disorder in Women*. London: Tavistock, 1978

7   Prudo R, Harris TO, Brown GW. Psychiatric disorder in a rural and an urban population: 3. Social integration and the morphology of affective disorder. *Psychol Med* 1984; **14**: 327–45

8   Gaminde I, Uria M, Padro D *et al*. Depression in three populations in the Basque country – a comparison with Britain. *Soc Psychiatry Psychiatr Epidemiol* 1993; **28**: 243–51

9   Paykel ES. Life events, social support and depression. *Acta Psychiatr Scand Suppl* 1994; **377**: 50–8

10 Brown GW, Harris TO, Hepworth C. Loss humiliation and entrapment among women developing depression: a patient and non-patient comparison. *Psychol Med* 1995; **25**: 7–21

11 Gilbert P, Andrews B., *Shame: Interpersonal Behaviour, Psychopathology and Culture*. Oxford: Oxford University Press, 1998

12 Price J, Sloman L, Gardner Jr R *et al*. The social competition hypothesis of depression. *Br J Psychiatry* 1994; **164**: 309–15

13 Brown GW, Adler Z, Bifulco A. Life events difficulties and recovery from chronic depression. *Br J Psychiatry* 1988; **152**: 487–98

14 Brown GW, Lemyre L, Bifulco A. Social factors and recovery from anxiety and depressive disorders: a test of the specificity hypothesis. *Br J Psychiatry* 1992; **161**: 44-=54

15 Leenstra AS, Ormel J, Giel R. Positive life change and recovery from anxiety and depression. *Br J Psychiatry* 1995; **166**: 333–43

16 Oldehinkel AJ, Ormel J, Neeleman J. The effect of positive life change on time to recovery from depression: some people benefit more than others. *J Abnorm Psychol* 2000; **109**: 299–307

17 Brown GW, Harris TO. The origins of life events and difficulties. In: Brown GW, Harris TO. *Life Events and Illness*. New York: Guilford, 1989

18 Harris TO, Brown GW. The origins of the life events preceding onset of depression: 1. Independence and humiliation/entrapment in a general population series. 2001; Submitted

19 Harkness LL, Monroe SM, Simons AD, Thase M. The generation of life events in recurrent and non-recurrent depression. *Psychol Med* 1999; **29**: 135–44

20 Xing-jia C, Vaillant GE. Antecedents and consequences of negative life events in adulthood: a longitudinal study. *Am J Psychiatry* 1996; **153**: 21–6

21 Adrian C, Hammen C. Stress exposure and stress generation in children of depressed mothers. *J Consult Clin Psychol* 1993; **61**: 354–9

22 Poulton RG, Andrews G. Personality as a cause of adverse life events. *Acta Psychiatr Scand* 1992; **85**: 35–8

23 Fergusson DM, Horwood LJ. Vulnerability to life events exposure. *Psychol Med* 1987; **17**: 739–49

24 Kendler KS, Neale M, Kessler R *et al*. A twin study of recent life events and difficulties. *Arch Gen Psychiatry* 1993; **50**: 789–96

25 Breslau N, Davis GC, Andreski P. Risk factors for PTSD-related traumatic events: a prospective analysis. *Am J Psychiatry* 1995; **152**: 529–35

26 Champion L, Goodall G, Rutter M. Behaviour problems in childhood and stressors in early adult life: 1. A twenty year follow-up of London school children. *Psychol Med* 1995; **25**: 231–46

27 Harris TO, Brown GW. The origins of the life events preceding onset of depression: 2 Personality disorder and contingent events in a patient series. 2001; Submitted

28 Plomin R, Perdersen NL, Lichtenstein P *et al*. Genetic influence on life events during the last half of the life span. *Psychol Aging* 1990; **5**: 25–30

29 Putnam R. Bowling alone: America's declining social capital. *J Democracy* 1995; **6**: 65–78

30 Kawachi I, Kennedy BP, Glass R. Social capital and self-rated health: a contextual analysis. *Am J Public Health* 1999; **89**: 1187–93

31 Schwartz S, The fallacy of the ecologic fallacy: the potential misuse of a concept and the consequences. *Am J Public Health* 1994; **84**: 825–9

32 Prince MJ, Harwood RH, Thomas A *et al*. A prospective population-based cohort study of the effects of disablement and social milieu on the onset and maintenance of late-life depression. The Gospel Oak Project VII. *Psychol Med* 1998; **28**: 337–50

33 Paykel ES. Recent life events and clinical depression. In: Gunderson EKE, Rahe RH. (eds) *Life Stress and Illness*. Springfield, IL: CC Thomas, 1974

34 Bebbington P, Tennant C, Hurry J. Adversity and the nature of psychiatric disorder in the community. *J Affect Disord* 1981; **3**: 345–66

35 Bebbington P, Brugha T, MacCarthy B *et al*. The Camberwell Collaborative Depression Study I. Depressed probands: adversity and the form of depression, *Br J Psychiatry* 1988; **152**: 754–65

36 Frank E, Anderson B, Reynolds CF *et al*. Life events and the research diagnostic criteria endogenous subtype. *Arch Gen Psychiatry* 1994; **51**: 519–24.

37 Brown GW, Harris TO & Hepworth C. Life events and 'endogenous' depression: a puzzle re-examined. *Arch Gen Psychiatry* 1994; **51**: 525–34

38 Post RM, Rubinow DR, Ballenger JC. Conditioning and sensitisation in the longitudinal course of affective illness. *Br J Psychiatry* 1986; **149**: 191–201

39 Brewin CR. Scientific status of recovered memories. *Br J Psychiatry* 1996; **169**: 131–4

40 Tennant C, Bebbington P, Hurry J. Parental death in childhood and risk of adult depressive disorders: a review. *Psychol Med* 1980; **10**: 289–99

41 Parker G. Parental 'affectionless control' as an antecedent to adult depression: a risk factor delineated. *Arch Gen Psychiatry* 1983; **40**: 956–60

42 Birtchnell J, Kennard J. How do the experiences of the early separated and early bereaved differ and to what extent do such differences affect outcome? *Social Psychiatry* 1984; **19**: 163–71

43 Harris T, Brown GW, Bifulco A. Loss of parent in childhood and adult psychiatric disorder: a tentative overall model. *Devel Psychopathol* 1990; **2**: 311–28

44 Bifulco A, Brown GW, Harris TO. Childhood experience of care and abuse CECA: a retrospective interview measure. *Child Psychol Psychiatry* 1994; **35**: 1419–35

45 Hill J, Pickles A, Burnside E. Child sexual abuse, poor parental care and adult depression: evidence for different mechanisms. *Br J Psychiatry* 2001; In press

46 Tousignant M, Habimana E, Biron C *et al*. The childhood experience of care and abuse (CECA), an exploration with adolescent refugees. In: Harris TO. (ed) *Where Inner and Outer Worlds Meet: Psychosocial Research in the tradition of George W. Brown*. London: Routledge, 2000; 195–209

47 Pathare S, Craig TKJ. Cross-gender sib-pair study of childhood adversity, substance use disorders. 2001: Submitted

48 Craig TKJ, Hodson S. Homeless youth in London: I. Childhood antecedents and psychiatric disorder. *Psychol Med* 1998; **28**: 1379–88. II Accommodation, employment and health outcomes at 1 year. *Psychol Med* 2000; **30**: 187–94

49 Herman DB, Susser ES, Struening L *et al*. Adverse childhood experiences: are they a risk factor for adult homelessness? *Am J Public Health* 1997; **87**: 249–55

50 Mullen PE, Martin JL, Anderson JC *et al*. The long-term impact of the physical, emotional and sexual abuse of children: a community study. *Child Abuse Neglect* 1996; **20**: 7–21

51 Fergusson DM, Horwood LJ, Lynskey MT. Childhood sexual abuse and psychiatric disorders in young adulthood. Part II. Psychiatric outcomes of sexual abuse. *J Am Acad Child Adolesc Psychiatry* 1996; **35**: 1365–74

52 Briere J, Runtz M. Differential adult symptomatology associated with three types of child abuse histories. *Child Abuse Neglect* 1990; **14**: 357–64

53 Brown J, Cohen P, Johnson JG *et al*. A longitudinal analysis of risk factors for child maltreatment: findings of a 17-year prospective study of officially recorded and self-reported child abuse and neglect. *Child Abuse Neglect* 1998; **22**: 1065–78

54 Brown GW, Moran P. Clinical and psychosocial origins of chronic depressive episodes. I: a community survey. *Br J Psychiatry* 1994; **165**: 447–56

55 Brown GW, Harris TO, Hepworth C, Robinson R. Clinical and psychosocial origins of chronic depressive episodes. II: a patient enquiry. *Br J Psychiatry* 1994; **165**: 457–65

56 Bifulco A, Brown GW, Lillie A *et al*. Memories of childhood neglect and abuse: corroboration in a series of sisters. *J Child Psychol Psychiatry* 1997; **38**: 365–74

57 Brewin CR, Andrews B, Gotlib IH. Psychopathology and early experience: a reappraisal of retrospective reports. *Psychol Bull* 1993; **113**: 82–98

58 Andrews B, Brown GW, Creasey L. Intergenerational links between psychiatric disorder in mothers and daughters: the role of parenting experiences. *J Child Psychol Psychiatry* 1990; **31**: 1115–29

59 Rutter M, Madge N. *Cycles of Disadvantage: A Review of Research*. London: Heinemann, 1976

60 Radke-Yarrow M. *Children of Depressed Mothers: From Early Childhood to Maturity*. Cambridge: Cambridge University Press, 1998

61 Murray L, Cooper PJ. *Post-partum Depression and Child Development*. New York: Guilford, 1997 for cited references see pp 202, 217–20

62 Brown GW, Andrews B, Harris TO, Adler Z, Bridge L. Social support, self-esteem and depression. *Psychol Med* 1986; **16**: 813–31

63 Bifulco A, Brown GW, Moran P *et al*. Predicting clinical depression in women: the role of past and present vulnerability. *Psychol Med* 1998; **28**: 39–50

64 Brown GW, Hepworth C. *Launching from Adolescence to Adulthood: A Study of the Impact of Family Life*. Report to the ESRC, Ref R000 23 2042, 1993 [mimeographed report]

65 Nazroo JY, Edwards AC, Brown GW. Gender differences in the onset of depression following a shared life event: a study of couples. *Psychol Med* 1997; **27**: 9–19

66 Edwards AC, Nazroo J, Brown GW. Gender differences in marital support following a shared life event. *Soc Sci Med* 1998; **46**: 1077–85

67 Brown GW, Moran P. Single mothers poverty and depression. *Psychol Med* 1997; **27**: 21–33

68 Sheppard M. Social work practice in child and family care: a study of maternal depression, *Br J Social Work* 1997; **27**: 814–5

69 Brugha T. (ed) *Social Support and Psychiatric Disorder: Research Findings and Guidelines for Clinical Practice*. Cambridge: Cambridge University Press, 1995

70 Okasha A, El Akabawi AS, Snyder AS *et al*. Expressed emotion, perceived criticism and relapse in depression: a replication in an Egyptian community. *Am J Psychiatry* 1994; **151**: 1001–5

71 Leff J, Vearnals S, Brewin CR. The London Depression Intervention Trial: randomised controlled trial of antidepressants v. couple therapy in the treatment and maintenance of people with depression living with a partner: clinical outcome and costs. *Br J Psychiatry* 2000; **177**: 95–100

72 Hayhurst H, Cooper Z, Paykel ES *et al*. Expressed emotion and depression: a longitudinal study. *Br J Psychiatry* 1997; **171**: 439–43

73 Bifulco AT, Moran PM, Ball C *et al*. Adult attachment style and depression: a new measure of the ability to make supportive relationships. 2001; Submitted

74 Parry G. Social support processes and cognitive therapy. In: Brugha T. (ed) *Social Support and Psychiatric Disorder: Research Findings and Guidelines for Clinical Practice*. Cambridge: Cambridge University Press, 1995

75 Mynors-Wallis LM, Gath DH, Lloyd-Thomas AR, Tomlinson D. Randomised controlled trial comparing problem solving treatment with amitryptyline and placebo for major depression in primary care, *BMJ* 1995; **310**: 441–5

76 Mynors-Wallis LM, Davies I, Gray A, Gath DH, Barbour F. Randomised controlled trial and cost analysis of problem-solving treatment for emotional disorders by community nurses in primary care. *Br J Psychiatry* 1997; **170**: 113–9

77 Mynors-Wallis LM, Gath DH, Day A, Baker F. Randomised controlled trial of problem solving treatment, antidepressant medication, and combined treatment for major depression in primary care. *BMJ* 2000; **320**: 26–30

78 Andrews G. Placebo response: boon of therapy, bane of research. *Br J Psychiatry* 2001; **178**: 192–4

79 Blanchard MR, Waterreus A, Mann A. The effect of primary care nurse intervention upon older people screened as depressed. *Int J Geriatr Psychiatry* 1999; **10**: 289–98

80 Harris TO, Brown GW, Robinson R. Befriending as an intervention for chronic depression among women in an inner city. I: Randomised controlled trial. *Br J Psychiatry* 1999; **174**: 219–25.

81 Harris TO, Brown GW, Robinson R. Befriending as an intervention for chronic depression among women in an inner city. III: The role of support: the befriending process and characteristics of the volunteers. 1999; In preparation

82 Harris TO, Brown GW, Robinson R. Befriending as an intervention for chronic depression among women in an inner city. II: Role of fresh-start experiences and baseline psychosocial factors in remission from depression. *Br J Psychiatry* 1999; **174**: 225–33

83 Seeley S, Murray L, Cooper PJ. The outcome for mothers and babies of health visitor intervention. *Health Visitor* 1996; **69**: 135–8

84 Fleming AS, Klein E, Corter C. The effects of a social support group on depression, maternal attitudes and behaviour in new mothers. *J Child Psychol Psychiatry* 1992; **33**: 685–98

85 Sandler IN, Wolchik SA, MacKinnon D *et al.* Developing links between theory and intervention in stress and coping processes. In: Wolchik SA, Sandler IN. (eds) *Handbook of Children's Coping: Linking Theory and Intervention.* New York: Plenum, 1997; 4–40

86 Kendler KS, Kessler R, Neale M *et al.* The prediction of major depression in women: toward an integrated etiologic model. *Am J Psychiatry* 1993; **150**: 1139–48

87 Kendler KS, Karkowski LM, Prescott CA. The assessment of dependence in the study of stressful life events: validation using a twin design. *Psychol Med* 1999; **29**: 1455–6

88 Kendler KS, Gardner CO. Monozygotic twins discordant for major depression: a preliminary exploration of the role of environmental experiences in the aetiology and course of illness. *Psychol Med* 2001; **31**: 411–23

89 Strickland P, Deakin W, Percival P, Dixon J, Gater R, Goldberg D. The bio-social origins of depression in the community: Interactions between social adversity, cortisol and serotonin transmission. Submitted

90 Goodyer I, Herbert J, Tamplin A *et al.* Recent life events, cortisol, dihydroepisandrosterone and the onset of major depression in high-risk adolescents. *Br J Psychiatry* 2000; **177**: 499–504

91 Harris TO, Borsanyi S, Messari S. Morning cortisol as a risk factor for subsequent major depressive disorder in adult women. *Br J Psychiatry* 2000; **177**: 505–10

Cultural factors and international epidemiology

Vikram Patel

London School of Hygiene and Tropical Medicine, UK and The Sangath Society, Goa, India

The debate on the role of culture on psychiatric epidemiology has evolved considerably in the past two decades. There is now a general consensus that the integration of the universalist and culturally relativist approaches, and their methodologies, is required to generate a truly international psychiatric epidemiology. The large body of research investigating the influence of culture on the epidemiology of depression has produced a number of key findings: the clinical presentation of depression in all cultures is associated with multiple somatic symptoms of chronic duration; psychological symptoms, however, are important for diagnosis and can be easily elicited. The diagnostic differentiation between depression and anxiety in general health care settings is not clinically valid. Culturally appropriate terminology for depression can be identified and their use may improve levels of recognition and treatment compliance. It is also evident that culture is only one factor in the difference between, and within, human societies which has a bearing on the epidemiology of depression. Other factors, which may interact with culture, such as gender and income inequality, are major risk factors for depression. Future international research must focus on two themes: (i) intervention studies including cost-effectiveness outcomes; and (ii) research aiming to bridge the gap between regional public health priorities and the concern that psychiatrists have about depression.

Correspondence to:
Dr Vikram Patel,
Sangath Centre,
841/1 Alto Porvorim,
Goa 403521, India

The debate on the extent and nature of the influence of cultural variables on psychiatric syndromes and mental health services has been extensively covered elsewhere[1–3]. In particular, this debate has focused on the theoretical rationales of the 'etic' and 'emic' approaches which emphasized either biological universality or cultural diversity, respectively. The assumption that mental illnesses as conceptualized by a dominantly biomedically based psychiatry was automatically valid in the rest of the world is the basis of the 'etic' approach. This approach underpins the bulk of epidemiological research world-wide. The effort to acknowledge and incorporate the profound role played by culture in the experience, expression, diagnosis and management of mental illness (the 'emic' approach) had its roots in the increasing role of medical anthropology in healthcare, particularly in non-industrialised countries.

The 'emic' approach suggested that psychiatric classifications in the West were as much a product of its own culture as the apparently exotic foreign conditions which were dumped into the miscellaneous categories of ICD. A general consensus emerged that both approaches had their limitations and strengths and that, for psychiatric research to be 'culturally and biologically correct', an integration of methods and concepts was required. As a result of this debate, culture became firmly ensconced as a key variable in psychiatric epidemiology, particularly when the research was based in non-Western societies.

As a researcher working in non-industrialised countries, the author was profoundly influenced by the theories of this 'new' cross-cultural psychiatry. These theories formed the basis of a series of ethnographic and epidemiological studies on depression in two, apparently culturally different, developing societies (Zimbabwe and India). This article uses this research evidence to question the actual contribution of culture on the international epidemiology of depression. The article proposes that culture is only one variable, and arguably not the most important one, which needs to be taken into account in international epidemiology of mental disorders. The health systems model provides a more relevant and pragmatic framework for the investigation of mental disorders from an international perspective[4].

The relevance of cross-cultural psychiatry: a critique

An important anomaly in cross-cultural psychiatry is that it is largely a specialty of interest to researchers and academics, particularly in industrialised countries. It is not accidental that the recent surge of interest in culture as an independent variable in the design and interpretation of psychiatric research coincides with the spectacular demographic change in the ethnic composition of many industrialised countries. The majority of research initiated by researchers in non-industrialised countries mimics the 'etic' approach and 'culture' is rarely considered as an independent variable. Another major anomaly is that whereas Western societies are considered 'multi-cultural' so that studies need to be conducted for different ethnic groups to ensure findings are 'culturally correct', non-industrialised societies are not offered the same privilege. It is common to see studies from vast, and hugely diverse, countries such as India or China being used to suggest that the findings are representative of the culture of the entire nation. Such naive assumptions have greatly limited the value of cross-cultural studies where the choice of country settings are used as a means of ensuring representativeness of cultural diversity. Furthermore, there is often an implicit assumption that non-Western cultures are, by definition, 'traditional' or 'non-scientific' in their explanatory models.

Research from Western cultures is considered to be of international significance whereas research from non-industrialised countries is of interest for its demonstration of the influence of culture on psychiatric disorders[5].

The main limitation of cross-cultural psychiatry, of course, is that it fails to recognize that cultures are dynamic, complex social constructs which defy easy definition or measurement. One definition of culture is that it is 'the customs, civilization and achievements of a particular time or people' (*Concise Oxford Dictionary*, 9th edn). This suggests that cultures are ever-changing; herein lies the key factor which influences the role of culture in international epidemiology. Globalization has been phenomenal in its impact on culture; no longer are cultures living in relative isolation from one another so that attitudes, practices and beliefs evolve separately in different cultures. Instead, cultures are integrating, with values and beliefs from one culture finding new homes in other cultures. While the process of globalization may work in diverse ways, in reality, the dominant cultures are those of industrialised societies because much of the mechanisms of globalization, such as the media, are largely controlled by these societies. The homogenization of cultures across the non-industrialised world in the past decade is a marker of the vulnerability of cultures to the onslaught of modern marketing and global media networks. In the face of this reality, one of the key rationales behind cross-cultural psychiatry is becoming rapidly redundant. Thus, this is an opportune time to consider a paradigm shift from cross-cultural psychiatry to an international psychiatry as discussed later. At this point, however, it would be fair to give due justice to the large and important body of work generated in the field of cross-cultural psychiatry. These studies have approached the international epidemiology of depression from a number of perspectives. The next section of this paper will consider some of the key questions posed and answered by cross-cultural psychiatric research on depression.

Culture and diagnosis of depression

Symptoms of depression

Several studies have described the clinical presentations of depression in primary and general health care settings. The commonest complaints are somatic, in particular tiredness and weakness, multiple aches and pains, dizziness, palpitations and sleep disturbances. However, psychological symptoms can be elicited relatively easily on inquiry. Thus, typical psychological symptoms such as loss of interest in daily or social activities, suicidal thoughts, poor concentration and anxiety or worry can are experienced by the majority of patients. Earlier theories suggested that somatic symptoms were the 'cultural' equivalent of depression and that somatization, the process by which psychological distress was 'converted' to somatic symptoms, was typical in non-industrialised countries. This hypothesis has now proven to be wrong in two respects. First, somatic symptoms are also the commonest presenting features of depression in industrialised societies[6,7]; second, the classic psychological symptoms of depression can often be elicited[8–10]. Acute presentations of depression are more likely to be somatic; as the illness becomes chronic the patient re-evaluates the illness and becomes more likely to present with psychological symptoms[11]. These, in turn, make them more likely to be detected by the physician. Thus, culture plays a limited role in the experience of common symptoms of depression; however, volunteering of these symptoms by patients in health care encounters may be influenced by stigma and awareness of depression as an illness category. Furthermore, some symptoms, such as visual hallucinations, may occur in the context of depression in some cultures[12]; these are, however, not crucial or central to the diagnosis of depression.

Culture and measurement of depression

A variety of screening questionnaires and interviews have been used internationally for the study of depression. Among the screening questionnaires, both locally developed measures and local versions of foreign measures have been used. Perhaps the most commonly used screening questionnaire is the *General Health Questionnaire*[13]. Cut-off scores for caseness have been found to vary considerably between centres[14]. Similarly, the 20 item *Self Reporting Questionnaire* (SRQ)[15], another widely used screening questionnaire in non-industrialised countries, was found to have a cut-off score in African countries often higher than the standard cut-off[16]. This re-affirms the need to evaluate the validity of screening questionnaires as an essential prerequisite of any study using them in a new population[14,17]. Short 5 item versions of the GHQ have been developed and evaluated in India and these investigations have shown that the shorter versions are as sensitive and specific as the longer versions[8,18]. In clinical settings, simple screening questions derived from such short questionnaires, focusing on loss of interest, sleep problems, tiredness and feelings of sadness may provide a sensitive method of identifying cases of depression[19]. Examples of locally developed screening questionnaire include the *Primary Care Psychiatric Questionnaire* (PPQ)[20] in India, the *Shona Symptom Questionnaire* in Zimbabwe[12], and the *Chinese Health Questionnaire*[21]. In general, the item composition of these indigenous measures share much with the questionnaires developed in the West, and there is a high degree of agreement in case classification[16]. Despite the high frequency of somatic symptoms, psychological symptoms have a higher sensitivity and specificity for the diagnosis of depression[8,22]. This may be due to the fact that somatic symptoms such as tiredness can also occur in a variety of chronic infectious and other diseases common in non-industrialised countries. Of the structured interviews, the *Revised Clinical Interview Schedule* (CISR), which was specifically developed for the measurement of common mental disorders in community and primary care settings[23], has been widely used in studies in the international context. The PSE and its successors, the SCAN and CIDI, has been used in the WHO multi-national studies. There are few examples of indigenous structured interviews, including the *Indian Psychiatric Survey Schedule*[24]. It is evident that the measurement of depression in the international context can be undertaken with similar instruments in different cultural settings, provided care is taken to ensure an adequate translation and validation of the cut-off score.

Culture and classification

Classification of depression remains a contentious issue. The first major issue is that diagnostic labels such as depression and phobias have no conceptually equivalent term in many non-European languages. These terms, derived from European cultures, have made the leap from common language to medical classifications and, in the process, acquired a biomedical significance. Thus, 'depression' in medicine is seen as being closely linked to mood changes. Using such labels in non-European cultures often leads to the mistaken belief that the experience of sadness is an essential presenting feature of the disorder. Terms such as common mental disorders, though offering some advantages over 'depression' because they do not imply a specific mood state, also have problems. The word 'mental' is associated with severe mental disorders and asylums. In settings where these are associated with a generally poor quality of care and outcome, patients and health care providers are understandably reluctant to stigmatise their patients as being 'mental' cases[25]. Thus, while the experience of dysphoric mood may be a universal human phenomenon, the concept of depressive disorder which focuses on the mood change as the primary or core feature of the disorder has evolved from within a Western culture and may not be universally applicable[26]. This problem is not just a semantic one and may account, in part, for the low recognition rates of depression (see below). Even in psychiatric settings, only a quarter of patients in one study attributed their symptoms to a mental illness, while 'nerves' was cited by half[27]. Arguably, a more acceptable alternative to any of the above terms would come through the identification of local concepts which bear some similarity to the construct of depression. Such constructs have been identified in several cultures, such as the construct of thinking too much or *kufungisisa* in the Shona language of Zimbabwe[28] and neurasthenia in China[29]. Another difficulty in the classification of depression refers to the clinical validity of the distinction between depression and anxiety. The recent WHO multinational study in general healthcare found that 'co-morbidity' of depression and anxiety exceeded 50%[30]. This considerable overlap, which agrees with other studies and clinical evidence that patients in primary care tend to have a general spectrum of anxiety and depressive symptoms[31], diminishes the validity of a meaningful distinction between these two constructs. In this instance, it would appear that it is the 'culture' of biomedical, tertiary-care oriented psychiatry which differs from the clinical reality of depression in culturally diverse populations.

Culture and aetiology of depression

Like most psychiatric disorders, the precise aetiology of depression remains unclear. The vast majority of international studies of depression have focused on sociodemographic and life-event risk factors for depression. These have conclusively shown the following findings: women, persons with less education, and persons who are less economically privileged are at significantly higher risk to suffer depression.

Gender and depression

Both community-based studies and studies of treatment seekers indicate that women are disproportionately affected by depression[32,33]. The obvious question thrown up by these findings are the reasons for this apparent vulnerability. There are a number of potential factors which may make women more vulnerable to suffer depression. Theories have ranged from biological perspectives with a focus on hormonal and physiological factors associated with reproduction, to the pervasive effects of oppression and lack of opportunities in all spheres of life as a result of gender inequality[34]. There is considerable evidence demonstrating that stressful life events are closely associated with depression and such events are more common in the lives of women[35]. Thus, women are far more likely to be victims of violence in their homes. Difficulties for women are encountered in a number of different areas such as their social position, aspirations and domestic problems. The reproductive roles of women, such as her expected role of bearing children, the consequences of infertility and the failure to produce a male child have been linked to wife battering and female suicide[33,34]. Women are far more likely to be denied educational and occupational opportunities and access to appropriate health care. Culture plays a profound role in determining the vulnerability posed by gender; for example, the pervasive influence of boy preference on gender status and the perceived life-roles for men and women in South Asia[36].

Poverty and depression

There is a large body of evidence demonstrating the association between poverty and depression in industrialised countries. In recent years, population-based research has demonstrated higher risk for depression and suicide in those who are unemployed[37–39], those who have relatively lower income[40], and those who have a relatively lower standard of living[41]. Such population-based data are also evident from non-industrialised countries. Five recent cross-sectional surveys of treatment seekers and community samples from Brazil, Zimbabwe, India and Chile were collated to examine the economic risk factors for depression. In all 5 studies, there was a consistent, and significant, relationship between low income and risk to suffer depression[32]. There was also a relationship between proxy indicators of impoverishment and depression; for example, those who had experienced hunger recently and those who were in debt were more likely to suffer depression. Other studies have demonstrated the relationship between depression and other indicators of poverty such as education and household amenities[22,42,43]. There is also evidence, from prospective longitudinal studies, that economic deprivation is associated with persistence and incidence of depression[44]. Culture plays a role in determining the vulnerability of the poor for depression in a number of ways, such as the caste system of South Asia which relegates a section of the population to subservient roles or the economic disadvantages faced by ethnic minorities in multicultural societies across the world.

Culture and management of depression

Pathways to care

In all parts of the world, the vast majority of depressed patients seen by biomedical health care professionals are in general or primary health care settings. The *International Pathways to Care Study* examined the referral pathways taken by patients referred to mental health services in

11 countries, including 7 non-industrialised countries in Asia, Africa and Latin America. Thus, the study was located in patients attending psychiatric care, which would be expected to reflect a small, and unrepresentative, fraction of the population suffering from any type of mental disorder. By far, the commonest route of referral was the general medical practitioner based in a family practice setting or in a hospital out-patient clinic setting[45]. A study from Harare, Zimbabwe described the pathways to primary care for patients with conspicuous common mental disorders attending primary care clinics and traditional medical clinics. Other than those patients with an acute illness, most patients consulted more than one care provider; three-quarters of those with a history of prior consultations had consulted both traditional and biomedical care providers. The first care provider sought for the illness was most often a biomedical carer. The finding is consonant with the cultural concepts of illness; thus, illness at onset is considered to be a 'normal' illness and is taken to a biomedical carer. If this treatment fails, or if the patients' expectations are not fulfilled, he will consult a traditional carer[46]. Depression is rarely considered to be a mental disorder in many non-industrialised countries and thus mental health professionals are perceived to have a limited role in its management[25,47]. Thus, attitudes and beliefs about illness causation, which are considerably influenced by culture, will determine the pathways to care.

Recognition and treatment

Primary care physicians recognize up to a third of psychological morbidity; this rate has been reported to be highly variable across centres being influenced by a number of factors such as the training of doctors[22,30,48]. In addition to low awareness or somatization, low recognition can be attributed to a number of other factors such as discomfort in recording distress states as a mental illness which were associated with considerable stigma and the perceived lack of personal skills in dealing with 'mental' problems.

There is robust evidence that antidepressants and brief psychological treatments such as problem-solving are efficacious treatments for depression[49,50], although virtually all the treatment evidence is from industrialised countries. The most typical treatment response by general physicians is to prescribe greater number of drugs (such as benzo-diazepines) and injectable vitamins[48]. The WHO *Multinational Study in General Health Care* reported that nearly 10% of primary care attenders in the Indian centre were prescribed psychotropic drugs, a figure similar to that of many European and North American centres[51]. However, the majority of prescriptions were for tranquilizers rather than antidepressant drugs; for example, while 50% of patients with anxiety disorders received tranquilizers, none received antidepressants. A similar, if less marked, imbalance was also recorded for patients with depressive syndromes. As might be expected, prescription of psychotropics was maximum in those patients whose mental disorder was recognised by the physician; recognition, in turn, was influenced by the severity of symptoms and the presence of overt psychological symptoms. A remarkable finding of the study was that nearly 80% of all prescriptions were for 'drugs of unproven clinical efficacy' such as tonics and tranquilizers[51]. These findings resonate with the earlier discussion on somatization in primary care[8]; thus, physicians are more likely to diagnose a mental illness when patients present with psychological symptoms, but tend to use inappropriate medications suggesting lack of knowledge or confidence in psychopharmacology as a key factor. The use of psychosocial and psychotherapeutic interventions is even lower[52]. Culture thus plays a role in the diagnosis of depression; however, the treatment of depression is more likely to be influenced by factors such as awareness and availability of effective interventions. Cultural factors may play a role in the acceptability of certain interventions, in particular psychological interventions in non-industrialised countries[53].

From cross-cultural epidemiology to international epidemiology

There is evidence that the prevalence of depressive illnesses is high in both industrialised and non-industrialised countries. Studies from diverse settings ranging from rural Lesotho, the slums of São Paulo and Santiago in South America and the urban general practices of India reveal prevalence figures of depression exceeding 30% in community samples and approaching 50% in primary care samples[9,24,54]. The high prevalence of depression is of concern for many reasons. First, the social factors known to be linked to depression are on the increase throughout the world as the formula for economic development adopted by most countries is leading to a reduction in public health expenditure, a rising inequality between the rich and poor, increased migration to urban areas with its attendant rise in urban squalor and rapid culture change as the great urban centres take on an international cosmopolitan flavour. Secondly, there is the much replicated association between depression and disability independent of any co-existing physical illness[55]. Thus, those who are already vulnerable due to their gender or social circumstances risk becoming ill with a disorder which will further disable them and render them less able to cope with the adverse circumstances that they already faced. Third, despite considerable epidemiological research from both multinational and local research initiatives, most individuals with a depression remain undiagnosed and untreated.

The priorities for international research on depression need to move well beyond its focus on examining cultural influences on depression to action-oriented research which serves to inform regional health policy and practice[4]. Health policy is unlikely to be influenced by research as long as the only evidence available are the astronomical numbers of persons with depression thrown up regularly by surveys, but no demonstrated affordable solutions for these problems. Due to considerable variations in cultural models, pharmacodynamic factors, health service variations and drug availability, there is a need for generating efficacy and cost-effectiveness evidence from different regions of the world. However, there is little evidence of this kind available today[53]. Thus a major research priority must be the evaluation of the efficacy and cost-effectiveness of health service interventions and treatments for various nervous systems disorders[56]. The second major research priority is examining the relationship between depression and other health priorities. Thus, in many non-industrialised countries, child development, poverty alleviation, reproductive health and violence are the main priorities. There are obvious mental health implications for these priorities; for example, learning disabilities are associated with poor school performance and drop-outs; poverty is linked to depression and suicide; reproductive health is associated with post-natal depression; and violence is associated with a range of adverse mental health outcomes. Such research, by working within the framework of existing priorities will lead to practical information which is of value to existing health programmes and which, in turn, is likely to make it more amenable for wider acceptance and implementation. Such research would be relatively cheap to implement since they could be 'piggy-backed' onto existing programmes of research.

An ethical imperative of international epidemiological research is empowerment of local health researchers to conduct and lead research programmes. Raising capacity must be a core element of all research in non-industrialised countries, most of all in the field of psychiatry where these skills are still extremely difficult to obtain. The 'dash-in-dash-out' research strategy where highly skilled researchers from industrialised countries 'collaborate' with economically and academically weaker colleagues in non-industrialised countries to conduct research programmes with little local capacity building has dubious ethical standards. Dissemination must be a multifaceted targeting, in addition to the academics, policy makers, health care providers and the general community.

Key points for clinical practice

- The clinical presentation of depression in all cultures is multiple somatic symptoms of chronic duration; psychological symptoms are important for diagnosis and can be easily elicited in most patients

- The diagnostic differentiation between depression and anxiety in general health care is not clinically useful since they typically occur together and the treatments are similar

- Awareness of culturally appropriate terminology for depression is a useful way of bridging the gap between lay and biomedical models of illness and may help improve levels of recognition and treatment compliance

- Women and the poor are at greater risk to suffer depression

- Treatment of depression should include antidepressants or problem-solving therapy, either of which can be delivered in general health care settings with relative ease and efficacy

Acknowledgements

The author wishes to acknowledge the Wellcome Trust, the MacArthur Foundation, IDRC and the Beit Trust which have supported his research on depression in Zimbabwe and India.

References

1   Kleinman A. Anthropology and psychiatry: the role of culture in cross-cultural research on illness. *Br J Psychiatry* 1987; **151**: 447–54
2   Littlewood R. From categories to contexts: a decade of the 'new cross-cultural psychiatry'. *Br J Psychiatry* 1990; **156**: 308–27
3   Patel V, Winston M. The 'universality' of mental disorder revisited: assumptions, artefacts and new directions. *Br J Psychiatry* 1994; **165**: 437–40
4   Patel V. Health systems research: a pragmatic model for meeting mental health needs in low-income countries. In: Andrews G, Henderson S. (eds) *Unmet Need in Psychiatry.* Cambridge: Cambridge University Press, 2000; 353–77
5   Patel V, Sumathipala A. International representation in psychiatric journals: a survey of 6 leading journals. *Br J Psychiatry*. 2001; **178**: 406–9
6   Bhatt A, Tomenson B, Benjamin S. Transcultural patterns of somatization in primary care: a preliminary report. *J Psychosom Res* 1989; **33**: 671–80
7   Katon W, Walker EA. Medically unexplained symptoms in primary care. *J Clin Psychiatry* 1998; **59 (Suppl 20)**: 15–21
8   Patel V, Pereira J, Mann A. Somatic and psychological models of common mental disorders in India. *Psychol Med* 1998; **28**: 135–43
9   Araya R, Robert W, Richard L, Lewis G. Psychiatric morbidity in primary health care in Santiago, Chile. Preliminary findings. *Br J Psychiatry* 1994; **165**: 530–2
10 Patel V, Gwanzura F, Simunyu E, Mann A, Lloyd K. The explanatory models and phenomenology of common mental disorder in Harare, Zimbabwe. *Psychol Med* 1995; **25**: 1191–9
11 Weich S, Lewis G, Donmall R, Mann A. Somatic presentation of psychiatric morbidity in general practice. *Br J Gen Pract* 1995; **45**: 143–7
12 Patel V, Simunyu E, Gwanzura F, Lewis G, Mann A. The Shona Symptom Questionnaire: the development of an indigenous measure of non-psychotic mental disorder in Harare. *Acta Psychiatr Scand* 1997; **95**: 469–75

13 Goldberg D, Williams P. *A User's Guide to the General Health Questionnaire.* Windsor: NFER-Nelson, 1988

14 Goldberg D, Oldehinkel T, Ormel J. Why GHQ threshold varies from one place to another. *Psychol Med* 1998; **28**: 915–21

15 Harding TW, De Arango MV, Baltazar J *et al.* Mental disorders in primary health care: a study of their frequency and diagnosis in four developing countries. *Psychol Med* 1980; **10**: 231–41

16 Patel V, Todd CH. The validity of the Shona version of the Self Report Questionnaire (SRQ) and the development of the SRQ8. *Int J Methods Psychiatr Res* 1996; **6**: 153–60

17 Sen B, Mari J. Psychiatric research instruments in the transcultural setting: experiences in India and Brazil. *Soc Sci Med* 1986; **23**: 277–81

18 Shamasundar C, Sriram T, Murali Raj G, Shanmugham V. Validity of a short 5-item version of the general health questionnaire (G.H.Q.). *Indian J Psychiatry* 1986; **28**: 217–9

19 Ballenger JC, Davidson JRT, Lecrubier Y *et al.* Consensus statement on the primary care management of depression from the International Consensus Group on Depression and Anxiety. *J Clin Psychiatry* 1999; **60 (Suppl 7)**: 54–61

20 Srinivasan TN, Suresh TR. Non-specific symptoms and screening of non-psychotic morbidity in primary care. *Indian J Psychiatry* 1990; **32**: 77–82

21 Cheng TA, Williams P. The design and development of a screening questionnaire (CHQ) for use in community studies of mental disorders in Taiwan. *Psychol Med* 1986; **16**: 415–22

22 Amin G, Shah S, Vankar GK. The prevalence and recognition of depression in primary care. *Indian J Psychiatry* 1998; **40**: 364–9

23 Lewis G, Pelosi A, Araya R, Dunn G. Measuring psychiatric disorder in the community: a standardized assessment for use by lay interviewers. *Psychol Med* 1992; **22**: 465–86

24 Shamasundar C, Krishna Murthy S, Prakash O, Prabhakar N, Subbakrishna D. Psychiatric morbidity in a general practice in an Indian city. *BMJ* 1986; **292**: 1713–5

25 Patel V. Recognizing common mental disorders in primary care in African countries: should 'mental' be dropped? *Lancet* 1996; **347**: 742–4

26 Bebbington P. Transcultural aspects of affective disorders. *Int Rev Psychiatry* 1993; **5**: 145–56

27 Channabasavanna SM, Raguram R, Weiss M, Parvathavardhini R, Thriveni M. Ethnography of psychiatric illness: a pilot study. *NIMHANS Jnl* 1993; **11**: 1–10

28 Patel V, Simunyu E, Gwanzura F. Kufungisisa (thinking too much): a Shona idiom for non-psychotic mental illness. *Cent Afr J Med* 1995; **41**: 209–15

29 Kleinman A, Kleinman J. Somatization: the interconnections in Chinese society among culture, depressive experiences, and the meanings of pain. In: Kleinman A, Good B. (eds) *Culture and Depression.* Berkeley, CA: University of California Press, 1985; 429–90

30 Goldberg D, Lecrubier Y. Form and frequency of mental disorders across cultures. In: Ustun TB, Sartorius N. (eds) *Mental Illness in General Health Care: An International Study.* Chichester: John Wiley, 1995; 323–34

31 Sen B, Williams P. The extent and nature of depressive phenomena in primary health care: a study in Calcutta, India. *Br J Psychiatry* 1987; **151**: 486–93

32 Patel V, Araya R, Lima MS, Ludermir A, Todd C. Women, poverty and common mental disorders in four restructuring societies. *Soc Sci Med* 1999; **49**: 1461–71

33 Dennerstein L, Astbury J, Morse C. Psychosocial and mental health aspects of women's health. Geneva: World Health Organization, 1993

34 Davar B. *The Mental Health of Indian Women: A Feminist Agenda.* New Delhi: Sage (India), 1999

35 Broadhead J, Abas M. Life events and difficulties and the onset of depression among women in a low-income urban setting in Zimbabwe. *Psychol Med* 1998; **28**: 29–38

36 Cohen A. Excess female mortality in India: the case of Himachal Pradesh. *Am J Public Health* 2001; **90**: 1369–71

37 Bartley M. Unemployment and ill health: understanding the relationship. *J Epidemiol Community Health* 1994; **48**: 333–7

38 Gunnell DJ, Peters TJ, Kammerling RM, Brooks J. Relation between parasuicide, suicide, psychiatric admissions, and socioeconomic deprivation. *BMJ* 1995; **311**: 226–30

39 Lewis G, Sloggett A. Suicide, deprivation and unemployment: record linkage study. *BMJ* 1998; **317**: 1283–6

40   Weich S, Lewis G. Poverty, unemployment and the common mental disorders: a population based cohort study. *BMJ* 1998; **317**: 115–9

41   Lewis G, Bebbington P, Brugha TS *et al*. Socioeconomic status, standard of living and neurotic disorder. *Lancet* 1998; **352**: 605–9

42   Bahar E, Henderson AS, Mackinnon AJ. An epidemiological study of mental health and socioeconomic conditions in Sumatera, Indonesia. *Acta Psychiatr Scand* 1992; **85**: 257–63

43   Mumford DB, Saeed K, Ahmad I, Latif S, Mubbashar M. Stress and psychiatric disorder in rural Punjab. A community survey. *Br J Psychiatry* 1997; **170**: 473–8

44   Todd C, Patel V, Simunyu E *et al*. The onset of common mental disorders in primary care attenders in Harare, Zimbabwe. *Psychol Med* 1999; **29**: 97–104

45   Gater R, De Almeida E Sousa B, Barrientos G *et al*. The pathways to psychiatric care: a cross-cultural study. *Psychol Med* 1991; **21**: 761–74

46   Patel V, Simunyu E, Gwanzura F. The pathways to primary mental health care in Harare, Zimbabwe. *Soc Psychiatry Psychiatr Epidemiol* 1997; **32**: 97–103

47   Patel V., Todd CH, Winston M *et al*. The outcome of common mental disorders in Harare, Zimbabwe. *Br J Psychiatry* 1998; **172**: 53–7

48   Patel V, Pereira J, Coutinho L, Fernandes R, Fernandes J, Mann A. Poverty, psychological disorder and disability in primary care attenders in Goa, India. *Br J Psychiatry* 1998; **171**: 533–6

49   Mynors-Wallis L, Gath D, Lloyd-Thomas A, Tomlinson D. Randomised controlled trial comparing problem solving treatment with amitryptiline and placebo for major depression in primary care. *BMJ* 1995; **310**: 441–5

50   Bech P, Cialdella M, Haugh MC *et al*. Meta-analysis of randomised controlled trials of fluoxetine vs placebo and tricyclic antidepressants in the short-term treatment of major depression. *Br J Psychiatry* 2000; **176**: 421–8

51   Linden M, Lecrubier Y, Bellantuono C, Benkert O, Kisely S, Simon G. The prescribing of psychotropic drugs by primary care physicians: an international collaborative study. *J Clin Psychopharmacol* 1999; **19**: 132–40

52   Channabasavanna SM, Sriram T, Kumar K. Results from the Bangalore Centre. In: Ustun TB, Sartorius N. (eds) *Mental Illness in General Health Care: An International Study*. Chichester: John Wiley, 1995; 79–97

53   Patel V. Why we need treatment evidence for common mental disorders in developing countries. *Psychol Med* 2000; **30**: 743–6

54   Hollifield M, Katon W, Spain D, Pule L. Anxiety and depression in a village in Lesotho, Africa: a comparison with the United States. *Br J Psychiatry* 1990; **156**: 343–50

55   Ormel J, Von Korff M, Ustun TB, Pini S, Korten A, Oldehinkel T. Common mental disorders and disability across cultures. *JAMA* 1994; **272**: 1741–8

56   Ustun TB. The global burden of mental disorders. *Am J Public Health* 1999; **89**: 1315–8

Depression, suicide and deliberate self-harm in adolescence

Richard Harrington

University Department of Child and Adolescent Psychiatry, Royal Manchester Children's Hospital, Manchester, UK

The past decade has seen important advances in research into the epidemiology, aetiology and treatment of depression and suicidal behaviour in the young. We are beginning to understand how risk factors combine to precipitate and maintain these problems. There is rarely a linear relationship between causes and outcomes. Rather, the cause is usually a combination of predisposing constitutional factors arising from genetic endowment or earlier experience and precipitating stressful events. These aetiological factors act through biochemical, psychological and social processes to produce the outcome. Progress has also been in the development of a range of effective treatments, such as 'here and now' psychological treatments and antidepressants. All depressed or suicidal young people require careful assessment. Some will require a brief intervention only. Others, however, will require more intensive and lengthy forms of treatment.

Depressive disorder

Assessment of depression

Defining the boundaries between extremes of normal behaviour and psychopathology is a dilemma that pervades all of psychiatry. It is especially problematic to establish the limits of depressive disorder in young people because of the cognitive and physical changes that take place during this time. Adolescents tend to feel things particularly deeply and marked mood swings are common during the teens. It can be difficult to distinguish these intense emotional reactions from depressive disorders. By contrast, young adolescents do not find it easy to describe how they are feeling and often confuse emotions such as anger and sadness. They have particular difficulty describing certain of the key cognitive symptoms of depression, such as hopelessness and self-denigration.

Assessment of young people who present with symptoms of depression must, therefore, begin with the basic question of diagnosis. This will mean interviewing the adolescent alone. It is not enough to rely on

Correspondence to:
Prof. Richard Harrington,
University Department of
Child and Adolescent
Psychiatry, Royal
Manchester Children's
Hospital, Pendlebury,
Manchester M27 4HA, UK

accounts obtained from the parents since they may not notice depression in their offspring, and may not even be aware of suicidal attempts. Indeed, it is now common practice to obtain information from several sources. Adolescents usually give a better account of symptoms related to internal experience whereas parents are likely to be better informants on overt behavioural difficulties. Accounts from young people and parents are usually supplemented by information from other sources, particularly teachers and direct observations.

Although the interviewing of multiple informants may yield much useful information, the diagnosis of depressive disorder in young people can still be very difficult. Standardised diagnostic systems such as the DSM-IV[1] and structured psychiatric interviews can help in deciding whether the patient has serious depressive symptomatology that requires treatment. Unfortunately, such diagnostic systems tend to be over-inclusive in this age group, and many dysphoric adolescents who meet criteria for major depression remit within a few weeks[2]. It is important, then, that careful inquiry is made about the impact the young person's symptoms have had on everyday functioning and about the presence of symptoms of unequivocal psychopathological significance, such as suicidal planning or marked weight loss. Probably the best single indicator of whether or not a young person has a serious depressive disorder is the duration of the problem. Polysymptomatic depressive states that persist for more than 6 weeks usually require intervention.

Assessment and differential diagnosis of other difficulties

Although the accurate diagnosis of depressive disorder is an important part of clinical management, assessment only starts with the diagnosis, it does not stop with it. Depressed adolescents usually have multiple problems, such as educational failure, impaired psychosocial functioning, and co-morbid psychiatric disorders. Indeed, it seems that most adolescents who meet research criteria for depressive disorder are given some other primary diagnosis by the clinicians involved in their care[3]. This overlap of depression and other psychiatric diagnoses has been one of the most consistent findings from research in referred clinical populations, where an association has been found with conditions as diverse as conduct disorder, anxiety states, learning problems, hyper-activity, anorexia nervosa and school refusal[4,5]. Moreover, depressed adolescents tend to come from families with high rates of psycho-pathology and may have experienced adverse life events[6]. All these problems need to be identified and the causes of each assessed.

The final part of the assessment involves the evaluation of the young person's personal and social resources. There is evidence that being successful at school or in other areas of life can protect young people from the effects of adverse life experiences[7]. The best guide to the child's ability to solve future problems is his or her record in dealing with difficulties in the past. The ability of the family to support the patient should also be evaluated.

Epidemiology

Rates of depressive disorder vary greatly between studies, depending on how it is defined. The one year prevalence is probably around 2% or less[8,9]. Almost all recent epidemiological research has found that depressive disorder is much less common among pre-adolescent children than among adolescents[10]. Pre-adolescent depression shows an equal gender ratio, but by mid-adolescence the female preponderance found in adult depression is established. The prevalence of depressive disorders may be increasing among young people[11], though most of the evidence of a secular trend comes from retrospective reports of age at onset of depression in family and community studies of depressed adults.

Aetiology

The aetiology of child and adolescent depressive disorders is likely to be multifactorial, including both genetic and environmental factors. Genetic factors account for a substantial amount of the variance in liability to bipolar illness in adults, but probably play a less substantial, though still significant, part in unipolar depressive conditions[12]. Interest in the genetics of depressive disorders arising in young people has been simulated by data from several sources. First, it seems that among adult samples, earlier age of onset is associated with an increased familial loading for depression[13]. Second, the children of depressed parents have greater than expected rates of depression[14]. Third, there are high rates of affective disorders among the first degree relatives of depressed child probands[15]. Moreover, there is some specificity in this linkage to the extent that the risk applies mainly to affective disturbances as opposed to non-affective disorders[16].

It will be appreciated that just because a disorder runs in families, it does not necessarily follow that the linkages are mediated genetically. It is likely that family environmental factors are also important. For instance, discordant intrafamilial relationships seem to be strong predictors of the course of depressive disorders among the young. Children with depression who have been admitted to hospital who return to families who show high levels of criticism and discord have a much worse outcome than children returning to more harmonious environments[17]. Stresses and acute life events outside of the family, such as friendship difficulties and bullying, are also likely to be relevant in this age group[18].

Current models of depression in young people also emphasize the importance of bi-directional influences. Depression and its associated symptoms such as irritability can be a cause of family and peer difficulties, as well as a consequence. It is possible that negative cycles of interaction are started, in which depression causes family environmental problems, which in turn lead to worsening of the depression[19].

The psychological and biological mechanisms that link these risk factors to depression remain poorly understood. The most influential of the psychological models (which have had important implications for treatment – see later) have been the so-called cognitive theories, which were first developed with adult cases of depression. The main idea behind these theories is that depressed people develop a distorted perception of the world (such as the expectation that things will always go wrong), which is caused by earlier adversity. When the child experiences current adversity, these negative cognitions become manifest and this then leads to depression. The occurrence of distorted negative cognitions has been documented in numerous studies of depressed young people though their causal role is still uncertain[20].

Biological theories have consisted, for the most part, of straight forward downward extensions of models first developed with adult cases. The best known theory is the amine hypothesis, which proposes that depression is caused by underactivity in cerebral amine systems. This hypothesis arose from studies of adults in which it was found that drugs that alter cerebral amine concentrations, such as imipramine, are also associated with changes in mood. Several studies of young people with depressive disorders have reported abnormalities of the biological markers that are thought to reflect the activity of these systems[21]. However, it is still not clear if these abnormalities cause depression.

Course and outcome

By comparison with non-depressed subjects, young people diagnosed as depressed are more likely to have subsequent episodes of depression[22]. This increased risk of recurrence extends into adulthood. Harrington and colleagues[3] followed up 63 depressed children and adolescents on average 18 years after their initial contact. The depressed group was 4 times more likely to have an episode of depression after the age of 17 years than a control group who had been matched on a large number of variables, including non-depressive symptoms. A preliminary report from a large follow-up study in the US has found increased rates of completed suicide in depressed adolescent patients[23].

Although the risk of recurrence of juvenile depression is high, it is important to know that the prognosis for the index episode is quite good. The available data suggest that the majority of children with major depression will recover within 2 years. For example, Kovacs and colleagues[24] reported that the cumulative probability of recovery from major depression by 1 year after onset was 74% and by 2 years was 92%.

It seems, then, that most young people with major depression will recover to a significant extent, but that a substantial proportion of those who recover will relapse.

Management

Initial management

The initial management of depressed young people depends greatly on the nature of the problems identified during the assessment. The assessment may indicate that the reaction of the child is appropriate for the situation. In such a case, and if the depression is mild, an early approach can consist of a few sympathetic discussions with the child and the parents, simple measures to reduce stress, and encouraging support. Around one-third of mild or moderately depressed adolescents will remit following this kind of brief non-specific intervention[25].

Cases that persist will require more specific and lengthy forms of treatment. First, however, the clinician should consider a number of issues. The first is whether the depression is severe enough to warrant admission to hospital. Indications for admission of depressed young people include severe suicidality, psychotic symptoms or refusal to eat or drink. A related question is whether the child should remain at school. When the disorder is mild, school can be a valuable distraction from depressive thinking. When the disorder is more severe, symptoms such as poor concentration and motor retardation may add to feelings of hopelessness. It is quite common to find in such cases that ensuring that the child obtains tuition in the home, or perhaps in a sheltered school, improves mood considerably.

The second issue is whether the depression is complicated by other disorders such as behavioural problems. If it is, then measures to deal with these other problems must be included in the treatment programme. In some cases, it is best to try to deal with co-morbid problems before embarking on therapy for depression. For instance, it is difficult to conduct psychological therapies for depression when a patient is very underweight because of co-morbid anorexia nervosa. In other cases, it may be possible to treat the co-morbid problem at the same time as the depression.

Managing the social context of depression

The third issue concerns the management of the stresses that are associated with many cases of major depression[26]. It is sometimes possible to alleviate these stresses. For example, bullying at school may be reduced by a discrete phone-call to the head teacher. However, in many cases, acute stressors are just one of a number of causes of the adolescent's depression. Moreover, such stressors commonly arise out of chronic difficulties such as family discord and may, therefore, be very hard to remedy. Symptomatic treatments for depression can, therefore, be helpful even when it is obvious that the depression occurs in the context of chronic adversity that is likely to persist.

Psychosocial interventions

The best studied of the psychological interventions is cognitive-behaviour therapy. Cognitive-behavioural treatment (CBT) programmes were developed to address the cognitive distortions and deficits identified in depressed adolescents (see above). Many varieties of CBT exist for adolescent depression, but they all have the following common characteristics. First, the adolescent is the focus of treatment (although most CBT programmes involve parents). Second, the adolescent and therapist collaborate to solve problems. Third, the therapist teaches the adolescent to monitor and keep a record of thoughts and behaviour. There is, therefore, emphasis on diary keeping and on homework assignments. Fourth, treatment usually combines several different procedures, including behavioural techniques (such as activity scheduling) and cognitive strategies (such as cognitive restructuring). A meta-analysis[25] of six randomised trials with clinically diagnosed cases of depressive disorder found that CBT was significantly superior to comparison conditions such as remaining on a waiting list or having relaxation training (pooled odds ratio of 2.2).

Two other psychological treatments have been evaluated in randomised trials with clinically depressed adolescents. Interpersonal psychotherapy, which like CBT is a brief time limited therapy, aims to help the adolescent to deal with the interpersonal problems that are strongly associated with adolescent depression. A randomised trial has shown significant benefits over non-specific counselling[27]. Family interventions are based on the reliable observation that adolescent depression often occurs in the context of family dysfunction (see above). There have been at least four randomised controlled trials of family therapy in adolescent depressive disorder. Two involved a family intervention only[2,28] and two examined the value of parental sessions given in parallel with individual CBT[29,30]. None has found a significant benefit of the family treatment. Therefore, until there is a firmer empirical basis for family therapy, other interventions will be the treatment of choice.

Biological treatments

Most of the research on pharmacotherapy has been with the tricyclic antidepressants (TCAs), especially imipramine and nortriptyline. The results from early open trials were encouraging but, with the exception of one study, the dozen or so randomized trials have found no significant differences between oral tricyclics and placebo. A meta-analysis of the tricyclic trials[31] found that the pooled response rate was around one-third, less than that generally found when tricyclics are given to depressed adults.

A randomised trial found that the serotonin specific re-uptake inhibitor (SSRI) fluoxetine may be of benefit in children and adolescents with major depression[32]. It is too early to say whether this finding is robust – a small trial with fluoxetine produced a negative result[33]. Nevertheless, it clearly raises the possibility that young people may be more responsive to antidepressants than previously thought, perhaps especially to drugs that act preferentially on serotonergic rather than noradrenergic systems[34].

Electroconvulsive therapy is very seldom used with adolescents, and then only for the most severe life-threatening depressions that have failed to respond to other treatments. For a review, see Walter *et al*[35].

Suicide

Official figures suggest that suicide is very uncommon in childhood and early adolescence. For example, there were no recorded suicides in children under 10 years between 1960 and 1990[36]. However, the rate increases markedly during middle adolescence: in 1990, the suicide rate for males aged 15–19 years was 57 per million, 4 times higher than that for females, at 14 per million. In the UK and US, the rate of suicide increased among male teenagers during the 1970s and 1980s. This increase is also reflected in the rates of 'accidental' and 'undetermined' deaths and is associated with an increase in more lethal methods such as hanging.

Pathways to suicide

Adolescent suicide sometimes occurs without any prior warning, but more commonly it is the endpoint of chronic problems. Figure 1 shows a pathway model of adolescent suicide[37], which postulates three kinds of contributing factor: individual disposition, proximate (trigger) factors, and the social milieu.

Psychological autopsy studies[38] suggest that the most significant predisposing factors are depressive disorder, previous attempts, antisocial behaviour, substance misuse and dependence, and personality traits such as impulsivity or obsessionality. There may be gender differences in the

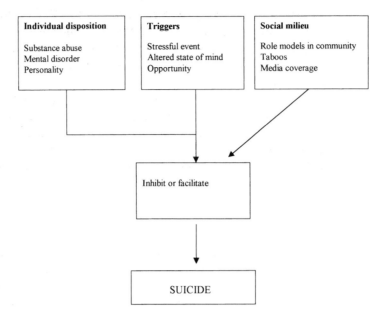

Individual disposition	Triggers	Social milieu
Substance abuse Mental disorder Personality	Stressful event Altered state of mind Opportunity	Role models in community Taboos Media coverage

Inhibit or facilitate

SUICIDE

Fig. 1 Pathway model of teenage suicide (adapted from Shaffer[37]).

ways that these risk factors lead to suicide. Conduct disorder and alcohol misuse are more common among males, but depression is more common among females.

Three factors, often in combination, can trigger a serious suicidal attempt among young people[37]. The first is an acute event such as a disciplinary crisis. An example would be an adolescent who has been caught stealing and who is told by the police that the family will be informed. Other acute stressors include humiliating events or breaking up with a girl or boy friend. The second trigger is any factor that alters the adolescent's state of mind. These include marked hopelessness, rage, or intoxication with drugs or alcohol. The third proximate factor is the opportunity for suicide. The method that young people use to kill themselves varies according to where they live, suggesting that it is in part determined by availability.

The wider social context, such as societal taboos or role models, can also influence the liability to suicidal behaviour. For example, portrayal of deliberate self-harm on television is associated with an increased risk presentation at hospital after deliberate self-poisoning[39].

Deliberate self-harm

Epidemiology

Little is known about the epidemiology of deliberate self-harm (DSH) among young people in the community. Rates of referral to hospital increased markedly during the 1960s and 1970s. The incidence seemed to level out during the 1980s, but may once again be on the increase[40]. The WHO/EURO multicentre hospital study of parasuicide found that the rates of DSH among 15–24-year-olds in the UK were amongst the highest in Europe[41].

Around 90% of DSH cases referred to hospitals involve self-poisoning. Whilst most of these overdoses pose little threat to life, an increasing proportion involve paracetamol, a worrying trend given the irreversible liver damage that it can cause. Self-poisoning is much more common in girls than boys, but laceration shows a less marked female preponderance.

Pathways to deliberate self-harm

DSH in young people is usually precipitated by stressful life problems. The most common are arguments with parents, other family problems, rejection by a boy or girl friend, or school problems such as bullying. These events often occur against a background of long-standing difficulties concerning family, school and behaviour. Adolescents who take overdoses have high rates of behavioural problems and illicit substance use. They have high rates of depressive symptoms, but few have sustained depressive disorders[2]. They tend to come from families that cannot communicate effectively[42]. Some of them, particularly those who repeatedly harm themselves, have been abused. They have often known someone who has harmed themselves.

Comparison between suicide attempters and completers

Although there is much overlap of risk factors for the two problems, there are also some dissimilarities. Suicide completers are more likely to be male, plan their attempts, use more dangerous methods and suffer from persistent mental disorders such as depression.

Assessment of young people after self-harm

The assessment is directed to four main questions. First, what are the immediate and subsequent risks of suicide? Second, what are the immediate and subsequent risks of self-harm? Third, what are the child and family's current problems and how have they led to self-harm? Fourth, what resources do the child and family have?

The assessment should include at least one interview with the young person alone. Adolescents aged 12 years and older can usually be interviewed in much the same way as adults. In younger children it is necessary to rely more on information from other sources. Whatever the age of the child, a background history should always be obtained from a relative. Information may also be required from other sources, such as the school or social services.

What are the immediate and subsequent risks of suicide?

Risk factors for completed suicide after an attempt include high suicidal intent, mood disorder and substance misuse. The interview should start with detailed enquiry into the days and hours leading up to the attempt. Circumstances suggesting high suicidal intent include planning in advance, precautions to avoid discovery, dangerous methods and a 'final act' such as a suicide note. The young person should always be asked whether they still intend to die. Careful enquiry should also be made into the patient's recent difficulties, and whether they have resolved. The more serious the problems that remain, the greater the risk of another attempt. Mental state exam should establish whether the young person has a depressive disorder and his or her degree of hopelessness.

The practitioner should now have the information required to establish if there is a continuing risk of suicide. It should be borne in mind, however, that a problem in identifying those young people who are most at risk of suicide is that even among high risk groups, such as attempters, suicide is rare (probably around 1% in the following year). Since even combinations of risk factors seldom predict with more than 80% accuracy, it is a mathematical certainty that many high risk cases must be treated to prevent one suicide. Moreover, suicide risk is not static, but changes over time. It is important, then, that suicide risk is re-assessed regularly.

What are the immediate and subsequent risks of deliberate self-harm?

Repetition of deliberate self-harm is common, being around 10–15% within 6 months, and about 20% over the next year or two.[2,43] Some cases repeat several times but only during a period of continuing problems. In others, repetition becomes a habitual response to stress. Factors that distinguish those who repeat from those who do not include depression, behavioural problems and continuing problems such as family discord.

What are the child and family's current problems and resources?

The next step is to bring all the information together into a formulation of the child and family's problems and how these have led to self-harm. Finally, it necessary to consider the strengths that the child and family have to deal with their problems. These include the child's intelligence, achievements and capacity to form relationships. The strengths of the family should also be assessed, as should other resources such as friends, other relatives or professionals.

Management of adolescents who deliberately harm themselves

The wide range of problems faced by young people who harm themselves demands a variety of different treatment strategies. The assessment will usually divide patients into four groups. The first group are those at very high risk of suicide, or with severe psychiatric disorders, or both. This group, which accounts for about 10% of cases, requires specialized psychiatric out-patient care or even admission. The second group comprise patients with long and often complex care histories, who are known to social services and who often present with repeated deliberate self-harm. This group, which also accounts for about 10% of cases, usually requires specialized multidisciplinary management from a team that includes an experienced social worker. The third group comprise patients in whom the overdose appears to have been a transient response to temporary difficulties and who have few other problems. This group usually requires little more than one follow-up appointment. The last group, which account for about 60% of cases, requires some help as described below.

Initial management

The first aim of management is to minimize the risk of further self-harm. The practitioner should identify an adult guardian or companion who can ensure the safety of the home environment by removing medications, sharp knives, and so on. It is common practice to arrange a means for the adolescent or family to receive help quickly if the urge to self-harm returns. The second aim it to engage the adolescent and their family in an intervention. Published reports suggest that close to a half of all adolescents who harm themselves fail to receive any formal intervention[44].

Psychological and social treatments

The main aims of treatment are first to help the patient and family to resolve the difficulties that led to self-harm, and secondly to help them to deal with future problems without recourse to self-harm. Treatment is psychological and social. Probably the most commonly used psychological technique with older adolescents is brief problem-orientated counselling. The patient is encouraged to produce a list of problems and to consider the steps needed to solve each. Many cases are associated with family problems and family counselling aimed at improving communication within the family may be of value.

The results of psychological or social treatment

There is little research evidence about which intervention practitioners should offer[45]. In adult patients, brief psychological therapies such as problem-solving therapy have some benefits on mood and social outcomes, though not on the risk of repetition[46]. Problem solving has a theoretical basis in adolescent self-harm because these patients are often poor problem solvers and because there is evidence that related techniques such as cognitive-behaviour therapy are effective in improving adolescent depression[25]. Family counselling may be of value in non-depressed adolescents who have harmed themselves, but does not reduce the risk of repetition[2]. Crisis cards do not seem to be effective[47].

Antidepressant medication

Although many adolescents who harm themselves have depressive symptoms, few have depressive disorders. However, if depression persists and does not respond to other measures, there may be a case for prescribing antidepressants. Tricyclics do not seem to be effective for child and adolescent depressions (see above) and are toxic in overdose. Serotonin specific re-uptake inhibitors are probably the first line medical treatment.

Primary prevention

Medical practitioners such as general practitioners and paediatricians may have a part to play in prevention. Indeed, their potential role is underlined by the finding in one study that a half of young people aged 25 years or less who committed suicide had had contact with a GP in the 3 months before death[48]. There are a number of potential preventive strategies that can be used in primary care. First, there should be systematic, on-going assessment of suicidal risk in high risk cases such as those who have just self-harmed or who have major depression. Second, it is important to recognize mental disorders, especially depression. Third, there should be prompt treatment of mental disorders, especially depression. Fourth, practitioners should limit access to dangerous methods, such as tricyclic anti-depressants.

References

1 American Psychiatric Association. *Diagnostic and Statistical Manual of Mental Disorders –* DSM-IV (4th edition). Washington, DC: American Psychiatric Association, 1994
2 Harrington RC, Kerfoot M, Dyer E *et al*. Randomized trial of a home based family intervention for children who have deliberately poisoned themselves. *J Am Acad Child Adolesc Psychiatry* 1998; 37: 512–8

3 Harrington RC, Fudge H, Rutter M, Pickles A, Hill J. Adult outcomes of childhood and adolescent depression: I. Psychiatric status. *Arch Gen Psychiatry* 1990; **47**: 465–73

4 Harrington RC, Fudge H, Rutter M, Pickles A, Hill J. Adult outcomes of childhood and adolescent depression: II. Risk for antisocial disorders. *J Am Acad Child Adolesc Psychiatry* 1991; **30**: 434–9

5 Brady EU, Kendall PC. Comorbidity of anxiety and depression in children and adolescents. *Psychol Bull* 1992; **111**: 244–55

6 Goodyer IM, Altham PME. Lifetime exit events and recent social and family adversities in anxious and depressed school-age children and adolescents – I. *J Affect Disord* 1991; **21**: 219–28

7 Garmezy N, Masten AS. Chronic adversities. In: Rutter M, Taylor E, Hersov L. (eds) *Child and Adolescent Psychiatry: Modern Approaches*, 3rd edn. Oxford: Blackwell Scientific, 1994; 191–208

8 Simonoff E, Pickles A, Meyer JM *et al*. The Virginia twin study of adolescent behavioral development. Influences of age, sex, and impairment on rates of disorder. *Arch Gen Psychiatry* 1997; **54**: 801–8

9 Lewinsohn PM, Rohde P, Seeley JR. Major depressive disorder in older adolescents: prevalence, risk factors, and clinical implications. *Clin Psychol Rev* 1998; **18**: 765–94

10 Meltzer H, Gatward R, Goodman R, Ford T. *Mental Health of Children and Adolescents in Great Britain*. London: The Stationery Office, 2000

11 Fombonne E. Time trends in affective disorders. In: Cohen P, Slomkoski C, Robins LN. (eds) *Historical and Geographical Influences on Psychopathology*. New Jersey: Lawrence Erlbaum, 1999; 115–39

12 Kendler KS, Kessler RC, Walters EE *et al*. Stressful life events, genetic liability, and onset of an episode of major depression in women. *Am J Psychiatry* 1995; **152**: 833–42

13 Strober M. Relevance of early age-of-onset in genetic studies of bipolar affective disorder. *J Am Acad Child Adolesc Psychiatry* 1992; **31**: 606–10

14 Radke-Yarrow M, Nottelmann E, Martinez P, Fox MB, Belmont B. Young children of affectively ill parents: a longitudinal study of psychosocial development. *J Am Acad Child Adolesc Psychiatry* 1992; **31**: 68–77

15 Harrington RC. Family-genetic findings in child and adolescent depressive disorders. *Int Rev Psychiatry* 1996; **8**: 355–68

16 Harrington RC, Fudge H, Rutter M, Bredenkamp D, Groothues C, Pridham J. Child and adult depression: a test of continuities with data from a family study. *Br J Psychiatry* 1993; **162**: 627–33

17 Asarnow JR, Goldstein MJ, Carlson GA, Perdue S, Bates S, Keller J. Childhood-onset depressive disorders. A follow-up study of rates of rehospitalization and out-of-home placement among child psychiatric inpatients. *J Affect Disord* 1988; **15**: 245–53

18 Goodyer IM, Wright C, Altham PME. Recent friendships in anxious and depressed school-age children. *Psychol Med* 1989; **19**: 165–74

19 Hammen C. *Depression Runs in Families. The Social Context of Risk and Resilience in Children of Depressed Mothers*. New York: Springer Verlag, 1991

20 Harrington RC, Wood A, Verduyn C. Clinically depressed adolescents. In: Graham P. (ed) *Cognitive Behaviour Therapy for Children and Families*. Cambridge: Cambridge University Press, 1998; 156–93

21 Yaylayan S, Weller EB, Weller RA. Neurobiology of depression. In: Shafii M, Shafii SL. (eds) *Clinical Guide to Depression in Children and Adolescents*. Washington, DC: American Psychiatric Press, 1992; 65–88

22 Kovacs M, Feinberg TL, Crouse-Novak M, Paulauskas SL, Pollock M, Finkelstein R. Depressive disorders in childhood. II. A longitudinal study of the risk for a subsequent major depression. *Arch Gen Psychiatry* 1984; **41**: 643–9

23 Rao U, Weissman MM, Martin JA, Hammond RW. Childhood depression and risk of suicide: preliminary report of a longitudinal study. *J Am Acad Child Adolesc Psychiatry* 1993; **32**: 21–7

24 Kovacs M, Feinberg TL, Crouse-Novak MA, Paulauskas SL, Finkelstein R. Depressive disorders in childhood. I. A longitudinal prospective study of characteristics and recovery. *Arch Gen Psychiatry* 1984; **41**: 229–37

25 Harrington R, Whittaker J, Shoebridge P, Campbell F. Systematic review of efficacy of cognitive behaviour therapies in child and adolescent depressive disorder. *BMJ* 1998; **316**: 1559–63

26 Hammen C, Rudolph K, Weisz J, Rao U, Burge D. The context of depression in clinic-referred youth: neglected areas in treatment. *J Am Acad Child Adolesc Psychiatry* 1999; **38**: 64–71

27 Mufson L, Weissman MM, Moreau D, Garfinkel R. Efficacy of interpersonal psychotherapy for depressed adolescents. *Arch Gen Psychiatry* 1999; **56**: 573–9

28 Brent D, Holder D, Kolko D *et al*. A clinical psychotherapy trial for adolescent depression comparing cognitive, family, and supportive treatments. *Arch Gen Psychiatry* 1997; **54**: 877–85

29 Lewinsohn PM, Clarke GN, Hops H, Andrews J. Cognitive-behavioural treatment for depressed adolescents. *Behav Ther* 1990; **21**: 385–401

30 Clarke GN, Rohde P, Lewinsohn PM, Hops H, Seeley JR. Cognitive-behavioural treatment of adolescent depression: efficacy of acute group treatment and booster sessions. *J Am Acad Child Adolesc Psychiatry* 1999; **38**: 272–9

31 Hazell P, O'Connell D, Heathcote D, Robertson J, Henry D. Efficacy of tricyclic drugs in treating child and adolescent depression: a meta-analysis. *BMJ* 1995; **310**: 897–901

32 Emslie GJ, Rush JA, Weinberg WA, Gullion CM, Rintelmann J, Hughes CW. Recurrence of major depressive disorder in hospitalized children and adolescents. *J Am Acad Child Adolesc Psychiatry* 1997; **36**: 785–92

33 Simeon JG, Dinicola VF, Ferguson HB, Copping W. Adolescent depression: a placebo-controlled fluoxetine treatment study and follow-up. *Prog Neuropsychopharmacol Biol Psychiatry* 1990; **14**: 791–95

34 Ryan ND, Varma D. Child and adolescent mood disorders-experience with serotonin-based therapies. *Biol Psychiatry* 1998; **44**: 336–40

35 Walter G, Rey JM, Mitchell PB. Practitioner review: electroconvulsive therapy in adolescents. *J Child Psychol Psychiatry* 1999; **40**: 325–34

36 McClure GMG. Suicide in children and adolescents in England and Wales 1960–1990. *Br J Psychiatry* 1994; **165**: 510–4

37 Shaffer D. Suicide and attempted suicide. In: Rutter M, Taylor E, Hersov L. (eds) *Child and Adolescent Psychiatry: Modern Approaches*, 3rd edn. Oxford: Blackwell Scientific, 1994; 407–24

38 Marttunen MJ, Aro HM, Lonnqvist JK. Adolescence and suicide: a review of psychological autopsy studies. *Eur Child Adolesc Psychiatry* 1993; **2**: 10–8

39 Hawton KSS, Deeks JJ, O'Connor S *et al*. Effects of a drug overdose in a television drama on presentations to hospital for self poisoning: time series and questionnaire study. *BMJ* 1999; **318**: 972–7

40 Hawton K, Fagg J, Simkin S, Bale E, Bond A. Deliberate self-harm in adolescents in Oxford, 1985–1995. *J Adolesc* 2000; **23**: 47–55

41 Schmidtke A, Bille-Brahe U, DeLeo D *et al*. Attempted suicide in Europe: rates, trends and sociodemographic characteristics of suicide attempters during the period 1989-1992. Results of the WHO/EURO Multicentre Study on Parasuicide. *Acta Psychiatr Scand* 1996; **93**: 327–38

42 Kerfoot M, Dyer E, Harrington V, Woodham A, Harrington RC. Correlates and short-term course of self-poisoning in adolescents. *Br J Psychiatry* 1996; **168**: 38–42

43 Spirito A, Brown L, Overholser J, Fritz G. Attempted suicide in adolescence: a review and critique of the literature. *Clin Psychol Rev* 1989; **9**: 335–63

44 Trautman PD, Stewart N, Morishima A. Are adolescent suicide attempters noncompliant with outpatient care? *J Am Acad Child Adolesc Psychiatry* 1993; **32**: 89–94

45 NHS Centre for Reviews and Dissemination. Deliberate self-harm. *Effect Health Care* 1998; **4**: 1–12

46 Hawton K, Arensman E, Townsend E *et al*. Deliberate self harm: systematic review of efficacy of psychosocial and pharmacological treatments in preventing repetition. *BMJ* 1998; **317**: 441–7

47 Cotgrove A, Zirinsky L, Black D, Weston D. Secondary prevention of attempted suicide in adolescence. *J Adolesc* 1995; **18**: 569–77

48 Hawton K, Houston K, Shepperd R. Suicide in young people. Study of 174 cases, aged under 25 years, based on coroners' and medical records. *Br J Psychiatry* 1999; **175**: 271–6

Depression – emerging insights from neurobiology

Vidita A Vaidya* and **Ronald S Duman†**

*Department of Biological Sciences, Tata Institute of Fundamental Research, Mumbai, India and †Department of Psychiatry and Pharmacology, Yale University, Connecticut Mental Health Center, New Haven, Connecticut, USA

An emerging hypothesis suggests that the pathogenesis and treatment of depression is likely to involve a plasticity of neuronal pathways. The inability of neuronal systems to exhibit appropriate, adaptive plasticity could contribute to the pathogenesis of depression. Antidepressant treatments may exert their therapeutic effects by stimulating appropriate adaptive changes in neuronal systems. Recent studies have demonstrated that chronic antidepressant administration up-regulates the cAMP signal transduction cascade resulting in an increased expression and function of the transcription factor CREB. Enhanced CREB expression leads to an up-regulation of specific target genes, including the neurotrophin BDNF. Chronic antidepressant treatments enhance BDNF expression within hippocampal and cortical neurons and can prevent the stress-induced decrease in BDNF expression. Stress has been shown to: (i) induce neuronal atrophy/death; and (ii) decrease neurogenesis of hippocampal neurons. Clinical studies indicate significant hippo-campal damage in cases of major, recurrent depression. It is possible that anti-depressant treatments through enhanced expression of growth and survival promoting factors like BDNF may prevent or reverse the atrophy and damage of hippocampal neurons. Indeed, studies have indicated that chronic antidepressant treatments enhance hippocampal neurogenesis, promote neuronal sprouting and prevent atrophy. The molecular mechanisms underlying the effects of antidep-ressant treatments including adaptations in the cAMP transduction cascade, CREB and BDNF gene expression, and structural neuronal plasticity are discussed.

Correspondence to:
Dr Vidita Vaidya,
Department of Biological
Sciences, Tata Institute of
Fundamental Research,
Homi Bhabha Road, Navy
Nagar, Colaba, Mumbai
400 005, India

Depression is a complex, heterogeneous disorder and several neuro-transmitter and neurohormonal pathways have been implicated in the pathophysiology of depression. The mechanisms underlying the pathogenesis of depression are not well understood. The serendipitous discovery of antidepressant treatments in the 1950s provided the first evidence of an inherent biochemical abnormality underlying the disorder. In the following 30–40 years research efforts concentrated on studying the mechanisms underlying antidepressant action thus attempting to gain insight into the dysfunction that results in depression.

These studies have led to the establishment of several theories not only for the mechanism of action of antidepressant drugs but also for the pathophysiology of depression. Amongst these has been the monoamine theory of depression. Both preclinical and clinical studies have clearly implicated the serotonin and norepinephrine neurotransmitter systems in antidepressant action. Although these studies have fuelled research efforts in the field and guided the development of novel therapeutic agents they have not been able to provide a clear model for the pathogenesis of depression. The monoaminergic hypothesis does not provide an adequate explanation for the number of patients who do not respond to current therapeutic agents and also does not solve the puzzle of the lag period in the therapeutic actions of antidepressants. Observations that monoamine depletion does not produce depressive symptoms in healthy individuals and that rapid elevation in monoamines is not correlated with quick antidepressant action has led to the need to revise the framework of existing theories[1,2].

An emerging hypothesis suggests that the pathogenesis and treatment of depression is likely to involve a plasticity of neuronal pathways[3,4]. Depression may arise when neuronal systems do not exhibit appropriate, adaptive plasticity in response to external stimuli such as stress. The dysfunction of adaptive pathways that control neuronal plasticity could contribute to the pathogenesis of depression. Antidepressant treatments may exert their therapeutic effects by either reversing this dysfunction or by independently stimulating an adaptive neuronal plasticity within the system. Despite the relatively rapid effects of antidepressant treatments on the monoamine system, their therapeutic actions emerge only after chronic administration. This supports the hypothesis that a plasticity or adaptation of neuronal systems following the acute effects of antidepressants underlies the therapeutic actions of these treatments. Initial research efforts focused on changes in monoamine neurotransmitter levels, receptors or receptor-coupled second messenger systems. Recent studies have demonstrated that the activation of intracellular cascades and the regulation of gene expression are likely to exert powerful effects on structural plasticity and neuronal survival. Our hypothesis is that these adaptive responses induced by antidepressant treatments may serve to reverse the underlying dysfunction induced by a genetic vulnerability or through exposure to stress and other aversive stimuli. In this review, we will discuss the recent advances that demonstrate a role for specific intracellular cascades, regulation of select target genes and structural neuronal plasticity in the action of antidepressants, as well as in the pathogenesis of depression.

Intracellular messenger cascades and depression

Regulation of intracellular messenger cascades exerts a powerful control on almost all aspects of neuronal function, inclusive of neuronal morphology, gene expression, activity and survival. It is these cascades that ultimately mediate the ability of neuronal systems to adapt in response to pharmacological and environmental stimuli[5]. Broadly, the intracellular signal transduction pathways can be classified into two categories, those that are regulated by G-protein receptor coupled second messengers (*e.g.* cAMP, Ca^{2+}, *etc*) and those that are regulated by receptors coupled directly or in close interaction with protein tyrosine kinases[6]. The former category is primarily regulated by neurotransmitters including the monoamines and neuropeptides, whereas the latter category is controlled by cytokines and growth factors including the neurotrophin family. It is our hypothesis that adaptations within these molecular cascades are likely to contribute eventually to the effects of antidepressant treatments on the plasticity of target neuronal populations within the brain.

Studies of cellular models of learning and activity-dependent plasticity have indicated that adaptations in response to stimuli include both enhanced synaptic strength as well as morphological changes, such as alterations in spine density, dendritic branching and axonal sprouting[7-9]. These forms of plasticity are mediated, in part, by underlying molecular adaptations in the intracellular signal transduction cascades[10,11]. Emerging insights from neurobiological research indicate that similar molecular and cellular adaptations arise in response to antidepressant treatments and may be relevant in the pathogenesis of depression.

Amongst the forms of molecular adaptations exhibited by intracellular signal transduction cascades are changes in functional status through alterations in phosphorylation state, changes in protein expression, or modified coupling to receptors. These forms of adaptations often result in either a positive or negative feedback. Positive feedback refers to the sensitization of a pathway leading to a stronger response in a system to the same stimulus. Negative feedback is observed when there is an enhancement or attenuation in the response of a cascade following decreased or increased stimulation, respectively. Antidepressants acting through diverse neurotransmitter systems may converge in their influences on adaptations within second messenger systems. Although these adaptations are complex and difficult to study, the realization of their importance has provided a strong incentive to examine their contribution to antidepressant action and in the pathophysiology of depression.

Antidepressant-induced adaptations of the cAMP signal transduction cascade

Amongst the second messenger cascades thought to play an important role in mediating the effects of antidepressant treatments is the cAMP cascade, which is regulated by both the serotonin and norepinephrine neurotransmitters. This signal transduction cascade represents a common target for several classes of antidepressants that differentially influence these two neurotransmitters acutely. Receptor activation (*e.g.* β_1AR, 5-HT$_{4,6,7}$) leads to the generation of cAMP via the stimulation of adenylyl cyclase by the G-protein subtype Gsα[12]. In addition, intracellular Ca^{2+} levels can also regulate certain subtypes of adenylyl cyclase. The generation of cAMP then results in the activation of cAMP-dependent protein kinase (PKA). The catalytic subunits of PKA are responsible for mediating effects on cellular function through the phosphorylation of specific target proteins. Amongst the substrates of PKA is the transcription factor cAMP response element binding protein (CREB), which in the dephosphorylated form constitutively regulates gene transcription and following phosphorylation exhibits a dramatic increase in its ability to regulate transcriptional activity[13].

Although results from earlier studies indicated that chronic antidepressant treatment down-regulated β_1AR and cAMP production, more recently evidence has mounted for an up-regulation of the cAMP cascade following chronic antidepressant administration. Postreceptor components of the cAMP signal transduction cascade are regulated at several levels. The coupling of the stimulatory G protein Gsα to adenylyl cyclase is enhanced following antidepressant treatment[14]. This enhanced coupling leads to increased adenylyl cyclase activity in response to several different classes of antidepressant treatments[15]. Besides regulation of enzyme activity, the expression of adenylyl cyclase types I and II is also enhanced following chronic treatment with lithium[16]. In addition to regulation of cAMP production, another target is the metabolism of cAMP. Breakdown of cAMP is catalyzed by the phosphodiesterases (PDEs). There are several different isoforms of these enzymes and accumulating evidence suggests a role for PDE4A and PDE4B in antidepressant action[17–19]. Support for the hypothesis that enhanced cAMP signalling may produce antidepressant effects comes from studies with the phosphodiesterase inhibitor rolipram, which has been reported to have antidepressant effects in clinical trials. Although rolipram is not in clinical use because of its unpleasant side effects, a rational target for drug design are selective PDE inhibitors that lack these side effects. The potential for PDE inhibitors in the treatment of refractory patients and to accelerate the lag phase with antidepressant drugs when used in combination therapy needs to be more carefully examined.

Levels and activity of cAMP-dependent protein kinase are reported to be influenced by antidepressant treatment. Chronic, but not acute, treatment with antidepressants leads to enhanced PKA activity in cerebral particulate fractions[20]. Reports also indicate an increase of PKA levels within the crude nuclear fraction suggesting a translocation of this enzyme into the nucleus following antidepressant administration[21].

Nuclear translocation of PKA would suggest that antidepressant treatments recruit the cAMP cascade to regulate gene expression. Although there are differences in the results of these studies, these are likely to be due to the problems of being unable to obtain pure subcellular fractions. Evidence clearly indicates that antidepressant treatment up-regulates several components of the cAMP signal transduction cascade.

Although recent studies indicate an up-regulation of the cAMP cascade, this is in contrast to previous work, which reported βAR down-regulation and a decreased ability of the receptor to stimulate cAMP production. This led to the genesis of the βAR subsensitivity hypothesis which postulated that depression is a consequence of overexpression of βAR and that the mechanism underlying antidepressant action is a down-regulation of these receptors. Considerable evidence against this hypothesis has been generated in addition to the reports which clearly indicate an up-regulated cAMP second messenger system. The down-regulation of βAR does not follow the therapeutic time course of antidepressant drugs. In addition, βAR antagonists do not demonstrate antidepressant effects as would be predicted by the subsensitivity hypothesis. In addition, enhanced βAR expression induced by thyroid hormone administration is thought to be associated with the ability of thyroid hormone treatment to augment antidepressant medication. The up-regulation of the cAMP cascade but the decreased expression of βAR in response to antidepressant treatment, as well as an associated attenuation in the ability of βAR to stimulate cAMP production, appear to be contradictory. However, an inherent problem with these studies is the methodology employed for the cAMP assays which uses exogenous agonists in a brain homogenate or in an *in vitro* brain slice system. Based on these studies, one cannot truly draw a conclusion of the *in vivo* situation. It is possible that *in vivo*, even though levels of βAR are reduced, there is a residual population of available receptors that are sufficient to produce a response to the enhanced norepinephrine available at the synapse following antidepressant treatment. If this is the case, then even though the levels of βAR are decreased relative to control levels, the enhanced levels of norepinephrine following antidepressant administration would be sufficient to drive the remaining receptors to up-regulate the cAMP system in contrast to control (Fig. 1). This may provide an explanation to the paradoxical findings of decreased βAR and enhanced cAMP signal transduction cascades following chronic antidepressant administration. Further studies will be required to address this paradox and examine whether the above hypothesis is true.

Up-regulation of the cAMP cascade and nuclear translocation of PKA suggest that antidepressant treatments regulate specific target genes, *i.e.* those that are likely to contain a functional cAMP response element

(CRE). A current area of research is to identify these candidate genes which are regulated in response to antidepressant treatment and to dissect out their significance in mediating the therapeutic effects of antidepressants.

Altered gene expression and depression

The property of neuronal plasticity which allows the brain to exert an adaptive response when faced with aversive stimuli is likely to arise through a programme of altered gene expression. It is these changes in gene expression which profoundly influence: (i) the metabolism of neurotransmitters; (ii) expression of receptors, channels, intracellular cascade components, growth factors and structural proteins; (iii) synaptic strength and neuronal activity;

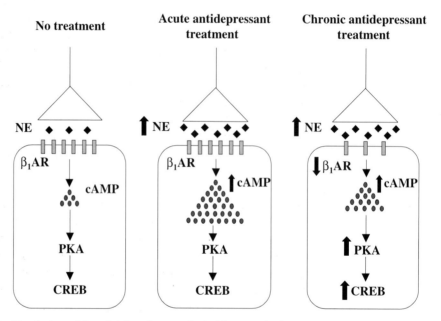

Fig. 1 A model explaining the paradoxical increase in the cAMP signal transduction cascade despite the down-regulation of βAR following chronic antidepressant treatment. In the absence of treatment, basal levels of norepinephrine (NE) stimulate the βAR-receptor coupled cAMP cascade, and levels of NE and cAMP are low. Following short-term administration of select antidepressants, there is an increase in NE levels leading to a corresponding increase in βAR-stimulated cAMP production. Chronic antidepressant administration leads to an increase in synaptic NE levels. Chronic treatment with several types of antidepressants results in a significant decrease in the β_1AR-binding sites available to stimulate cAMP production. This in turn causes a decrease in the maximal level of βAR-stimulated cAMP production. However, the residual population of βARs is sufficient to respond to the elevated levels of NE and drive an increase in cAMP production relative to the cAMP levels observed with no treatment. This model proposes a hypothetical mechanism, which requires further testing, to explain the enhanced cAMP cascade even though levels of βAR are decreased following chronic antidepressant treatment.

and (iv) morphology and survival of neurons, thus eventually contributing to an adaptive response being mounted by the brain in response to stimuli which perturb homeostatic balance. It is likely that aberrant programmes of gene expression, which lead to a dysfunction in neuronal plasticity, contribute to the pathogenesis of depression. Antidepressant treatments through their influence on intracellular signal transduction cascades serve to regulate specific transcription factors thus orchestrating long-term adaptations through the regulation of specific genes[22,23]. Adaptations resulting from antidepressant-induced changes in gene expression may then serve to reverse or ameliorate the dysfunction in neuronal plasticity. A major goal of current research efforts is to identify the target genes which are regulated by several classes of antidepressant treatments and to examine their role in the therapeutic effects of antidepressant action.

The regulation of transcription factors by different classes of antidepressants may serve as a common target for antidepressant drugs stimulating diverse receptor-coupled signal transduction cascades. Antidepressant induced regulation of transcription would then feed forward to the regulation of a number of target genes. Although this suggests that antidepressants may broadly influence the expression of several genes, it is likely that several additional factors would determine the target genes eventually regulated by antidepressant treatment. There is a differential regulation of intracellular cascades by antidepressant treatments within the brain, which would bring about a spatial restriction in the regulation of transcription factors and target genes. In addition, the control of gene expression will also depend upon a complex interplay between different transcription factors in the promoter region, eventually determining the influence of antidepressant treatment on a particular gene. The regulation of transcription factors by antidepressant treatments is of great interest since these factors may serve as common intracellular targets for different second messenger system cascades. Transcription factors are uniquely suited to integrate signals from distinct signal transduction cascades and mediate the effects of diverse classes of antidepressant treatments on gene expression. We will discuss the regulation of the transcription factor CREB as a potential common postreceptor target for antidepressant treatments. The regulation of CREB suggests that antidepressant treatments influence the regulation of specific genes containing CRE regulatory elements. We will describe the regulation of one such target gene of interest the growth factor brain-derived neurotrophic factor (BDNF).

Antidepressant regulation of CREB expression

Studies demonstrating an antidepressant-induced increase in (i) activity of the cAMP cascade and (ii) the nuclear translocation of PKA, suggest

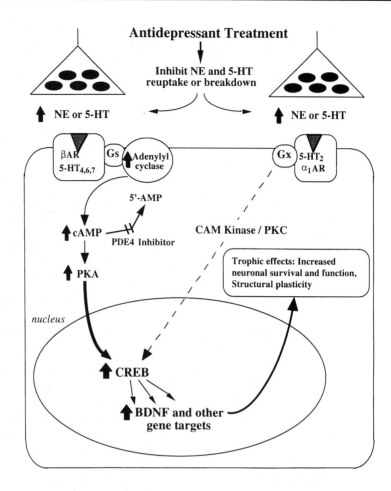

Fig. 2 A model describing the influence of antidepressant administration on the cAMP signal transduction cascade. Chronic treatment with different classes of antidepressants results in an up-regulation of the several postreceptor components of the cAMP cascade. Chronic antidepressant administration results in an increased coupling of Gs and adenylyl cyclase, increased expression of specific types of adenylyl cyclase, cAMP dependent protein kinase (PKA), and increased expression of cAMP response element binding protein (CREB). Taken together, these studies suggest that the cAMP cascade may serve as a common postreceptor target for diverse classes of antidepressant drugs. In addition, to up-regulation of CREB by norepinephrine (NE) and serotonin (5-HT) receptors (βAR, 5-HT$_{4,6,7}$) coupled to the cAMP intracellular pathway, CREB is also a target for calcium-dependent protein kinases and receptors coupled to activation of these pathways (5-HT$_2$, α$_1$AR). Up-regulation of the cAMP cascade may serve as a common target for different classes of antidepressants with diverse acute sites of action. Preclinical and clinical studies demonstrating the antidepressant effects of specific cAMP phosphodiesterase (PDE4) inhibitors support the possibility that up-regulation of the cAMP pathway may contribute to antidepressant action. Up-regulation of CREB by chronic antidepressant treatments suggests that specific target genes are likely to be regulated in response to antidepressant administration. Amongst these target genes is brain-derived neurotrophic factor (BDNF), which is known to play an important role in neuronal plasticity, survival and function.

that antidepressant treatment may regulate the cAMP responsive transcription factor CREB thus influencing gene expression. Recent studies clearly indicate that chronic, but not acute, administration of several distinct classes of antidepressant treatments up-regulates CREB mRNA expression within the hippocampus[24]. The antidepressants studied belong to diverse classes including selective norepinephrine and serotonin re-uptake inhibitors, non-selective tricyclic monoamine re-uptake inhibitors, monoamine oxidase inhibitors, and electroconvulsive seizure administration. This suggests that CREB may serve as a common target for antidepressant drugs with very different primary sites of action (Fig. 2). In addition to an up-regulation of CREB mRNA, corresponding increases in CREB protein as well as an increased level of CRE binding is observed following antidepressant treatment. CREB induction follows a time-course that is consistent with the therapeutic actions of anti-depressant treatments (*i.e.* 10–21 days of treatment)[24]. In addition to these studies demonstrating an up-regulation of CREB expression, a recent study reports that the phosphorylation and transcriptional activity of CREB is also increased by antidepressant treatment[25]. This study used a transgenic mouse line that expresses a gene containing a tandem of CRE elements attached to a reporter (*LacZ*). Chronic antidepressant administration increased levels of CRE-mediated *LacZ* expression, as well as phosphorylation of CREB. Future studies are now needed to determine the functional consequences of altered CREB levels. This can be accomplished with inducible transgenic mice that express CREB, or a dominant negative mutant of CREB, in a region- and time-specific manner.

The mechanisms which underlie the enhanced expression of CREB mRNA and protein are not clearly understood *in vivo*. However, evidence from *in vitro* systems implicates activation of the cAMP system in this regulation[26]. This would reflect a positive feed-forward mechanism that controls expression of CREB in response to antidepressant treatments. It is likely that the cAMP system also plays a role in the antidepressant-mediated induction of CREB mRNA and protein. As has been described earlier, antidepressant treatments augment the functioning of the cAMP signal transduction cascade and PKA which is responsible for phosphorylation of CREB is translocated to the nucleus following chronic antidepressant administration. There are distinct CRE elements within the up-stream promoter region of the CREB gene, which have been shown to up-regulate CREB transcription[27,28]. However, studies in a cell culture system have demonstrated that activation of the cAMP signal transduction cascade leads to a down-regulation of CREB expression[29]. This suggests that the regulation of CREB by the cAMP cascade is likely to be region specific and will also be influenced by the tissue specific expression of cAMP response modulator (CREM) and inducible cAMP early repressor (ICER) proteins which bind to the CRE element and repress transcription.

Different classes of antidepressant treatments are likely to recruit distinct norepinephrine and serotonin receptor subtypes and evidence indicates that the signal transduction cascades activated by these diverse receptors may converge on CREB as a common postreceptor target (Fig. 2). Several norepinephrine and serotonin receptors (βAR, 5-HT$_{4,6,7}$) are coupled to the cAMP cascade and could contribute to up-regulation of CREB transcriptional activity through phosphorylation by PKA. In addition, specific classes of serotonin and norepinephrine receptors (α_1AR and 5-HT$_2$) are coupled to the phosphatidylinositol second messenger cascade inducing the release of Ca^{2+} from intracellular stores. The enzymes Ca^{2+}/calmodulin dependent protein kinase, and protein kinase C are both activated by Ca^{2+} and have been shown to phosphorylate and activate CREB[27]. Changes in Ca^{2+} signalling induced by ion channels may also eventually up-regulate CREB activity. CREB can also be phosphorylated and activated by an enzyme termed rsk or CREB kinase which is stimulated by signalling through the MAP kinase cascade. It is likely then that signalling through diverse signal transduction cascades in response to a variety of antidepressant treatments may converge to up-regulate CREB activity, which in a positive feedforward mechanism would lead to an up-regulation of CREB mRNA expression.

Antidepressant treatments through adaptations in intracellular cascades induce a powerful regulation in gene expression of the transcription factor CREB. It is possible that an up-regulation in CREB may contribute to the actions of antidepressant treatments through effects on specific target genes. Inability to regulate expression or function of CREB and thus induce adaptive gene expression may contribute to the pathogenesis of depression. Support for this hypothesis comes from recent evidence that CREB expression is decreased within the temporal cortex of depressed patients and this decrease is reversed by antidepressant treatment in keeping with data from preclinical studies[30]. A goal of future studies is to determine the target genes that are regulated by CREB and to characterize their role in the actions of antidepressant treatments. One such candidate gene is the neurotrophic factor, BDNF.

Antidepressant regulation of BDNF expression

Brain derived neurotrophic factor, BDNF, belongs to the NGF family of growth factors referred to as the neurotrophins. BDNF is known to exert a powerful influence on the development, survival, maintenance and plasticity of neurons within the immature and adult nervous system and has recently been shown to also elicit rapid action potentials thus influencing neuronal excitability[31,32]. Neurotrophic factors mediate their effects on cellular function and plasticity through the stimulation of specific tyrosine kinase coupled receptors, referred to as trks, which signal through MAP kinase signalling cascades. Studies have clearly indicated that BDNF serves as a target for antidepressant treatment (Fig. 2). Chronic, but not acute, administration of various classes of antidepressant drugs increases the expression of BDNF and its receptor trkB within the hippocampus[33]. This up-regulation follows the time course for the therapeutic action of antidepressant treatments. Pretreatment with antidepressants can also block the stress-induced down regulation of hippocampal BDNF mRNA[33].

Regions exhibiting an up-regulation of BDNF in response to antidepressant administration overlap closely with the regions that show an up-regulation of CREB. This spatial correlation suggests that CREB may contribute to the antidepressant induced increase in hippocampal BDNF expression. A role for the cAMP system in mediating the antidepressant-induced increase in BDNF expression is supported by studies with the PDE inhibitors papaverine and rolipram[24]. PDE inhibitors have been shown to enhance BDNF expression (Fig. 2) and to accelerate the induction of BDNF when co-administered with an antidepressant. In addition, culture studies indicate that activation of the cAMP or Ca^{2+} signalling systems up-regulates BDNF expression[34,35]. Studies indicate that there is a CRE-like element within the promoter region of exon III of BDNF. Further studies are required to dissect the role of CREB in mediating the up-regulation of BDNF expression following chronic anti-depressant treatment. In addition to regulation of BDNF expression through the cAMP/Ca^{2+} signalling and CREB system, an alternate pathway may involve βAR or 5-HT$_2$ receptor internalization. Receptor internaliz-ation recruits Ras and the MAP kinase intracellular cascade and may thus influence BDNF expression independent of the cAMP signalling cascade.

There are several lines of evidence that suggest a role for BDNF in the action of antidepressant treatment and in the pathogenesis of depression. First, chronic, but not acute, antidepressant treatment increases hippocampal BDNF mRNA with the induction following the time-course observed for the therapeutic effects of antidepressant treatments. In addition, pre-administration of antidepressants prevents stress-induced decreases in hippocampal BDNF mRNA. Second, direct infusion of BDNF protein into the midbrain exerts antidepressant effects in two models of depression, i.e. the forced swim and learned helplessness models[36]. Third, BDNF exerts a strong trophic effect on serotonergic and noradrenergic neurons regulating morphology, neurotransmitter metabolism and firing patterns of these neuronal populations[37,38]. Fourth, chronic stress is known to result in neuronal damage and death. Decreased BDNF expression as a consequence of stress may play a role in stress-induced neuronal damage. We hypothesize that enhanced BDNF expression resulting from chronic antidepressant administration may play an important role in reversing or preventing neuronal damage that is a consequence of exposure to sustained stress or other aversive stimuli. Taken together, these studies indicate that antidepressants up-regulate BDNF expression and BDNF itself exerts an antidepressant effect. Moreover, antidepressant treatment can reverse the down-regulation of the BDNF expression induced by stress and antidepressant induced BDNF expression may serve to ameliorate stress-induced neuronal damage.

These studies provide evidence for a neurotrophic basis to the pathogenesis of depression. Further studies are required to characterize the role of CREB and BDNF in the influence of antidepressant treatments on neuronal plasticity including changes in neuronal structure and function. These studies will make it possible to design novel therapeutic agents for the treatment of depression rationally. A strategy for new drug development could focus on synthetic agonists for the trk receptors, as well as drugs that activate specific components of the cAMP pathway. We have described here only the cAMP cascade and gene expression likely to be regulated as a result of activation of the cAMP cascade. It is unlikely that only this intracellular pathway is involved. Preclinical and clinical studies are required to elucidate the role of other intracellular cascades, transcription factors and candidate genes in the pathophysiology and treatment of depression.

Structural plasticity and depression

Stress-induced neuronal atrophy and cell death suggest that antidepressants, through adaptive influences on neuronal plasticity, may serve to reverse or block the deleterious effects of stress on neuronal morphology and survival. Amongst the primary targets of stress is the hippocampus. Hippocampal CA3 neurons show neuronal atrophy or death following sustained exposure to stress[39]. Although mature dentate gyrus granule cell neurons are relatively resistant to stress-induced damage, stress is known to decrease on-going adult neurogenesis within the subgranular zone of the dentate gyrus[40]. Adult neurogenesis has been reported in rodents, tree shrews, non human primates and in humans[41]. The functional significance of neurogenesis is unclear, but studies indicate that hippocampal-dependent learning tasks and exposure to enriched environment enhance neurogenesis. These studies suggest that this form of structural plasticity may contribute to hippocampal functions such as learning. Stress-induced neuronal atrophy, cell death and inhibition of neurogenesis may then serve to contribute to a functional deficit of the hippocampus.

Recent clinical studies have clearly indicated a decrease in hippocampal volume in patients suffering from recurrent, major depression. This decrease in hippocampal volume appears to be correlated with the duration of depressive episodes[42]. Hippocampal fast feedback inhibition of the hypothalamo-pituitary-adrenocortical (HPA) axis is deficient in depressed patients[43]. A decrease in feedback inhibition of the HPA axis would lead to elevated levels of cortisol and a further endangerment of hippocampal neurons through exposure to sustained high levels of stress steroids. Clinical and preclinical studies both suggest that exposure to prolonged stress and aversive stimuli can result in hippocampal damage. Hippocampal damage is seen in patients suffering from major depression, although the sites of damage within the hippocampus are as yet unclear. In addition, recent studies also report damage within the prefrontal cortex, through a reduction in neuronal and glial number, in patients suffering from depression[3,44]. Taken together, these studies suggest that the pathogenesis of depression may involve the atrophy and damage of specific neuronal populations. Antidepressants may mediate their therapeutic effects by exerting trophic actions on these vulnerable neuronal populations. The therapeutic effects of antidepressant treatments could arise from an ability to block/reverse neuronal damage or through direct influences on neuronal architecture, survival and function. In support of this hypothesis, several studies have indicated that antidepressants appear to block stress-induced damage and positively influence structural plasticity (Fig. 3). Most of these studies have focused on the hippocampus and need to be extended to examine the influence of antidepressants on other brain regions.

Antidepressant treatment, neuronal atrophy and sprouting

Chronic antidepressant treatment has been shown to block the stress-induced atrophy of CA3 hippocampal pyramidal neurons (Fig. 3)[3,39]. These studies demonstrated a blockade of stress-induced neuronal atrophy following chronic administration of the atypical antidepressant tianeptine, but not the serotonin selective re-uptake inhibitor fluoxetine. Tianeptine is known to enhance serotonin re-uptake. It is interesting to speculate that decreased availability of serotonin during stress may prevent the atrophy of hippocampal neurons. Our studies indicate that in part, stress decreases hippocampal BDNF expression through activation of the 5-HT$_{2A}$ receptor[45]. It is possible that chronic pretreatment with tianeptine may act to block the decrease in BDNF and thus the atrophy of CA3 neurons. Based on these studies, one would predict that blockade of the 5-HT$_{2A}$ receptor, which is a known target of

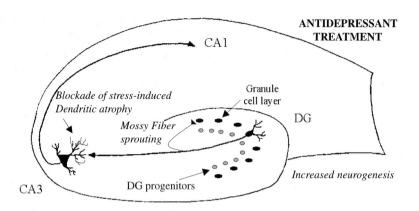

Fig. 3 Schematic diagram of the hippocampus and the influence of chronic anti-depressant treatment on different hippocampal subfields. The CA1, CA3 and dentate gyrus (DG) comprise the main hippocampal anatomical subfields. DG granule cell neurons project to the CA3 region via the mossy fibre pathway. Exposure to stressful stimuli leads to CA3 dendritic atrophy and in severe cases loss of CA3 pyramidal neurons. In addition, stress is known to suppress of on-going neurogenesis in the DG. Pretreatment with specific antidepressants blocks the ability of stress to induce CA3 dendritic atrophy. Chronic treatment with several classes of antidepressants results in an increased neurogenesis within the DG. This increase in neurogenesis is due to a marked increase in proliferation of DG progenitors. Chronic administration of a powerful antidepressant treatment (electroconvulsive seizure) results in sprouting of the mossy fibre pathway axons. Although the mechanisms underlying this form of structural re-organization are not clear, up-regulation of BDNF has been implicated. Structural plasticity within specific neuronal populations may play an important role in the therapeutic actions of antidepressant treatments.

certain antidepressant drugs, would block the atrophy of CA3 neurons. Further studies are required to test this hypothesis and to examine the influence of different classes of antidepressant drugs on stress-induced hippocampal atrophy.

We have also found that chronic administration of a potent form of antidepressant treatment, namely electroconvulsive seizure (ECS), induces axonal sprouting of dentate granule cell neurons (Fig. 3)[46]. This effect is dependent on chronic administration and is fairly long-lasting, persisting 6 months after the last treatment. The increase in sprouting follows a time course that parallels the therapeutic effects appearing 10–12 days after chronic administration of ECS. This form of sprouting, in contrast to the mossy fibre sprouting seen in animal models of epilepsy, does not appear to arise as an adaptation to death of target neurons as there is no evidence of cell death following chronic ECS treatment. ECS induced sprouting is significantly attenuated in BDNF heterozygote knockout mice, which show significantly decreased levels of BDNF in contrast to wild-type mice[46]. However, infusion of BDNF alone is not sufficient to induce mossy fibre sprouting suggesting that BDNF may be necessary, but not sufficient, to induce spouting of granule cell neurons. Chronic administration of antidepressant drugs does not produce sprouting of the mossy fibre pathway suggesting that this effect may be specific to ECS treatment. Further studies are required to examine the functional consequences of enhanced neuronal sprouting.

Antidepressant treatment and hippocampal neurogenesis

Antidepressant treatment could oppose the effects of stress on hippocampal neurogenesis through an increase in the proliferation of dentate granule cell neuron progenitors (Fig. 3). Recent studies have clearly demonstrated that chronic, but not acute, administration of several different classes of antidepressant treatments increases the proliferation of progenitor cells within the subgranular zone of the dentate gyrus (Fig. 4)[47]. Administration of non-antidepressant, psychotropic drugs did not enhance neurogenesis indicating that neurogenesis appears to be a common, selective target for diverse classes of antidepressant treatments. Proliferating progenitors mature and become neurons, as determined by double labelling with neuronal- or

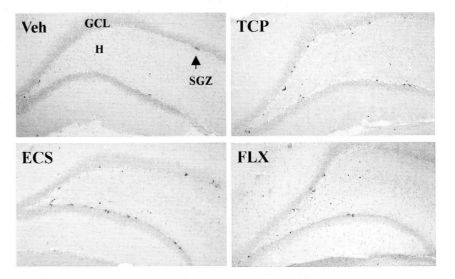

Fig. 4 Chronic antidepressant treatment increases the number of BrDU positive cells within the dentate gyrus region of the hippocampus. Rats received BrDU injection 4 days after the last electroconvulsive (ECS) seizure (10 days) or drug treatment (fluoxetine FLX or tranylcypromine TCP, 14–21 days) and were sacrificed 24 h after the last BrDU injection. Representative photomicrographs demonstrating the increase in BrDU immunolabelling following chronic ECS, FLX, TCP are shown. BrDU labelled progenitors are localised primarily within the subgranular zone (indicated by an arrow in the vehicle section) between the granule cell layer (GCL) and the hilus (H) of the dentate gyrus.

glial-specific markers indicating an increase in hippocampal neurogenesis. Preliminary studies[48] suggest that the 5-HT$_{1A}$ receptor subtype may be important in mediating the influence of antidepressant treatments on hippocampal neurogenesis. The underlying mechanisms which contribute to the effects of antidepressant treatment on neurogenesis are not yet clearly understood. Enhanced cAMP signal transduction cascades and regulation of trophic factors like BDNF may play a role in increased proliferation of neuronal precursors in the hippocampus following antidepressant treatment. Overall, these studies suggest a possibility that enhanced neurogenesis may be a potential mechanism via which antidepressant treatments reverse stress-induced hippocampal neuronal damage/death and exert their therapeutic effects.

Conclusions

Emerging insights from neurobiology suggest that chronic antidepressant treatment leads to an augmentation of the cAMP signal transduction cascade. One of the functional consequences of enhanced cAMP signalling is an increase in the expression and activity of the transcription factor CREB. Studies indicate that enhanced CREB function regulates diverse target genes one of which is the trophic factor BDNF. Several lines of evidence support a role for the growth factor BDNF in antidepressant action, and BDNF itself appears to exert antidepressant effects in certain animal models. Extensive preclinical and clinical studies have indicated a damage of hippocampal neuronal systems in animal models of chronic stress and in patients suffering from recurrent, major depression. This has lead to the model that neuronal atrophy and cell death of specific neuronal populations, within the hippocampus and prefrontal cortex, may play a role in the aetiology of depression. Individual variability in the vulnerability to stress and depression may arise from inherent genetic or environmental exposure differences that could predispose certain individuals to an enhanced susceptibility to depression, in response to stress or other pre-cipitating factors. Chronic antidepressant treatments, through regulation of the cAMP cascade, CREB and BDNF, could exert their therapeutic effects by reversing or preventing neuronal damage and atrophy of damaged or vulnerable neuronal populations. Although the initial acute targets for antidepressants are distinct, these treatments could converge following chronic administration on specific signalling cascades and candidate genes to stimulate an adaptive form of neuronal plasticity. The validity of this unifying hypothesis needs to be tested through preclinical and clinical studies.

Although the regulation of CREB and BDNF may be important to antidepressant action, it would be naive to imply that these are unique targets of antidepressant treatment. Mechanisms underlying antidepressant action are likely to involve a complex interplay between different signal transduction pathways and different target genes. Further studies are required to elucidate the interactions of different signalling pathways and candidate genes, which play an important role in mediating neuronal plasticity in response to antidepressant treatments.

References

1   Schildkraut JJ. The catecholamine hypothesis of affective disorders: a review of supporting evidence. *Am J Psychiatry* 1965; **122**: 509–22

2   Heninger GR, Delgado PL, Charney DS. The revised monoamine theory of depression: a modulatory role for monoamines, based on new findings from monoamine depletion experiments in humans. *Pharmacopsychiatry* 1996; **29**: 2–11

3   Duman RS, Malberg J, Thome J. Neural plasticity to stress and antidepressant treatment. *Biol Psychiatry* 1999; **46**: 1181–91

4   Duman RS, Heninger GR, Nestler EJ. A molecular and cellular theory of depression. *Arch Gen Psychiatry* 1997; **54**: 597–606

5   Duman RS, Heninger GR, Nestler EJ. Adaptations of receptor-coupled signal transduction pathways underlying stress- and drug-induced neural plasticity. *J Nerv Ment Dis* 1994; **182**: 692–700

6   Manji HK, Potter WC, Lenox RH. Signal transduction pathways. *Arch Gen Psychiatry* 1995; **52**: 531–43

7   Bliss TVP, Collingridge G. A synaptic model of memory: long-term potentiation in the hippocampus. *Nature* 1993; **361**: 31–9

8   Han EB, Stevens CI. Of mice and memory. *Learning Memory* 1999; **6**: 539–541

9   Thoenen H. Neurotrophins and neuronal plasticity. *Science* 1995; **270**: 593–8

10 Abel T, Nguyen PV, Barad M, Deuel TAS, Kandel ER, Bourtchouladze R. Genetic demonstration of a role for PKA in the late phase of LTP and in hippocampus-based long-term memory. *Cell* 1997; **88**: 615–26

11 Impey S, Smith DM, Obrietan K, Donahue R, Wade C, Storm DR. Stimulation of cAMP response element (CRE)-mediated transcription during contextual learning. *Nat Neurosci* 1998; **1**: 595–601

12 Nestler EJ, Duman RS. G-Proteins and cyclic nucleotides in the nervous system. In: Siegel G, Agranoff B, Albers RW, Molinoff P. (eds) *Basic Neurochemistry*, 5th edn. New York: Raven, 1994; 429–48

13 Duman RS, Nestler EJ. Signal transduction pathways for catecholamine receptors. In: Meltzer H. (ed) *Psychopharmacology: The Fourth Generation of Progress*. New York: Raven, 1995: 303–20

14 Ozawa H, Rasenick MM. Chronic electroconvulsive treatment augments coupling of the GTP-binding protein Gs to the catalytic moiety of adenylyl cyclase in a manner similar to that seen with chronic antidepressant drugs. *J Neurochem* 1991; **56**: 330–8

15 Menkes DB, Rasenick MM, Wheeler MA, Bitensky MW. Guanosine triphosphate activation of brain adenylate cyclase: enhancement by long-term antidepressant treatment. *Science* 1983; **129**: 65–7

16 Colin SF, Chang HC, Mollner S *et al*. Chronic lithium regulates the expression of adenylate cyclase and Giα in rat cerebral cortex. *Proc Natl Acad Sci USA* 1991; **88**: 10634–7

17 Suda S, Nibuya M, Ishiguro T, Suda H. Transcriptional and translation regulation of phosphodiesterase type IV isozymes in rat brain by electroconvulsive seizure and antidepressant drug treatments. *J Neurochem* 1998; **71**: 1554–63

18 Ye Y, Conti M, Houslay MD, Faroqui SM, Chen M, O'Donell JM. Noradrenergic activity differentially regulates the expression of rolipram-sensitive, high-affinity cyclic AMP phosphodiesterase (PDE4) in rat brain. *J Neurochem* 1997; **69**: 2397–404

19 Takahashi M, Terwilliger R, Lane C, Mezes PS, Conti M, Duman RS. Chronic antidepressant administration increases the expression of cAMP phosphodiesterase 4A and 4B isoforms. *J Neurosci* 1999; **19**: 610–8

20 Perez J, Tinelli D, Brunello N, Racagni G. cAMP-dependent phosphorylation of soluble and crude microtubule fractions of rat cerebral cortex after prolonged desmethylimipramine treatment. *Eur J Pharmacol* 1989; **172**: 305–16

21 Nestler EJ, Terwilliger RZ, Duman RS. Chronic antidepressant administration alters the subcellular distribution of cyclic AMP-dependent protein kinase in rat frontal cortex. *J Neurochem* 1989; **53**: 1644–7

22 Peiffer A, Veilleaux S, Barden N. Antidepressant and other centrally acting drugs regulate glucocorticoid receptor messenger RNA levels in the rat brain. *Psychoneuroendocrinology* 1991; **16**: 505–15

23 Brady LS, Gold PW, Herkenham M, Lynn AB, Whitfield HJ. The antidepressants fluoxetine, Idahoan and phenelzine alter corticotrophin-releasing hormone and tyrosine hydroxylase mRNA levels in the rat brain: therapeutic implications. *Brain Res* 1992; **572**: 117–25

24 Nibuya M, Nestler EJ, Duman RS. Chronic antidepressant administration increases the expression of cAMP response element binding protein (CREB) in rat hippocampus. *J Neurosci* 1996; **16**: 2365-72

25 Thome J, Impey S, Storm D, Duman RS. cAMP-response element-mediated gene transcription is upregulated by chronic antidepressant treatment. *J Neurosci* 2000; **20**: 4030–6

26 Walker WH, Fucci L, Habener JF. Expression of the gene encoding transcription factor cyclic adenosine 3',5'-monophosphate (cAMP) response element-binding protein (CREB): regulation by follicle stimulating hormone induced cAMP signaling in primary rat Sertoli cells. *Endocrinology* 1995; **136**: 3534–45

27 Lee KAW, Masson N. Transcriptional regulation by CREB and its relatives. *Biochim Biophys Acta* 1993; **1174**: 221–33

28 Meyer T, Habener J. Cyclic adenosine 3',5'-monophosphate response element binding protein (CREB) and related transcription-activating deoxyribonucleic acid binding proteins. *Endocrine Rev* 1993; **14**: 269–90

29 Widnell KL, Russell DS, Nestler EJ. Regulation of expression of cAMP response element binding protein in the locus coeruleus *in vivo* and in a locus coeruleus-like cell line *in vitro*. *Proc Natl Acad Sci USA* 1994; **91**: 10947–51

30 Dowlatshahi D, Macqueen GM, Wang JF, Young LT. Increased temporal cortex CREB concentrations and antidepressant treatment in major depression. *Lancet* 1998; **352**: 1754-5

31 Kafitz KW, Rose CR, Thoenen H, Konnerth A.. Neurotrophin-evoked rapid excitation through TrkB receptors. *Nature* 1999; **401**: 918–21

32 Thoenen H. Neurotrophins and neuronal plasticity. *Science* 1995; **270**: 593–98

33 Nibuya M, Morinobu S, Duman RS. Regulation of BDNF and trkB mRNA in rat brain by chronic electroconvulsive seizure and antidepressant drug treatments. *J Neurosci* 1997; **15**: 7539–47

34 Tao X, Finkbeiner S, Arnold DB, Shaywitz AJ, Greenber ME. Ca^{2+} influx regulates BDNF transcription by a CREB family transcription factor-dependent mechanism. *Neuron* 1998; **20**: 709–26

35 Shieh PB, Hu SC, Bobb K, Timmusk T, Ghosh A. Identification of a signaling pathway involved in calcium regulation of BDNF expression. *Neuron* 1998; **20**: 727–40

36 Siuciak JA, Lewis DR, Wiegand SJ, Lindsay RM. Antidepressant-like effect of brain derived neurotrophic factor. *Pharmacol Biochem Behav* 1996; **56**: 131–7

37 Sklair-Tavron L, Nestler EJ. Opposing effects of morphine and the neurotrophins, NT-3, NT-4 and BDNF, on locus coeruleus neurons in vitro. *Brain Res* 1995; **702**: 117–25

38 Mamounas LA, Blue ME, Siuciak JA, Anthony AC. BDNF promotes the survival and sprouting of serotonergic axons in the rat brain. *J Neurosci* 1995; **15**: 7929–39

39. McEwen BS. Stress and hippocampal plasticity. *Annu Rev Neurosci* 1999; **22**: 105–122

40. Gould E, Tanapat P, McEwen BS, Flugge G, Fuchs E. Proliferation of granule cell precursors in the dentate gyrus of adult monkeys is diminished by stress. *Proc Natl Acad Sci USA* 1998; **95**: 3168–71

41 Erickson PS, Perfilieva E, Bjork-Erikkson T *et al.* Neurogenesis in the adult human hippocampus. *Nat Med* 1998; **4**: 1313–7

42 Sheline YI, Wang P, Gado MH, Csernansky JG, Vannier MW. Hippocampal atrophy in recurrent major depression. *Proc Natl Acad Sci USA* 1996; **93**: 3908–13

43 Young EA, Haskett RF, Murphy-Weinberg V, Watson SJ, Akil H. Loss of glucocorticoid fast feedback in depression. *Arch Gen Psychiatry* 1991; **48**: 693–9

44 Rajkowska G, Miguel-Hidalgo JJ, Wei J *et al.* Morphometric evidence for neuronal and glial prefrontal pathology in major depression. *Biol Psychiatry* 1999; **45**: 1085–98

45 Vaidya VA, Terwilliger RZ, Duman RS. Role of 5-HT$_{2A}$ receptors in the down regulation of BDNF by stress. *Neurosci Lett* 1999; **287**: 1–4

46 Vaidya VA, Siuciak JA, Du F, Duman RS. Mossy fiber sprouting and synaptic reorganization induced by chronic administration of electroconvulsive seizure: role of BDNF. *Neuroscience* 1999; **89**: 157–62

47 Malberg JE, Eisch AJ, Nestler EJ, Duman RS. Chronic antidepressant treatment increases neurogenesis in adult rat hippocampus. *J Neurosci* 2000; **20**: 9104–10

48 Jacobs B, Tanapat P, Reeves A, Gould E. Serotonin stimulates the production of new hippocampal granule neurons via the 5-HT$_{1A}$ receptor in the adult rat. *Soc Neurosci Abstr* 1998; **23**: 1992

Depression and sexual dysfunction

David S Baldwin

Community Clinical Sciences Research Division, Faculty of Medicine, Health and Biological Sciences, University of Southampton, Southampton, UK

Adequate sexual expression is an essential part of many human relationships, and may enhance quality of life and provide a sense of physical, psychological and social well-being. Epidemiological and clinical studies show that depression is associated with impairments of sexual function and satisfaction, even in untreated patients. Most antidepressant drugs have adverse effects on sexual function, but accurate identification of the incidence of treatment-emergent dysfunction has proved troublesome, as disturbances of the sexual response can only be detected in a reliable fashion when systematic enquiries are made before and during the course of treatment. Growing awareness of the adverse effects of many antidepressants on sexual function has led to attempts to resolve dysfunction though adjuvant or substitution treatment approaches. There is a need for further studies of the effects of antidepressants on sexual function.

Interest in human sexual function has increased considerably in recent years. Western societies are more open about sexual matters and sexual images are used in advertising and entertainment. These shifts in social attitudes may increase the number of people who wonder whether their sexual performance is less than ideal, and increase the number who consult health professionals[1]. The introduction of sildenafil (Viagra), the first orally active drug for male erectile disorder, created wide-spread comment and increased public awareness of sexual dysfunction, which is now often regarded as a medical condition that can be treated by a doctor.

Sexual dysfunction can arise from physical conditions (*e.g.* circulatory disorders may cause erectile dysfunction in men) and from psychological factors (*e.g.* unsatisfactory interpersonal relationships, psychiatric illness). Many drugs can cause sexual dysfunction, including antihypertensives[2], antipsychotics[3], and antidepressants[4,5]. However, it can be difficult to separate drug-induced adverse effects from consequences of illness, particularly in psychiatric disorders with major effects on interpersonal relationships. There is relatively little scientific information on the incidence of antidepressant-induced sexual dysfunction, even though this may be important to the patient and contribute to non-compliance with treatment.

Correspondence to:
Dr David S Baldwin,
University Department of
Mental Health, Royal
South Hants Hospital,
Brintons Terrace,
Southampton
SO14 0YG, UK

The human sexual response and sexual dysfunctions

The normal human sexual response cycle is conventionally divided into four phases. Disorders of the sexual response can occur at one or more of these phases.

1   *Desire*: typically this consists of fantasies about, and the desire to have, sexual activity.

2   *Excitement*: the subjective sense of sexual pleasure and accompanying physiological changes, namely penile tumescence and erection in men, and pelvic vasocongestion, swelling of the external genitalia, and vaginal lubrication and expansion in women.

3   *Orgasm*: sexual pleasure peaks, with release of sexual tension and rhythmic contraction of the perineal muscles and reproductive organs. In men, the sensation of ejaculatory inevitability is followed by ejaculation of semen. In women, contractions of the outer third of the vaginal wall occur.

4   *Resolution*: the sense of muscular relaxation and general well-being. Men are physiologically refractory to erection and orgasm for a variable period, whereas women may be able to respond to further stimulation.

The tenth edition of the *International Classification of Mental and Behavioural Disorders* (ICD-10)[6] uses the term 'sexual dysfunction' to cover the ways in which an individual is unable to participate in a sexual relationship as he or she would wish. The ICD-10 classification of sexual dysfunction, not caused by organic disorder or disease is as shown below. The fourth edition of the *Diagnostic and Statistical Manual of Mental Disorders* (DSM-IV)[7] uses a broadly similar classificatory scheme.

    F52.0   Lack or loss of sexual desire
    F52.1   Sexual aversion and lack of sexual enjoyment
    F52.2   Failure of genital response
    F52.3   Orgasmic dysfunction
    F52.4   Premature ejaculation
    F52.5   Non-organic vaginismus
    F52.6   Non-organic dyspareunia
    F52.7   Excessive sexual drive
    F52.8   Other sexual dysfunction, not caused by organic
            disorder or disease
    F52.9   Unspecified sexual dysfunction, not caused by organic
            disorder or disease

Some types of dysfunction occur in both men and women, although women tend to present with complaints about the subjective quality of sexual experience (*e.g.* lack of interest or enjoyment) whereas men often describe the failure of a specific response such as erection, whilst reporting a continuing sexual appetite. It has been argued[8] that the categorical approach to sexual dysfunction adopted by the ICD-10 and DSM-IV simply serves 'to obscure the varied and often unique ways in which individuals and couples present with sexual problems'. When one aspect of the sexual response is affected, other aspects are also likely to be impaired, and it is important to 'look beyond' any presenting complaint, to find the most appropriate diagnosis.

Epidemiology of sexual dysfunction

This area has not been studied extensively (Table 1). In an attempt to derive prevalence data for sexual dysfunctions as defined in DSM-III, Nathan surveyed 22 studies of sexual behaviour in the general population, but concluded that methodological problems in the surveys meant that only broad estimates could be made[9]. The prevalence of inhibited sexual desire was 16% for men, 35% for women; erectile dysfunction and premature ejaculation, 10–20% and 35% of men, respectively; and female orgasmic difficulties had a prevalence of 5–15%.

A recent study in the US has shown that sexual dysfunction in the general population is more prevalent in women (43%) than men (31%)[1]. Using latent class analysis, symptoms of sexual dysfunction during the previous 12 months could be grouped into three categories. For women, these were low sexual desire (22% prevalence), arousal problems (14%), and sexual pain (7%). The categories in men were premature ejaculation (21%), erectile dysfunction (5%) and low sexual desire (5%).

Rates of sexual dysfunction vary considerably between studies, probably reflecting differences in study population and types of dysfunction being assessed. The studies which provided data for both genders show a higher prevalence of sexual dysfunction in women than men[1,10,11]. Among men, the most commonly encountered sexual dysfunction appears to be premature ejaculation, whereas women are more likely to complain of reduced sexual desire, or difficulties in getting excited and reaching orgasm.

Many factors influence the reported incidence of sexual dysfunction. First, the method of enquiry; for example, in a prospective study of depressed out-patients, the incidence of sexual dysfunction was 14% when relying on spontaneous reporting, but 58% when patients were questioned directly by doctors[14]. Second, the expectations people have of their sexual performance and their willingness to discuss problems varies widely between different cultures[15]. Third, many terms used to define sexual dysfunction are subjective and dependent on ideas of what is normal. Finally, temporal trends can occur as increased awareness of sexual matters and availability of medical treatments increase the number who perceive themselves as suffering from sexual dysfunction.

Table 1 Sexual dysfunction in the general population

Study	Population	No. subjects (M/F)	Dysfunctions assessed	Prevalence (%)
Laumann et al 1999[1]	Representative cohort aged 19–59 years, from National Health and Social Life Survey	1410/1749	Overall	
			Men	31
			Women	43
Dunn et al 1998[11]	Stratified random sample of the adult general population	789/979	Overall	
			Men	34
			Women	41
Ernst et al 1993	29-year-old men 30-year-old women	197/218	Men	
			Difficulties/dissatisfaction	21
			Impaired interest	7
			Erectile dysfunction	0
			Premature ejaculation	4
			Women	
			Difficulties/dissatisfaction	21
			Impaired interest	16
			Orgasmic difficulties	7
			Pain/dyspareunia	6
Osborn et al 1988[13]	35–59-year-old Oxford women	0/521	Impaired interest	17
			Orgasmic difficulties	16
			Pain/dyspareunia	8
Garde et al 1980[12]	40 year-old Danish women	0/324	Difficulties/dissatisfaction	35.4
			Impaired interest	41.8
			Orgasmic difficulties	36.7
			Pain/dyspareunia	1.3

Sexual dysfunction in depressed patients

Depression is characterised by loss of interest, reduction in energy, lowered self-esteem and inability to experience pleasure: irritability and social withdrawal may impair the ability to form and maintain intimate relationships. This constellation of symptoms may be expected to produce difficulties in sexual relationships, and depression has long been associated with sexual problems[16]. In 132 patients with depressive disorders, loss of sexual interest, characterised by loss of libido or decrease of sexual desire or potency, was reported by 72% of patients with unipolar depression, and 77% of patients with bipolar depression[17]. Conversely, loss of sexual desire may be the presenting complaint of some patients, who only after direct questioning are found to have significant depressive symptoms. In others, low sexual desire may precede the onset of depression[18].

Comparative studies reveal higher levels of sexual dysfunction in depressed patients than in non-depressed controls (Table 2). The specific

Table 2 Comparative studies of sexual dysfunction in depressed patients and controls

Study	Depressed subjects	Control subjects	Dysfunctions assessed	Prevalence in depressed (%)	Prevalence in controls (%)
Casper et al 1985[17]	Hospitalised for major depressive disorder Unipolar $n = 85$ Bipolar $n = 47$	Age- and sex-matched $n = 80$	Loss of sexual interest (derived from scores on item 14 of HDS, 32 of VIBES, 5 of HSCL and) 230 of SADS-C	Unipolar 72 Bipolar 77	5[a]
Mathew & Weinman 1982[19]	51 drug-free depressed patients	51 age- and sex-matched controls	Loss of libido (defined as desire to have sex)	31	6[b]
			Excessive libido	22	0[b]
			Impotence	35	0 NS
			Premature ejaculation	38	0 NS
			Delayed ejaculation	47	6 NS
			Lack of orgasm	34	11 NS
Angst 1998[20]	Random selection from a population scoring above 85th percentile on SCL-90-R. Includes MDD, dysthymia and RBD ($n = 126$)	Randomly selected from population scoring below 85th percentile on SCL-90-R ($n = 365$)	Males		
			Increased libido	23	7 ND
			Decreased libido	26	11 ND
			Sexual dysfunction	11	7 ND
			Emotional problems	16	7 ND
			Any sexual problem	48	18 ND
			Females		
			Increased libido	9	2 ND
			Decreased libido	35	32 ND
			Sexual dysfunction	26	18 ND
			Emotional problems	19	15 ND
			Any sexual problem	51	32 ND

Terminology is taken from the source.
HDS, Hamilton Depression Scale; VIBES, Video Interview Behaviour Evaluation Scale; HSCL, Hopkins Symptom Checklist; SADS-C, Schedule for Affective Disorders and Schizophrenia Change form; SCL-90-R, Symptom Checklist 90-R; MDD, major depressive disorder; RBD, recurrent brief depression.
[a]$P < 0.00$; [b]$P < 0.05$; NS, no significant difference; ND, not determined.

type of sexual dysfunctions vary in incidence, but loss of sexual desire may be more common than disorders of arousal and orgasm: in a comparative study, changes in libido were significantly more common in depressed patients than controls, but differences in the prevalence of impotence, orgasmic or ejaculatory problems were not[19]. The prospective Zurich cohort study shows that the prevalence of sexual problems in depressed subjects (including those with major depression, dysthymia and recurrent brief depression) is approximately twice that in controls (50% *versus* 24%). This difference encompassed emotional problems, sexual dysfunction, and both decreased and increased libido. The data in this study are from a group of young people (28–35 years) and may not be applicable to older age groups[20].

The Zurich study provides comparative data on the prevalence of sexual problems in untreated depressed patients and depressed patients receiving either medication (50% benzodiazepines, 50% antidepressants) or psychotherapy. Sexual problems were more prevalent in the 78 depressed patients who received treatment (62%) than in the 122 who did not (45%), and both groups had a higher prevalence of sexual dysfunction than controls (26%). However, there were no statistically significant differences in the prevalence of any type of sexual dysfunction between patients treated with medication (62%) or psychotherapy alone (63%)[20].

Sexual dysfunction associated with antidepressants

Papers for this review were identified by searching the Medline, Toxline, Embase, Biosis, DDFU, Scisearch, PsychLit and ADIS Newsletter databases. Sexual dysfunction was used as an index term, and combined with names of antidepressant drugs. Further papers were obtained from *Current Contents* 1995–1999. These were supplemented by papers identified from reference lists, abstracts presented at congresses, and through scanning library copies of relevant journals. Studies were included if they were published in English, reported an incidence of sexual dysfunction in patients receiving antidepressant medication and if there were 10 or more subjects. All studies reporting data on drug-associated sexual dysfunction were assessed on the following criteria: design (randomised, prospective, double-blind); comparative; type of control (placebo-controlled and/or baseline-controlled); use of defined diagnostic criteria; use of validated rating scale for assessing sexual dysfunction.

Although the high prevalence of sexual dysfunction in the general population and in depressed patients can make evaluation difficult, treatment-emergent sexual dysfunction can occur with tricyclic antidepressants (TCAs), selective serotonin re-uptake inhibitors (SSRIs) and monoamine oxidase inhibitors (MAOIs)[5,21]. Some antidepressants (bupropion, mirtazapine, moclobemide, reboxetine, nefazodone) may be associated with a relatively lower incidence of sexual dysfunction[4,22], but most data for these newer drugs come from reviews of clinical trial adverse event databases or work with healthy volunteers.

Studies which made no direct comparison between antidepressants

Table 3 lists studies conducted in mixed populations of patients receiving antidepressants for depressive or anxiety disorders. The prevalence of sexual dysfunction may not differ according to diagnosis[23,24]. One study found no significant difference between patients undergoing drug or non-

Table 3 Studies of sexual dysfunction which made no direct comparison between antidepressant drugs

Study	Diagnosis	Sexual dysfunction assessment	No. and drug dose (mg)	Sexual dysfunction prevalence	Design	Placebo or baseline control
Ashton et al. 1997[23]	MDD, dysthymia, bipolar disorder, OCD, panic	Open question	596 Fluoxetine, paroxetine, sertraline, venlafaxine Doses not stated	16.3% No difference between drugs	Retrospective chart review Non-randomised Non-blinded	None
Balon et al. 1993[24]	Mood or anxiety disorder (DSM-III-R)	Questionnaire developed for the study	60 Imipramine 20–300 Fluoxetine 20–60 Trazodone 75–200 Desipramine 60–150 Nortriptyline 60–125 Doxepin 20–50 Clomipramine 150–275	43.3%	Non-randomised Non-blinded Baseline function assessed retrospectively	None
Karp et al 1994[25]	Recurrent MDD (RDC criteria)	Subscales of HRSD and SAS	Imipramine 150-300 ($n = 44$) Non-drug therapy ($n = 46$)	SAS score[a]: 1.63 (SD 1.19) 1.77 (SD 1.42)	Prospective Randomised Non-blinded	Placebo, analysed with non-drug therapy
Labbate et al. 1998[68]	MDD	Visual analogue scale	30 Fluoxetine 5–30 Paroxetine 20 Sertraline 50–200	Significant worsening in orgasm delay and orgasm quality	Prospective Non-randomised Non-blinded	No placebo Baseline-adjusted
Clayton et al. 1995[61]	MDD	CSFQ	7 Paroxetine (dose not stated)	43%	Prospective Non-randomised Non-blinded	No placebo Baseline controlled
Patterson 1993[27]	MDD, panic, OCD	Specific query about delayed or absent ejaculation	60 Fluoxetine 20	75%	Prospective Non-randomised Non-blinded	None
Zajecka et al. 1991[28]	Depression	Spontaneous reports of orgasm dysfunction	77 Fluoxetine 20–80	8%	Prospective Non-randomised Non-blinded	None
Jacobsen 1992[67]	MDD (DSM-III-R)	Open question	160 Fluoxetine 20–40	34%	Non-randomised Non-blinded Baseline function assessed retrospectively	None
Zajecka et al 1997[72]	Depression with/without OCD	RSI	42 Fluoxetine 20–60 Sertraline 50–200 Paroxetine 20	Males 60% Females 57%	Prospective Non-randomised Non-blinded	No placebo Baseline-adjusted

[**Table 3** continued on p88]

Table 3 (*Continued*) Studies of sexual dysfunction which made no direct comparison between antidepressant drugs

Study	Diagnosis	Sexual dysfunction assessment	No. and drug dose (mg)	Sexual dysfunction prevalence	Design	Placebo or baseline control
Kennedy et al. 1996[42]	Healthy volunteers	Sexual Function Questionnaire	Moclobemide 300 (n = 26) Placebo (n = 25)	No difference on any parameter	Prospective Randomised Double-blind	Placebo Baseline
Mucci 1997[70]	Depression	Adverse event report of impotence in men	Reboxetine (n = 373) Placebo (n = 373)	5% 0%	Prospective Randomised Double-blind	Placebo No baseline
Montgomery 1995[69]	Moderate or severe depression	Adverse event report of decreased libido in men	Mirtazapine (n = 359) Placebo (n = 328)	4% 7%	Prospective Randomised Double-blind	Placebo No baseline
Feighner 1994[64]	MDD	Adverse event report of abnormal ejaculation in men	Venlafaxine (n = 836) Placebo (n = 609)	12% 0%	Prospective Randomised Double-blind	Placebo No baseline
Baldwin & Birtwistle 1988[56]	Major depression	Spontaneous reports	Milnacipran < 100 mg Milnacipran 100 mg Milnacipran >100 mg	0.8% 2.7% 6.5%	Prospective	No baseline

Terminology is taken from source.
Prevalence of sex-specific problems is calculated as a percentage of patients of the appropriate sex.
HRSD, Hamilton Rating Scale for Depression; SAS, Social Adjustment Scale; CSFQ, Changes in Sexual Functioning Questionnaire; RSI, Rush Sexual Inventory; MDD, major depressive disorder; OCD, obsessive-compulsive disorder.
[a]Sexual problems subscale.

drug therapy, across a range of sexual function variables assessed using the Social Adjustment Scale (SAS) and Hamilton Rating Scale for Depression (HRSD)[25]. Few data have been published on sexual dysfunction occurring with TCAs, although anorgasmia was common in a study of clomipramine in patients with obsessive-compulsive disorder[26].

The majority of the studies assess sexual dysfunction with SSRIs. It is difficult to interpret these findings, as the study populations include patients with varying degrees of depression and/or anxiety, and no two studies used the same method of assessing sexual dysfunction. Few studies assessed sexual function at baseline (4 studies), and 8 of the studies involved fewer than 100 subjects. Large patient populations and placebo control were mainly confined to controlled clinical trials, which invariably failed to include a baseline control. Fluoxetine had both the highest (75%) and the lowest (8%) reported prevalence of treatment-emergent sexual dysfunction, one figure derived from specific questioning about abnormal ejaculation[27], the other derived from spontaneous reports of orgasmic problems[28].

Studies which made direct comparisons between antidepressants

Table 4 summarises studies which directly compared two or more active agents. As with the non-comparative studies, the methodology varies considerably. Several are not true comparisons, but report differences between drugs in manufacturers' databases[29,30], adverse events spontaneously reported to a national body[31,32] or hospital monitoring scheme[33]. These evaluations are troublesome to interpret, through differences in coding of adverse events, possible bias in reporting, and inadequate data on dosage and number of exposed patients.

Comparative studies of SSRIs have generally found no significant differences between drugs[14,34,35], but one study reported more sexual dysfunction with sertraline than fluvoxamine[36]. Bupropion may be associated with a low incidence of sexual adverse effects, being significantly superior to sertraline in one study[37] and to SSRIs in another[34]. A comparative study with nefazodone found it to be significantly superior to sertraline on some measures of sexual function[38]. All the studies had some methodological flaw. Only two[39,40] used a recognised rating scale for sexual dysfunction (the Sexual Function Questionnaire), the others relying on patients reporting adverse events. Only two[37,39] used a baseline assessment and placebo control.

The findings of a randomised controlled trial comparing moclobemide (a reversible inhibitor of monoamine oxidase type A) with the TCA doxepin suggest that moclobemide is relatively free of adverse effects on sexual function[41]. This is supported by a study in healthy volunteers[42] and post-marketing surveillance[43].

Augmentation or switching studies

Several studies have investigated whether SSRI-associated sexual dysfunction can be resolved by adding, or changing to, a different antidepressant. For example, a retrospective review of 16 patients who complained of sexual dysfunction during SSRI treatment found that 11/16 (69%) rated their sexual function as much or very much improved when buspirone was added to the drug regimen: however, buspirone was associated with increased irritability in 4 (25%) of patients[44].

Mirtazapine may be a useful alternative in depressed patients who develop sexual dysfunction with SSRIs. In a study of 20 patients with

Table 4 Studies directly comparing sexual dysfunction with two or more antidepressant drugs

Study	Definition of sexual dysfunction	Drug and dose (mg)	n	Prevalence of sexual dysfunction	Statistical significance	Diagnosis	Sexual dysfunction assessment	Design	Controlled Placebo	Controlled Baseline
Hekimian et al. 1978[66]	Impotence or loss of libido	Amoxapine 126–210 Amitriptyline 64–107	30 31	27% 10%	ND	Moderate to severe depression	a.e.r.	Prospective Randomised Double-blind	No	No
Harrison et al. 1986[39]	Decrease in sexual function during treatment	Imipramine 200–300 Phenelzine 60–90 Placebo	82 overall	30% 40% 6%	P < 0.02 vs placebo P < 0.002 vs placebo NS between active treatments	Major, minor or intermittent depression (RDC)	s.f.q.	Prospective Randomised Double-blind	Yes	Yes
Grohmann et al. 1999[33]	Impaired sexual function	TCAs SSRIs	48,564 overall	~1% ~3%	ND	All in-patients receiving psychotropic drugs in 19 hospitals	a.d.r.r.	Naturalistic data-gathering in clinical practice	No	No
Reimherr et al. 1990[71]	Male sexual dysfunction	Sertraline 50–200 Amitriptyline 50–150 Placebo	149 149 150	21.4% 7.7% 1.4%		P ≤ 0.05 vs placebo P ≤ 0.05 vs sertraline	MDD (DSM-III)	Prospective Randomised Double-blind	Yes	No
ADRAC 1996[32]	Various sexual dysfunctions	Fluoxetine Sertraline Paroxetine	Not stated	19 reports 22 reports 61 reports	ND	Not stated	Spontaneous a.d.r.r.	Adverse reaction reports to national drug monitoring body	No	No
Merino et al, 2000	Various dysfunctions	Clomipramine Moclobemide Nefazodone Paroxetine Venlafaxine	20 20 20 20 20	10–40% 0% 0–15% 15–80% 10–45%	Hard to interpret	Depressive episode or recurrent depressive disorder or dysthymia				
Montejo-González et al 1997[14]	Decreased libido, delayed or absent orgasm delayed or absent ejaculation, impotence, sexual satisfaction	Fluoxetine 23[a] Paroxetine 23[a] Fluvoxamine 114[a] Sertraline 89[a]	160 85 42 57	54% 65% 59% 56%	NS	MDD, dysthymia, panic, OCD, GAD, bulimia, personality disorder	quest	Prospective Non-randomised Open	No	No

[Table 4 continued next page]

Table 4 (*continued*) Studies directly comparing sexual dysfunction with two or more antidepressant drugs

Study	Definition of sexual dysfunction	Drug and dose (mg)	n	Prevalence of sexual dysfunction	Statistical significance	Diagnosis	Sexual dysfunction assessment	Design	Controlled Placebo	Baseline
Grimsley & Jann 1992[30]	Sexual dysfunction	Paroxetine Sertraline Fluvoxamine Fluoxetine	2683 861 24,624 1034	3% 17% < 0.1% 0%	ND	Not stated	a.e.r.	Pooled data from manufacturers' clinical trial databases	Not stated	Not stated
Kiev & Feiger 1997[35]	Impotence in men Ejaculatory abnormality in men Decreased libido	Paroxetine 20–50 Fluvoxamine 50–150 Paroxetine 20–50 Fluvoxamine 50–150 Paroxetine 20–50 Fluvoxamine 50–150	30 30 30 30 30 30	21% 14% 21% 7% 17% 13%	NS paroxetine vs fluvoxamine for all parameters	Moderate or severe MDD (DSM-III-R)	a.e.r.	Prospective Randomised Double-blind	No	No
Nemeroff et al 1995[36]	Ejaculatory abnormality in men, decreased libido, anorgasmia or impotence	Fluvoxamine 50–150 Sertraline 50–200	49 48	10% 28%	P = 0.047 vs sertraline	MDD (DSM-III-R)	s.q.	Prospective Randomised Double-blind	No	No
Price et al 1996[31]	Male sexual dysfunction	Fluoxetine Fluvoxamine Paroxetine Sertraline	Not stated	Incidence highest with paroxetine, no data presented	ND		Spontaneous a.d.r.r	Adverse reaction reports to national drug monitoring body	No	No
Fava et al 1998[63]	Sexual dysfunction	Paroxetine 20–50 Fluoxetine 20–80 Placebo	55 54 19	25% 7% 0%	(P < 0.005) NS after Benferroni correction	Moderate to severe depression (DSM-III-R)	a.e.r.	Prospective Randomised Double-blind	Yes	No
Ekselius et al 1997[62]	Increased sexual desire Decreased sexual desire Ejaculatory dysfunction Orgasmic dysfunction	Sertraline 50–150 Citalopram 20–60 Sertraline 50–150 Citalopram 20–60 Sertraline 50–150 Citalopram 20–60 Sertraline 50–150 Citalopram 20–60	145 163 145 163 145 163 145 163	2.5% 3.5% 3.5% 6.5% 10.5% 14.5% 5.0% 7.0%	NS	MDD	UKU	Prospective Randomised Double-blind	No	Yes

*[**Table 4** continued next page]*

Table 4 *(continued)* Studies directly comparing sexual dysfunction with two or more antidepressant drugs

Study	Definition of sexual dysfunction	Drug and dose (mg)	n	Prevalence of sexual dysfunction	Statistical significance	Diagnosis	Sexual dysfunction assessment	Design	Controlled Placebo	Controlled Baseline
Montgomery 1995[69]	Decreased libido	Mirtazepine Amitriptyline	463 466	6% M, 6% F 14% M, 6% F	NS vs amitriptyline	Not stated	a.e.r.	Pooled data from comparative clinical trials	No	No
Philipp et al. 1993[41]	Increased sexual desire	Doxepin 32–137 Moclobemide 240–580	119 118	6% 18%	P = 0.038 vs moclobemide	MDD (RDC)	UKU	Prospective Randomised Double-blind	No	Yes
Preskorn 1995[29]	Abnormal ejaculation/ orgasm Decreased libido	Nefazodone Paroxetine Sertraline Venlafaxine Bupropion Fluoxetine Nefazodone Paroxetine Venlafaxine	393 421 861 1033 323 1730 393 421 1033	0.6% 13% 13% 12% 1.5% 1.6% 1.1% M 0.3% F 3.3% 2%	ND Rates are placebo-adjusted	Not stated	a.e.r.	Placebo-adjusted data from placebo-controlled trials	Yes	No
Modell et al. 1997[34]	Change in libido Change in arousal Change in intensity of orgasm Change in duration of orgasm	Bupropion SSRIs Bupropion SSRIs Bupropion SSRIs Bupropion SSRIs	22 85 22 85 22 85 22 85	50% I, 14% D 14% I, 55% D 57% I, 0% D 11% I, 50% D 38% I, 0% D 14% I, 42% D 48% I, 0% D 18% I, 36% D	P < 0.001 bupropion vs SSRIs NS between SSRIs	MDD, panic, OCD, adult attention-deficit disorder	quest	Retrospective Non-randomised Non-blind	No	Patients assessed baseline functioning retrospectively
Croft et al. 1999[37]	Orgasm dysfunction	Bupropion 150–400 Sertraline 50–200 Placebo	120 119 121	~15% ~40% ~10%	P < 0.001 vs sertraline P < 0.001 vs placebo	Depression	s.i.	Prospective Randomised Double-blind	Yes	Yes
Feighner et al. 1991[65]	Impotence Anorgasmia Libido decrease	Fluoxetine 20–80 Bupropion 225–400	60 60	4.2% 1.7% 1.7% Not stated	ND	MDD (DSM-III-R)	a.e.r.	Prospective Randomised Double-blind	No	No

Table 4 *(continued)* Studies directly comparing sexual dysfunction with two or more antidepressant drugs

Study	Definition of sexual dysfunction	Drug and dose (mg)	n	Prevalence of sexual dysfunction	Statistical significance	Diagnosis	Sexual dysfunction assessment	Design	Controlled Placebo	Baseline
Feiger et al 1996[38]	**Men**					MDD (DSM-III-R)	quest	Prospective Randomised Double-blind	No	Yes
	Difficulty with ejaculation	Sertraline 50–200	27	67%	P < 0.01 vs nefazodone					
		Nefazodone 100–600	27	19%	P < 0.01 vs nefazodone					
	Delayed ejaculation	Sertraline 50–200	27	Score 2.63	P < 0.01 vs nefazodone					
	Ability to enjoy sex	Nefazodone 100–600	27	Score 4.04[b]						
	Satisfaction with sexual function	Sertraline 50–200	27	Score 2.25	P < 0.01 vs nefazodone					
		Nefazodone 100–600	27	Score 1.56						
	Women									
	Difficulty achieving orgasm	Sertraline 50–200	27	Score 3.43	P < 0.01 vs nefazodone					
		Nefazodone 100–600	27	Score 2.44						
	Satisfaction with achieving orgasm	Sertraline 50–200	23	Score 3.09	P < 0.03 vs nefazodone					
		Nefazodone 100–600	23	Score 4.09[b]	P < 0.04 vs nefazodone					
		Sertraline 50–200	23	Score 2.83						
		Nefazodone 100–600	23	Score 2.13						

Terminology is taken from the original source.

Prevalence of sex-specific problems (*e.g.* ejaculation disorder in men) is calculated as a percentage of the number of patients of the appropriate sex.

RDC, Research Diagnostic Criteria; M, male; F, female; I, increase; D, decrease; NS, no significant difference; ND, not determined; MDD, major depressive disorder; OCD, obsessive-compulsive disorder; GAD, generalised anxiety disorder.

[a]Mean drug dosage; [b]High score indicates better functioning.

Current prevalence estimate.

6-month prevalence estimate.

4-year prevalence estimate.

a.e.r., adverse event report; s.f.q., sexual function questionnaire; a.d.r.r., adverse drug reaction report; quest, questionnaire; s.q., specific questionnaire; UKU, adverse agent rating; s.i, structured interview.

SSRI-associated sexual dysfunction who switched to mirtazapine, sexual function improved in 9 of 12 patients (75%) who completed at least 6 weeks' treatment, although 6 patients developed irritability and 9 reported sedation[45]. A second study in 11 patients who stopped SSRIs because of sexual problems found that mirtazapine treatment did not result in the re-emergence of sexual dysfunction[46]. These observations are supported by recent findings in a group of 25 depressed out-patients, indicating that mirtazapine treatment had beneficial effects on sexual function[47].

The largest body of data is for bupropion. Adjunctive treatment improved sexual dysfunction in 31 of 47 (66%) patients previously treated with SSRIs, but 7 (15%) discontinued bupropion because of anxiety and tremor[48]. In another study, switching to bupropion improved sexual function in 24 of 28 men who had experienced sexual dysfunction during treatment with TCAs or MAOIs[49]. Similar effects have been reported in 31 patients (men and women) who developed anorgasmia or delayed orgasm while taking fluoxetine: after switching to bupropion for 8 weeks, orgasm dysfunction completely or partially resolved in 29 patients (94%), and libido was much or very much increased in 25 (81%)[50]. However, not all data with bupropion are consistent: a retrospective review in 27 patients found that sexual dysfunction occurred in 11 patients (41%) when they were receiving combination bupropion-SSRI treatment, not significantly different to the rate (52%) when they were taking either agent alone[51].

All of these studies were of open design, none had a placebo-control or double-blind design, or a baseline assessment, all had fewer than 40 patients, and only one[45] used a validated scale for measuring sexual dysfunction. The results, therefore, need to be replicated in controlled clinical studies.

Method for assessing sexual dysfunction

Studies investigating antidepressant drug-induced sexual dysfunction must be especially stringent, in order to differentiate between normal variations in sexual function, sexual problems related to depression or anxiety, and sexual dysfunction associated with antidepressant treatment. Ideally, these studies should be prospective, randomised, double-blind, placebo-controlled and conducted in a defined diagnostic population. The studies should make direct comparisons between different drugs, and the dose ranges should be of equivalent efficacy.

Sexual dysfunction should be assessed using a rating scale administered to all patients, rather than relying on spontaneous reporting or open questions which may be interpreted differently by different patients. The rating scale chosen should be valid and reliable, able to discriminate between normal variations in sexual behaviour and sexual dysfunction, and sensitive to change. A baseline measure of sexual dysfunction is needed to identify treatment-emergent changes, and in comparative studies groups should be balanced according to degree of sexual function at baseline. Many sexual functioning questionnaires exist, but most have not been thoroughly tested and remain unvalidated[52]. Some of the most well-known scales are the Sexual Function Questionnaire[39], the Sexual Functioning Questionnaire[53], and the Arizona Sexual Experience Scale (ASEX)[54]. The latter has been validated for multiple comparisons, but is not yet used widely[55].

Treatment of sexual dysfunction

Sexual dysfunction occurring in a depressed patient should be assessed sensitively, and treatment tailored to individual needs and circumstances. Several strategies may be beneficial in the management of treatment-associated sexual dysfunction in depression[56], including:

* behavioural strategies to improve sexual technique
* waiting for the development of tolerance
* reduction in dosage
* delaying drug intake until after sexual activity
* 'drug holidays'
* adjuvant treatments
* changing to a different antidepressant

Drug holidays, involving brief interruptions of treatment, have been advocated as an approach to SSRI-induced sexual dysfunction[57]. However, this approach can put the patient at risk of discontinuation symptoms and possible relapse of depression: furthermore, a drug holiday is only possible with drugs with a short half-life and not with fluoxetine, where sexual side effects may not resolve until a few weeks after stopping treatment[21]. Many adjuvant compounds have been advocated for the treatment of psychotropic drug-induced sexual dysfunction, including buspirone, cyproheptadine, mianserin, yohimbine, neostigmine, amantadine and dexamphetamine[56]. However, there have been very few double-blind placebo-controlled studies of these drugs[58], and it is wise to be cautious when using unfamiliar treatments. Finally, it seems likely that sildenafil may come to have a role in relieving sexual dysfunction in depression. In a sub-group of 136 depressed patients included within the placebo-controlled clinical trial database, 76% described improvements with sildenafil, compared to 18% of the group receiving placebo[59]: in a second report, sildenafil was effective in 10 of 14 patients with antidepressant drug-induced sexual dysfunction[60].

Conclusions

Accurate assessment of sexual function in depression is subject to many difficulties, including the little data on prevalence of sexual dysfunction in the general population, and the effects of antidepressant drugs. Obtaining accurate data on an intimate subject is potentially prone to under-reporting unless careful attention is paid to the method of data collection. Until data from rigorous, controlled, comparative studies are available, the perceived likelihood of sexual side effects should not unduly influence the choice of antidepressant drug, and prescribing decisions should be made on an assessment of the overall balance of the benefits and risks of treatment.

Acknowledgements

Thanks are due to Jon Birtwistle for his help with the literature search, and to Stuart Montgomery and Alan Riley for shared discussions regarding the assessment of sexual dysfunction in depression.

References

1   Laumann EO, Park A, Rosen RC. Sexual dysfunction in the United States: prevalence and predictors. *JAMA* 1999; **281**: 537–44
2   Fogari R, Zoppi A, Corradi L, Mugellini A, Poletti L, Lusardi P. Sexual function in hypertensive males treated with lisinopril or atenolol: a cross-over study. *Am J Hypertens* 1998; **11**: 1244–7
3   Baldwin DS, Birtwistle J. Schizophrenia, antipsychotic drugs and sexual function. *Prim Care Psychiatry* 1997; **3**: 115–23
4   Baldwin DS, Thomas SC, Birtwistle J. Effects of antidepressant drugs on sexual function. *Int J Psychiatr Clin Pract* 1997; **1**: 47–58
5   Goldstein BJ, Goodnick PJ. Selective serotonin reuptake inhibitors in the treatment of affective disorders – III. Tolerability, safety and pharmacoeconomics. *J Psychopharmacol* 1998; **12** (**Suppl B**): S35–87
6   World Health Organization. *The ICD-10 Classification of Mental and Behavioural Disorders*. Geneva: World Health Organization, 1992
7   American Psychiatric Association. *Diagnostic and Statistical Manual of Mental Disorders, 4th edn*. Washington, DC: American Psychiatric Association, 1994
8   Bancroft J. *Human Sexuality and its Problems*. Edinburgh: Churchill Livingstone, 1989
9   Nathan SG. The epidemiology of the DSM-III psychosexual dysfunctions. *J Sex Marital Ther* 1986; **12**: 267–81
10 Ernst C, Foldenyi M, Angst J. The Zurich Study: XXI. Sexual dysfunctions and disturbances in young adults. *Eur Arch Psychiatry Clin Neurosci* 1993; **243**: 179–88
11 Dunn KM, Croft PR, Hackett GI. Sexual problems: a study of the prevalence and need for health care in the general population. *Fam Pract* 1998; **15**: 519–24

12 Garde K, Lunde I. Social background and social status: influence on female sexual behaviour. A random sample of 40 year old Danish women. *Maturitas* 1980: **2**: 241–6

13 Osborn M, Hawton K, Gath D. Sexual dysfunction among middle aged women in the community. *BMJ* 1988; **296**: 959–62

14 Montejo-González AL, Liorca G, Izquierdo JA *et al.* SSRI-induced sexual dysfunction: fluoxetine, paroxetine, sertraline and fluvoxamine in a prospective, multicenter, and descriptive clinical study of 344 patients. *J Sex Marital Ther* 1997; **23**: 176–94

15 Bhugra D, De Silva P. Sexual dysfunction across cultures. *Int Rev Psychiatry* 1993; **5**: 243–52

16 Baldwin DS. Depression and sexual function. *J Psychopharmacol* 1996; **10 (Suppl. 1)**: S30–4

17 Casper RC, Redmond E, Katz MM, Schaffer CB, Davis JM, Koslow SH. Somatic symptoms in primary affective disorders: presence and relationship to the classification of depression. *Arch Gen Psychiatry* 1985; **42**: 1098–104

18 Schreiner-Engel P, Schiavi RC. Lifetime psychopathology in individuals with low sexual desire. *J Nerv Ment Dis* 1986; **174**: 646–51

19 Mathew RJ, Weinman ML. Sexual dysfunctions in depression. *Arch Sex Behav* 1982; **11**: 323–5

20 Angst J. Sexual problems in healthy and depressed patients. *Int Clin Psychopharmacol* 1998; **13 (Suppl 6)**: S1–3

21 Lane RM. A critical review of selective serotonin reuptake inhibitor-related sexual dysfunction: incidence, possible aetiology and implications for management. *J Psychopharmacol* 1997; **11**: 72–82

22 Mir S, Taylor D. Sexual adverse events with new antidepressants. *Psychiatr Bull* 1998; **22**: 438–41

23 Ashton AK, Hamer R, Rosen RC. Serotonin reuptake inhibitor-induced sexual dysfunction and its treatment: a large scale retrospective study of 596 outpatients. *J Sex Marital Ther* 1997; **23**: 165–76

24 Balon R, Yeragani VK, Pohl R, Ramesh C. Sexual dysfunction during antidepressant treatment. *J Clin Psychiatry* 1993; **54**: 209–12

25 Karp JF, Frank E, Ritenour A, McEachran A, Kupfer DJ. Imipramine and sexual dysfunction during the long term treatment of recurrent depression. *Neuropsychopharmacology* 1994; **11**: 21–7

26 Monteiro WO, Noshirvani HF, Marks IM, Leliott PT. Anorgasmia from clomipramine in obsessive-compulsive disorder: a controlled trial. *Br J Psychiatry* 1987; **151**: 107–12

27 Patterson WM. Fluoxetine-induced sexual dysfunction. *J Clin Psychiatry* 1993; **54**: 71

28 Zajecka J, Fawcett J, Schaff, M, Jeffriess H, Guy C. The role of serotonin in sexual dysfunction: fluoxetine-associated orgasm dysfunction. *J Clin Psychiatry* 1991; **52**: 66–8

29 Preskorn SH. Comparison of the tolerability of bupropion, fluoxetine, imipramine, nefazodone, paroxetine, sertraline, and venlafaxine. *J Clin Psychiatry* 1995; **56 (Suppl 6)**: S12–21

30 Grimsley SR, Jann MW. Paroxetine, sertraline and fluvoxamine: new selective serotonin reuptake inhibitors. *Clin Pharm* 1992; **11**: 930–57

31 Price JS, Waller PC, Wood SM, Mackay AV. A comparison of the post-marketing safety of four selective serotonin re-uptake inhibitors including the investigation of symptoms occurring on withdrawal. *Br J Clin Pharmacol* 1996; **42**: 757–63

32 ADRAC. SSRIs and genitourinary disorders. *Aust Adv Drug Reac Bull* 1996; **15**: 11

33 Grohmann R, Ruther E, Engel RR, Hippius H. Assessment of adverse drug reactions in psychiatric inpatients with the AMSP drug safety program: methods and first results for tricyclic antidepressants and SSRI. *Pharmacopsychiatry* 1999; **32**: 21–8

34 Modell JG, Katholi CR, Modell JD, DePalma RL. Comparative sexual side effects of bupropion, fluoxetine, paroxetine, and sertraline. *Clin Pharmacol Ther* 1997; **61**: 476–87

35 Kiev A, Feiger A. A double-blind comparison of fluvoxamine and paroxetine in the treatment of depressed outpatients. *J Clin Psychiatry* 1997; **58**: 146–52

36 Nemeroff CB, Ninan PT, Ballenger J *et al.* Double-blind multicenter comparison of fluvoxamine versus sertraline in the treatment of depressed outpatients. *Depression* 1995; **3**: 163–9

37 Croft H, Settle Jr E, Houser T, Batey SR, Donahue RM, Ascher JA. A placebo-controlled comparison of the antidepressant efficacy and effects on sexual functioning of sustained-release bupropion and sertraline. *Clin Ther* 1999; **21**: 643–58

38 Feiger A, Kiev A, Shrivastava RK, Wisselink PG, Wilcox CS. Nefazodone versus sertraline in outpatients with major depression: focus on efficacy, tolerability and effects on sexual function and satisfaction. *J Clin Psychiatry* 1996; **57** (Suppl 2): S53–62

39 Harrison WM, Rabkin JG, Ehrhardt AA *et al*. Effects of antidepressant medication on sexual function: a controlled study. *J Clin Psychopharmacol* 1986; **6**: 144–9

40 Merino M-J, Gonzalez P, Muniz J, Bobes J. Sexual dysfunction in depressed patients undergoing treatment with antidepressants. *Int J Psychiatr Clin Pract* 2000; **4**: 311–7

41 Philipp M, Kohnen R, Benkert O. A comparison study of moclobemide and doxepin in major depression with special reference to effects on sexual dysfunction. *Int Clin Psychopharmacol* 1993; **7**: 123–32

42 Kennedy SH, Ralevski E, Davis C, Neitzert C. The effects of moclobemide on sexual desire and function in healthy volunteers. *Eur Neuropsychopharmacol* 1996; **6**: 177–81

43 Phillip M, Delini-Stula A, Baier D, Kohnen R, Scholz H-J, Laux G. Assessment of sexual dysfunction in depressed patients and reporting attitudes in routine practice: results of postmarketing surveillance studies with moclobemide, a reversible MAO-A inhibitor. *Int J Psychiatr Clin Pract* 1999; **4**: 257–64

44 Norden MJ. Buspirone treatment of sexual dysfunction associated with selective serotonin reuptake inhibitors. *Depression* 1994; **2**: 109–12

45 Gelenberg AJ, Laukes C, McGahuey C *et al*. Mirtazapine substitution in SSRI-induced sexual dysfunction. *Biol Psychiatry* 1998; **43**: 104S

46 Koutouvidis N, Pratikakis M, Fotiadou A. The use of mirtazapine in a group of 11 patients following poor compliance to selective serotonin reuptake inhibitor treatment due to sexual dysfunction. *Int Clin Psychopharmacol* 1999; **14**: 253–5

47 Boyarsky BK, Haque W, Rouleau MR, Hirschfeld RMA. Sexual functioning in depressed outpatients taking mirtazapine. *Depression Anxiety* 1999; **9**: 175–9

48 Ashton AK, Rosen RC. Bupropion as an antidote for serotonin reuptake-induced sexual dysfunction. *J Clin Psychiatry* 1998; **59**: 112–5

49 Gardner EA, Johnston JA. Bupropion: an antidepressant without sexual pathophysiological action. *J Clin Psychopharmacol* 1985; **15**: 24–9

50 Walker PW, Cole JO, Gardner EA *et al*. Improvement in fluoxetine-associated sexual dysfunction in patients switched to bupropion. *J Clin Psychiatry* 1993; **54**: 459–65

51 Bodkin JA, Lasser RA, Wines JD, Gardner DM, Baldessarini RJ. Combining serotonin reuptake inhibitors and bupropion in partial responders to antidepressant monotherapy. *J Clin Psychiatry* 1997 **58**, 137–45

52 Davidson JRT. Sexual dysfunction and antidepressants. *Depression* 1995; **2**: 233–40

53 Burke MA, McEvoy JP, Ritchie JC. A pilot study of a structured interview addressing sexual function in men with schizophrenia. *Biol Psychiatry* 1994; **35**: 32–5

54 McGahuey CA, Gelenberg AJ, Laukes CA *et al*. The Arizona sexual experience scale: validity and reliability. *150th Annual Meeting of the American Psychiatric Association: New Research Program and Abstracts*. Washington DC: American Psychiatric Association, 1997

55 McGahuey CA, Delgado PL, Gelenberg AJ. Assessment of sexual dysfunction using the Arizona Sexual Experiences Scale (ASEX) and implications for the treatment of depression. *Psychiatr Ann* 1999; **29**: 39–45

56 Baldwin DS, Birtwistle J. Antidepressant drugs and sexual function: improving the recognition and management of sexual dysfunction in depressed patients. In: Briley M, Montgomery S. (eds) *Antidepressant Therapy at the Dawn of the Third Millennium*. London: Martin Dunitz, 1998; 231–54

57 Rothschild AJ. Selective serotonin reuptake inhibitor-induced sexual dysfunction: efficacy of a drug holiday. *Am J Psychiatry* 1995; **152**: 514–6

58 Michelson D, Bancroft J, Targum S, Kim Y, Tepner R. Female sexual dysfunction associated with antidepressant administration: a randomized, placebo-controlled study of pharmacologic intervention. *Am J Psychiatr* 2000; **157**: 239–43

59 Price D. Sildenafil citrate (Viagra®) efficacy in the treatment of erectile dysfunction in patients with common concomitant conditions. In: Padma-Nathan, ed. Selected Proceedings fron the 8th World Meeting of the International Society for impotence Research, Amsterdam, 24–28 August 1996. *Int J Clin Pract* 1999; (Suppl 102): 21–3, June

60 Fava M, Rankin MA, Alpert JE, Nierenberg AA, Worthington JJ. An open trial of sildenafil in antidepressant-induced sexual dysfunction. *Psychother Psychosom* 1998; **67**: 328–31

61 Clayton AH, Owens JE, McGarvey EL. Assessment of paroxetine-induced sexual dysfunction using the Changes in Sexual Functioning Questionnaire. *Psychopharmacol Bull* 1995; **31**: 397–413

62 Ekselius L, von Knorring L, Eberhard G. A double-blind study comparing sertraline and citalopram in patients with major depression treated in general practice. *Eur Neuropsychopharmacol* 1997; **7 (Suppl 2)**: S147

63 Fava M, Amsterdam JD, Deltito JA, Salzman C, Schwaller M, Dunner DL. A double-blind study of paroxetine, fluoxetine, and placebo in outpatients with major depression. *Ann Clin Psychiatry* 1998; **10**: 145–50

64 Feighner JP. The role of venlafaxine in rational antidepressant therapy. *J Clin Psychiatry* 1994; **55 (Suppl A)**: 62–8

65 Feighner JP, Gardner EA, Johnston JA *et al*. Double-blind comparison of bupropion and fluoxetine in depressed outpatients. *J Clin Psychiatry* 1991; **52**: 329–35

66 Hekimian LJ, Freidhoff AJ, Deever E. A comparison of the onset of action and therapeutic efficacy of amoxapine and amitriptyline. *J Clin Psychiatry* 1978; **39**: 633–7

67 Jacobsen FM. Fluoxetine-induced sexual dysfunction and an open trial of yohimbine. *J Clin Psychiatry* 1992; **53**: 119–22

68 Labbate LA, Grimes J, Hines A, Oleshansky MA, Arana GW. Sexual dysfunction induced by selective serotonin reuptake antidepressants. *J Sex Marital Ther* 1998; **24**: 3–12

69 Montgomery SA. Safety of mirtazapine: a review. *Int Clin Psychopharmacol* 1995; **10 (Suppl 4)**: 37–45

70 Mucci M. Reboxetine: a review of antidepressant tolerability. *J Psychopharmacol* 1997; **11 (Suppl)**: S33–7

71 Reimherr FW, Chouinard G, Cohn CK *et al*. Antidepressant efficacy of sertraline: a double-blind, placebo- and amitriptyline-controlled, multicenter comparison study in outpatients with major depression. *J Clin Psychiatry* 1990; **51 (Suppl B)**: 18–27

72 Zajecka J, Mitchell S, Fawcett J. Treatment-emergent changes in sexual function with selective serotonin reuptake inhibitors as measured with the Rush Sexual Inventory. *Psychopharmacol Bull* 1997; **33**: 755–60

Cognitive therapy for depression

Jan Scott

University Department of Psychological Medicine, Gartnavel Royal Hospital, Glasgow, UK

There is considerable empirical support for the use of cognitive therapy in the treatment of mild to moderately severe acute major depression. More recent research has focused on the utility of this approach in severe or chronic depressive disorders, in relapse prevention and also on the potential benefits of combining cognitive therapy with medication. This paper attempts to clarify the empirical data on these important issues in order to identify further the role of cognitive therapy in day-to-day clinical practice. It also provides an overview of findings regarding predictors of response to cognitive therapy and the possible mediators of its effects.

The American Psychological Association Task Force[1] published list of empirically validated treatments reports that cognitive therapy (CT) for depression meets all the criteria for designation as a 'well-established psychological treatment'. Nevertheless, there are still a significant number of unanswered questions regarding the appropriate place of CT in the treatment of depressive disorders. This paper will assess the role of CT through a review of research data published in the last decade. It takes as its starting point the large scale National Institute of Mental Health (NIMH) randomized controlled trial of the treatment of depression[2]. This study represents an important landmark in depression research that influenced thinking about CT, shaping both the research agenda and advice given in clinical guidelines on the treatment of depression[3,4]. However, before embarking on the review of subsequent outcome studies, it is useful to recap briefly the basic premises of the cognitive theory and therapy of depression.

Brief overview of cognitive theory and therapy

Correspondence to:
Prof. Jan Scott, University
Department of
Psychological Medicine,
Gartnavel Royal Hospital,
Glasgow G12 0XH, UK

Beck's[5] cognitive theory of depression represents a stress-diathesis model. It postulates that some individuals may be vulnerable to depression because they develop dysfunctional beliefs as a result of early learning experiences. These beliefs may be latent for long periods, but become primed by events that carry a specific meaning for that individual. Beck[6] suggests that the underlying beliefs that render an individual vulnerable to depression may be broadly categorized into beliefs about being helpless or unlovable. Thus events that are deemed uncontrollable or involve relationship difficulties may re-activate these beliefs and be important in the genesis of depressive symptoms. Negative cognitions about the self, world and future are concomitants of depression but serve to re-inforce the core underlying dysfunctional beliefs. The negative automatic thoughts that dominate the thinking of many depressed patients are sustained through systematic distortions of information processing (*e.g.* focusing only on negative aspects of an interpersonal interaction) and contribute to further depression of affect. Beck[7] clearly states that whilst the vicious cycle of low mood enhancing negative thinking leading to further lowering in mood may represent a causal theory in some cases, it represents a maintenance model for other depressions. However, he proposes that intervention in the cycle can be effective in alleviating acute depressive symptoms in the latter group.

Cognitive therapy is a collaborative 'hypothesis-testing' approach that uses guided discovery to identify and re-evaluate distorted cognitions and dysfunctional beliefs. However, the common misconception that CT simply uses a fixed set of behavioural (*e.g.* activity scheduling) and cognitive (*e.g.* challenging automatic thoughts) techniques is unfortunate. The therapy is not simply technique driven. The interventions are selected on the basis of a cognitive conceptualization that uniquely identifies the likely core negative beliefs of that individual and explains the onset and maintenance of their depression. If the patient shows a low level of functioning, behavioural techniques may be used to improve activity levels and improve mood, but the goal is still to identify and modify negative cognitions and maladaptive underlying beliefs. Verbal interventions are initially employed to re-evaluate negative cognitions. Between session experiments, frequently focused on inter-personal functioning, are used to re-evaluate ideas. Later, when the patient has developed his or her cognitive and behavioural skills, these interventions are used to try to modify underlying dysfunctional beliefs. This is critical to the process as the expressed goal of CT is to reduce vulnerability to future depressive relapse.

This brief overview has two aims. First, it highlights the key elements of the cognitive theory that should be assessed in research on the unique mechanisms of action of CT. This is important if we are to understand how CT produces its effect or wish to abbreviate the intervention. Second, the overview clarifies the key components of the therapy. This allows a comparison of CT with other brief psychotherapies (*e.g.* interpersonal therapy [IPT], behavioural family therapy) for depression. Scott[8] noted that whilst the emphasis of each approach varies, the brief therapies all assume that cognitive, behavioural, emotional and interpersonal domains are related factors associated with the maintenance of depression and that these are the key targets for change.

Table 1 Shared characteristics of effective brief therapies

- The therapy offers a specific formulation of the individual's problems
- The model of therapy is shared openly with the patient
- There is rational use of techniques in a logical sequence
- There is an emphasis on skill development and transfer of learning outside of therapy sessions
- Change is attributed to the patient's rather than the therapist's efforts

Not only do brief interventions overlap in their objectives, Teasdale[9] reported that brief psychotherapies of proven effectiveness in depression demonstrate similarities in their core clinical characteristics (Table 1).

The potential implication of the above is that there will be no specific link between the empirical status of a cognitive or interpersonal theory of depression and the respective clinical effectiveness of CT, IPT or variants of these approaches. Furthermore, we may not be able to demonstrate differences in the efficacy of CT, IPT, or similar interventions. This is important to note. Although CT is the most widely researched brief therapy, there are a number of plausible alternatives that may become equally well established in the future.

Outcome research

The NIMH study[2] represents an important landmark in depression research. It was the largest ($n = 239$) multi-model intervention trial of acute depressive disorders ever undertaken. It compared antidepressant medication (ADM) and structured clinical management (CM), with pill-placebo plus CM, CT and IPT. Although the trial confirmed that CT was an effective treatment of mild-to-moderate major depressive disorders, it suggested CT was not an effective treatment for severely depressed out-patients. The trial reported equivocal findings about the effect of CT as compared with ADM in preventing relapse, but noted that chronic symptomatology was a predictor of poor outcome with any intervention. Although previous research data did not concur with all of the findings of Elkin and colleagues[2], the study greatly influenced published treatment guidelines for depression[3,4]. These documents emphasized that CT was best targeted at mild-to-moderate depression. The authors went on to document that there was no robust evidence of any additional benefits of combining CT with ADM, although they recognized that many clinicians would value advice on when to employ this approach in practice. Empirical data are now explored on the role of CT in each of these situations to clarify our current understanding.

Severe depressive disorders

The NIMH study suggested that ADM plus CM outperformed CT in severe depression (defined as a Hamilton Depression Rating Scale score > 21). However, further exploration of the NIMH results revealed that, overall, only 26 subjects with severe depression received CT across three study sites and that ADM was more effective than CT with severely depressed patients at only one centre[10]. Furthermore, a similar study by Hollon and colleagues[11] did not demonstrate any advantage for ADM in severe depression. A meta-analysis has recently been undertaken[12] to integrate these conflicting data. Outcomes were compared for subjects with severe depression who were treated with ADM (n = 102) or CT (n = 62) from four randomised controlled trials. Response rates to both CT and ADM were over 50% and the overall effect sizes demonstrated no significant differences between treatments (in fact the trends consistently favoured CT). Dropout rates were also comparable (ADM = 39%; CT = 31%).

These findings suggest that CT is as effective as ADM in severe depressive disorders. However, before revising clinical practice guidelines, it is important to note that because an intervention is effective does not automatically make it a treatment of choice. Whilst DeRubeis and colleagues[12] have demonstrated that CT can be an effective alternative to ADM, the findings of two other research groups, led by Thase in the US and by Shapiro in the UK, provide important caveats about the use of CT in severe depression that may also influence a clinician.

In a series of studies, Thase and colleagues demonstrated that individuals with severe depressions, sometimes accompanied by abnormal Dexamethasone Suppression Test (DST) or delayed Rapid Eye Movement (REM) sleep latency, showed a parallel but slower rate of response to CT than those with less severe depressions[13,14]. The results suggested a significant dose-response relationship and it was suggested that individuals with severe depression required a more intensive course of CT. Scott and DeRubeis[15] noted a similar phenomenon and commented that CT therapists treating individuals with severe depression tend to target behavioural activation for a prolonged period, rather than cognitive techniques, such as hypothesis testing. This may mean that, in time-limited trials of CT, more severely depressed patients may receive less of the therapy components that are particularly associated with improvement.

Shapiro and colleagues[16] separately pursued this issue, exploring the impact of different lengths of treatment with CT (8 or 16 sessions) on outcome for mild (Beck Depression Inventory [BDI] score < 21), moderate (BDI = 21–26) and severe (BDI > 26) depression. They demonstrated a significant interaction between initial symptom severity and duration of therapy. Individuals with mild or moderately severe

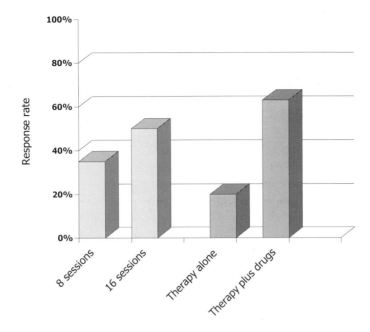

Fig. 1 Effect of longer duration of cognitive therapy or use of combined therapy and medication on response rates in severe depression.

depression did equally well with either eight or 16 sessions of CT (50–53% response rate). However, individuals with severe depression demonstrated a significantly improved response rate with 16 sessions (50%) as compared to eight sessions (35%) of CT (Fig. 1).

Whilst extending the course of therapy may improve the response of severe depressive disorders to CT, an alternative approach is to combine CT with ADM. Previous analyses[3] of combined CT and ADM for depression were inconclusive, suggesting that the overall efficacy of the combination (response rate 54–63%) was not significantly different from either treatment alone. However, these analyses did not differentiate outcomes according to initial severity of depression. Thase and colleagues[17] assessed the potential benefits of the combined treatment in less and more severe depressions through a meta-analysis of 595 subjects allocated to different standardized treatment groups including CT or IPT alone (n = 243) or brief therapy in combination with ADM (n = 352). The results demonstrated that the combination of brief therapy with ADM was no more effective than either IPT or CT alone in less severe recurrent depressions. However, in severe recurrent depressive disorders (Fig. 1), the overall response rate to combined therapy (63%) was 3 times higher than to brief psychotherapy alone (20%). An analysis of rate of response also demonstrated no additional benefit of combined versus single therapy in less severe depression – just over 50% of subjects responded to either approach by 16 weeks. However, in severe recurrent depression, 50% of subjects receiving combined treatment responded by 16 weeks as compared to only 26% of those receiving psychological interventions alone.

The above studies only explored the use of brief therapy alone compared with brief therapy plus ADM. Hollon and colleagues[10,11] explored the benefit of CT plus ADM versus either ADM or CT alone in a sample of subjects with moderate and severe depressions. They report a consistent modest advantage in response rates (a 10–15% increment in absolute terms) for combined treatment compared with ADM alone.

Depressive relapses

A common argument for the selective role of CT in the treatment of acute episodes of depression is that a course of therapy is more expensive than a course of ADM. This contention has some validity, but would obviously be weakened if CT had a significant effect on relapse rates. The trend in the NIMH study was for CT to reduce relapse rates[18]. Indeed, at 12-month follow-up the relapse rate for CT (9%) was only a third of that of individuals who received ADM plus CM (28%). Furthermore, of the patients who recovered during the treatment phase of the study, only 5% of CT subjects sought further treatment, compared with 38% of IPT and 39% of ADM subjects. Although these differences may be significant, the data are hard to interpret. Like most CT studies of relapse, it comprised a naturalistic follow-up of treatment responders from previously published acute depression studies, sometimes without adequate ADM continuation. An exception is the prospective follow-up[19] of the cohort of subjects treated in the randomised controlled trial of CT and ADM conducted by Hollon *et al*[10]. The relapse rate in the CT group (20%) was not significantly different from that in the ADM continuation treatment group (27%), but was less than half that of subjects whose ADM was withdrawn at the time their depression remitted (50%). Given the strong tendency for individuals to stop taking ADM when they feel better, it is interesting to note that CT appears to have a durable effect beyond the end of a course of treatment.

The use of continuation or maintenance psychotherapy to prevent relapse is a new concept in psychological treatment studies. In two sequential cohort studies, Jarett *et al*[20] demonstrated that, compared with acute phase CT, acute phase CT plus 10 sessions of continuation CT reduced relapse rates over 24 months by an additional 30%. Likewise, in a small 24 month pilot study of atypical depression[21], subjects who continued to receive phenelzine (relapse rate = 57%) or CT (40%) were significantly less likely to relapse than those who, after initially responding to treatment, stopped receiving either phenelzine (relapse rate = 75%) or CT (83%). In the largest study so far, Blackburn and Moore[22] allocated 75 subjects with recurrent major depression to 16 weeks of acute treatment and 2 years of maintenance treatment. The group treatments comprised ADM alone, CT alone or ADM followed by maintenance CT. All three groups improved in the acute phase and there were no between-group differences in relapse rates in the maintenance phases. The authors suggested that maintenance CT is a viable alternative to maintenance medication.

Chronic, residual or treatment refractory depressive disorders

At least 20% of people with an initial episode of major depressive disorder do not recover within 2 years, and those with residual depressive symptoms have a 50–80% risk of a further relapse. The poor response of chronic depression to treatment with ADM alone is not fully understood, but was frequently quoted as a reason for the use of psychotherapy. Unfortunately, a review of nine early psychotherapy studies revealed poor research designs and limited benefits from this alternative[15]. Three randomized controlled trials published in the last few years give greater insight into the effectiveness of CT in this patient population. The studies differ in the model of CT used (standardized CT, well-being therapy, cognitive behavioural analysis system psychotherapy) and the samples studied, but together they provide important data on acute, 18 month and longer term (6 year) outcome of chronic depressive disorders.

Keller *et al*[23] reported a comparison of the efficacy of a single ADM (nefadazone) and a modified version of CT (cognitive behavioural analysis system psychotherapy) given alone, or in combination in a sample of over 650 patients with chronic depressive disorders. The groups were well matched for severity and chronicity of depression at baseline, but more than 20% of those randomized had not received any treatment for their disorder prior to entry into the study and many others had received sub-therapeutic doses of ADM. After 12 weeks, the group receiving the combined treatment had a significantly greater overall reduction in depressive symptoms (an increment of about 25%) as compared with single therapies. Furthermore, almost twice as many people receiving both ADM and CT (42%) met remission criteria as compared to those receiving either ADM or CT alone (22–24%). The study supports the view that the rate of change, *i.e.* the trajectory of improvement, is faster in people who received a combined as compared with a single therapy. However, this study does not indicate whether response rates continue to improve in those treated with ADM or CT alone, nor whether there were any long-term differences in outcome for subjects in each group.

The other two trials evaluated relapse rates following treatment of chronic depression. Paykel *et al*[24] assessed 158 subjects with residual treatment refractory depressive symptoms throughout 20 weeks of treatment and for a year afterwards. Subjects received ADM plus CM or ADM plus CM plus CT. At 18-month follow-up, relapse rates in the CT group (29%) were reduced by 45–50% compared with the control group and the CT group also showed significantly greater reductions in hopelessness, pessimism, guilt and self-esteem. Subjects who received additional CT showed significantly greater improvements in social adjustment than those receiving ADM plus CM[25]. Furthermore, those allocated to CT and ADM plus CM had significantly fewer visits with their psychiatrist than the control group. Such findings are clearly important when considering the overall benefits and costs of treatment.

Fava *et al*[26] reported the 6 year outcome of 40 subjects randomly allocated to either CT (a model of called well-being therapy) or to CM. Unlike the other studies of chronic depression, ADM was gradually tapered off, so that most subjects were medication-free during the follow-up phase. At 2 and 4 years, relapses in the CT group were significantly lower than in the CM group. This trend continued at 6 years (CT relapses = 50%; CM = 75%), but was no longer significant. However, subjects in the CT group experienced significantly fewer new episodes of depression (mean = 0.8) than those receiving CM (mean = 1.7) over the 72 months of the study.

Predictors of response

Predictors of response can be divided into patient factors and therapy/therapist factors.

Individual characteristics

A critical issue for clinicians is to try to identify not just which depressed patients may benefit from CT, but which individuals will **differentially** respond to CT as compared with ADM. Research attempts to characterize this latter group of CT responders have been disappointing. For example, work suggesting certain cognitive variables such as learned resourcefulness or dysfunctional attitudes may predict specific response to CT have not been replicated[27,28]. Currently, it is easier to define demographic or clinical limitations to the effectiveness of CT[29].

No demographic factors have consistently predicted poor response to CT. Age, gender, ethnicity, IQ and educational status do not appear to be predictors. However, there are some data suggesting that being married may predict a better response to CT than being single[27]. Also, attrition rates may be higher in younger males of lower socio-economic status[30].

As noted previously, severity and chronicity of depression may predict less favourable response to psychological or pharmacological treatments. However, the evidence regarding level of depressive symptoms and response to CT suggests that it may be the nature of the depression (endogenous/melancholic) that predicts poorer response to CT independent of severity[28].

The data on the outcome of depression associated with co-morbid personality disorder are equivocal[27,32]. Recent studies have clarified that the beliefs held by individuals with certain personality types are more specific predictors of outcome than traditional diagnoses of personality disorder. For example, the NIMH study found that high levels of perfectionism predicted poor outcome of depression with any treatment[33]. In a study of 162 subjects with major depressive disorders who were treated with CT, Kuyken and colleagues[34] demonstrated that maladaptive avoidant and paranoid beliefs rather than personality disorder status predicted a significant proportion of the variance in depression outcome.

Cognitive variables, such as high pretreatment levels of dysfunctional attitudes may predict poor outcome with ADM or CT[27], but the role of other variables such as learned resourcefulness is uncertain[28]. Addis and Jacobson[35] demonstrated that a stronger match between an individual's model of the cause of his or her depression and the treatment offered predicts better response to treatment. This parallels the findings of Fennel and Teasdale[36] who showed that individuals who reported a negative reaction to being depressed (referred to as 'depression about depression') responded more rapidly to CT than individuals who did not endorse this view.

Therapy factors

An apparently suitable candidate for CT may fail to respond if the therapy is not carried out competently[29]. Pooled data from 15 psychotherapy studies suggests there is a significant relationship between the therapist's level of training or experience, the degree of adherence to the treatment manual, the type of therapy used (CT being superior to psychodynamic therapies) and patient outcome[37]. Gortner and colleagues demonstrated a significant correlation between ratings of competency and patient outcome[38]. In a study of CT in 185 depressed patients, individuals treated by senior therapists (> 4 years' CT experience) showed significantly greater improvement than those treated by novice therapists[32]. The experience of the therapist is a particularly important determinant of outcome when treating more severe or complex cases[29]. DeRubeis and Feeley[39] demonstrated a significant correlation ($r = 0.53$) between adherence to symptom focused CT techniques and patient outcome. However, technical fidelity and competency are not the only important 'intra-therapy' factors, therapist empathy[32] and the therapeutic alliance[11,16] both significantly influence outcome of depression treated with CT.

Mediators of effect

Although there is robust evidence that CT can be an effective treatment of acute depressive disorders and emerging evidence of its prophylactic effect, the process through which CT achieves these effects is not well understood. For example, individuals with good outcome from depression treated with ADM or CT all show reductions in post-treatment levels of dysfunctional attitudes[29]. Data on changes in depressogenic attributional style (a tendency to attribute negative events to internal, stable, global causes) produced by CT are also equivocal. The lack of evidence for specific cognitive mediators led Persons[40] to propose that the key therapeutic process may not lead to the cognitive change but be the acquisition of compensatory skills that allowed the individual to cope with isolated depressive symptoms and prevented the symptoms evolving into a depressive episode. However, a recent study[41] sheds new light on cognitive mediation of relapse prevention demonstrating that CT reduced relapse via changes in the style rather than the content of thinking. Good outcome from CT was achieved via reductions in absolutist, dichotomous thinking. Individuals with persistent extreme response styles to depression related material (relapse rate = 44%) were more than 2.5 times as likely to experience early relapse as compared with individuals without this extreme style (relapse rate = 17%). This suggests that training individuals to change the way that they process depression related material, rather than changing their belief in depressive thought content may be a critical component of CT.

Conclusions

Cognitive therapy is the most widely researched brief psychological therapy for depression with over 80 randomized controlled trials assessing its utility in the acute and longer-term outcome of this disorder. Despite empirical data supporting its efficacy, there are still problems in gaining access to CT in clinical practice. As highlighted in the National

Service Framework, the psychotherapies of proven effectiveness are not necessarily the most readily available in the mental health services. Given the relative scarcity of CT therapists, it is inevitable that clinicians ask for advice on who should be referred to CT. Previous guidelines suggested that individuals with mild-to-moderately severe depressive disorders are the best candidates for CT. However, it can be argued that, as these individuals are equally likely to respond to ADM and show no additional benefit from combined treatment, their treatment should be either ADM or CT. In mild or moderate depression, referral to brief therapy could be restricted to those who cannot be prescribed or will not adhere to ADM regimens. Given the minimal additional benefit (only a 3% increase in overall response rates) of extended courses of CT (16 sessions) over brief CT in this population, it would be worthwhile monitoring the duration of therapy offered to this patient population and asking therapists to justify extensions of CT beyond 8 sessions. This notion is not intended to be draconian, but rather to ensure that the lessons of research are implemented in day-to-day practice.

This review suggests that clinical practice guidelines on the use of CT in severe depression can now be revised to take into account recent research findings. The data suggest that CT could be used alone in severe disorders if there was a particular contra-indication to medication, provided an extended course of therapy is planned. However, progress with CT alone would be slow and a more acceptable trajectory of change in depressive symptoms (equivalent to that of mild and moderate depression) can be achieved by combining CT with ADM.

Perhaps one of the most important roles of CT in the future will be the treatment of individuals with persistent symptoms that have not responded fully to ADM. Thus the recent studies of CT in management of chronic or residual depressive symptoms are particularly important. There appears to be a significant additional health gain from providing CT as an adjunct to medication in this population that not only improves the rate of improvement, but also reduces specific symptoms that appear to be less amenable to change with ADM (such as hopelessness and self-esteem). Most importantly, the addition of CT to usual treatment appears to protect against future relapse in individuals known to be at high risk of repeated episodes of depression. This durable effect of CT beyond the point of treatment termination is critical to grasp – this is not an effect demonstrated for any ADM. Medication only works for as long as it is prescribed or taken. Furthermore, evidence that 16 sessions of CT prevent relapse in the long-term radically changes the balance between the cost and benefits of this intervention.

It is too early to judge whether continuation or maintenance CT will prove a cost-effective intervention. The clinical imperative for this approach is clear as many individuals with severe and complex disorders benefit from longer-term support. Interestingly, this may be a particularly useful treatment for individuals with bipolar depression. There are accumulating data suggesting that the cognitive style of individuals with bipolar depression is indistinguishable from that of individuals with unipolar depression. Furthermore, there is tentative evidence that CT may be as useful or more useful than ADM in reducing bipolar depressive symptoms without the risk of precipitating hypomania[42].

References

1 Chambless DL, Baker MJ, Baucom DH *et al*. Update on empirically validated therapies, II. *Clin Psychol* 1998; **51**: 3–16

2 Elkin I, Shea MT, Watkins A *et al*. National Institute of Mental Health Treatment of Depression Collaborative Research Programme: general effectiveness of treatment. *Arch Gen Psychiatry* 1989; **46**: 971–82

3 Agency for Health Care Policy and Research. Depression Guideline Panel. *Depression in Primary Care: Volume 1. Detection and Diagnosis: Volume 2. Treatment of Major Depression.* [Clinical Practice Guideline Number 5] Rockville, MD: USDHHS, Public Health Service, 1993

4 American Psychiatric Association. Practice guideline for major depressive disorder in adults. *Am J Psychiatry* 1993; **150 (Suppl 4)**: 1–26

5 Beck AT. *Depression: Clinical, Experimental, and Theoretical Aspects.* New York: Harper and Row, 1967

6 Beck AT. *Cognitive Therapy: Basics and Beyond.* New York: Guildford, 1995

7 Beck AT. Beyond belief: a theory of modes, personality, and psychopathology. In: Salkovskis PM. (ed) *Frontiers of Cognitive Therapy.* New York: Guildford, 1996; 1–25

8 Scott J. Invited editorial: treatment of chronic depression. *N Engl J Med* 2000; **342**: 1518–20

9 Teasdale JD. Psychological treatments for depression: how do they work? *Behav Res Ther* 1985; **23**: 157–65

10 Hollon SD, Shelton RC, Davis DD. Cognitive therapy for depression: conceptual issues and clinical efficiency. *J Consult Clin Psychol* 1993; **62**: 270–5

11 Hollon SD, DeRubeis RJ, Evans MD *et al*. Cognitive therapy and pharmacotherapy for depression: singly or in combination. *Arch Gen Psychiatry* 1992; **49**: 774–81

12 DeRubeis RJ, Gelfand LA, Tang TZ, Simons AD. Medications versus cognitive behaviour therapy for severely depressed outpatients: mega-analysis of four randomised comparisons. *Am J Psychiatry* 1999; **156**: 1007–13

13 Thase ME, Simons AD, Cahalane JF, McGeary J, Harden T. Severity of depression and response to cognitive behaviour therapy. *Am J Psychiatry* 1991; **148**: 784–9

14 Thase ME, Simons AD, Cahalane JF, McGeary J. Cognitive behaviour therapy of endogenous depression. Part 1: an outpatient clinical replication series. *Behav Res Ther* 1991; **22**: 457–67

15 Scott J, Derubeis RJ. Cognitive therapy and psychosocial interventions in chronic and treatment-resistant mood disorders. In: Amsterdam J, Neirberg N. (eds). *Treatment Refractory Mood Disorders.* Cambridge: Cambridge University Press, 2001

16 Shapiro DA, Barkham M, Rees A, Hardy GE, Reynolds S, Startup M. Effects of treatment duration and severity of depression on the effectiveness of cognitive/behavioural and psychodynamic/ interpersonal psychotherapy. *J Consul Clin Psychol* 1994; **62**: 522–34

17 Thase ME, Greenhouse JB, Frank E *et al*. Treatment of major depression with psychotherapy or psychotherapy-pharmacotherapy combinations. *Arch Gen Psychiatry* 1997; **54**: 1009–15

18 Shea MT, Elkin I, Imber SD *et al*. Course of depressive symptoms over follow-up: findings from the National Institute of Mental Health Treatment of Depression Collaborative Research Program. *Arch Gen Psychiatry* 1992; **49**: 782–7

19 Evans I, Shea MT, Watkins JT *et al*. National Institute of Mental Health Treatment of Depression Collaborative Research Programme: general effectiveness of treatment. *Arch Gen Psychiatry* 1989; **46**: 971–82

20 Jarrett RB, Basco MR, Risser R *et al.* Is there a role for continuation phase cognitive therapy for depressed outpatients? *J Consult Clin Psychol* 1998; **66**: 1036–40

21 Jarrett RB, Kraft D, Schaffer M *et al.* Reducing relapse in depressed outpatients with atypical features: a pilot study. *Psychother Psychosom* 2000; **69**: 232–9

22 Blackburn IM, Moore RG. Controlled acute and follow-up trial of cognitive therapy and pharmacotherapy in outpatients with recurrent depression. *Br J Psychiatry* 1997; **171**: 328–34

23 Keller M, McCullough J, Klein D *et al.* The acute treatment of chronic depression: a comparison of nefazadone, cognitive behavioural analysis system of psychotherapy, and their combination. *N Engl J Med* 2000; **342**: 1462–70

24 Paykel ES, Scott J, Teasdale JD *et al.* Prevention of relapse in residual depression by cognitive therapy: a controlled trial. *Arch Gen Psychiatry* 1999; **56**: 829–35

25 Scott J, Teasdale J, Paykel ES *et al.* The effects of cognitive therapy on psychological symptoms and social functioning in residual depression. *Br J Psychiatry* 2000; **177**: 440–6

26 Fava GA, Rafanelli C, Grandi S, Canestrari MD, Morphy MA. Six year outcome for cognitive behavioural treatment of residual symptoms in major depression. *Am J Psychiatry* 1998; **155**: 1443–5

27 Sotsky SM, Glass DR, Shea MT *et al.* Patient predictors of response to psychotherapy and pharmacotherapy: findings of the NIMH Treatment of Depression Collaborative Research Program. *Am J Psychiatry* 1991; **148**: 997–1008

28 Whisman AM. Mediators and moderators of change in cognitive therapy of depression. *Psychol Bull* 1993; **114**: 248–65

29 Scott J. Cognitive therapy of affective disorders: a review. *J Affect Disord* 1996; **37**: 1–11

30 Schulberg H, Pilkonis P, Houck P. Treating major depression in primary care practice: eight month clinical outcomes. *Arch Gen Psychiatry* 1998; **53**: 913–38

31 Scott AI, Freeman CP. Edinburgh primary care depression study: treatment outcome, patients satisfaction and cost after 16 weeks. *BMJ* 1992; **304**: 883–7

32 Burns DD, Nolen-Hoeksema S. Therapeutic empathy and recovery from depression in cognitive-behavioural therapy: a structural equation model. *J Consult Clin Psychol* 1992; **60**: 441–9

33 Blatt SJ, Zuroff DC, Bondi CM, Sanislow CA, Pilkonis PA. When and how perfectionism impedes the brief treatment of depression: further analysis of the National Institute of Mental Health Treatment of Depression Collaborative Research Program. *J Consult Clin Psychol* 1998; **66**: 423–8

34 Kuyken W, Kurzer N, DeRubeis RJ, Beck AT, Brown GK. Response to cognitive therapy in depression: the role of maladaptive beliefs and personality disorders. *J Consult Clin Psychol* 2001; In press

35 Addis ME, Jacobson NS. Reasons for depression and the process and outcome of cognitive-behavioural psychotherapies. *J Consult Clin Psychol* 1996; **64**: 1417–24

36 Fennel MJV, Teasdale JD. Cognitive therapy for depression: individual differences and the process of change. *Cog Ther Res* 1987; **11**: 253–71

37 Crits-Christoph P, Baranackie K, Kurcias JS *et al.* Meta-analysis of therapist effects in psychotherapy outcome studies. *Psychother Res* 1991; **1**: 81–91

38 Gortner ET, Gollan JK, Dobson KS, Jacobson NS. Cognitive behavioural treatment for depression: relapse prevention. *J Consult Clin Psychol* 1998; **66**: 377–84

39 DeRubeis RJ, Feeley M. Determinants of change in cognitive therapy for depression. *Cog Ther Res* 1990; **14**: 469–82

40 Persons JB. The process of change in cognitive therapy: schema change or acquisition of compensatory skills? *Cog Ther Res* 1993; **17**: 123–37

41 Teasdale JD, Scott J, Moore RG, Hayhurst H, Pope M, Paykel ES. How does cognitive therapy prevent relapse in residual depression – evidence from a controlled trial. *J Consult Clin Psychol* 2001; In press

42 Scott J, Garland A, Moorhead S. A pilot study of cognitive therapy for bipolar disorders. *Psychol Med* 2001;30: 467–72

Counselling and interpersonal therapies for depression: towards securing an evidence-base

Michael Barkham* and **Gillian E Hardy*,†**

*Psychological Therapies Research Centre, School of Psychology, University of Leeds, Leeds, UK and †Clinical Psychology Unit, Department of Psychology, University of Sheffield, Sheffield, UK

Both generic counselling (delivered by BACP level counsellors in primary care settings) and the interpersonal therapies place a central value on the role and function of relationships – both within and outside the practice setting – as a vehicle for understanding and treating people presenting with depression. Recent studies have compared generic counselling with antidepressant medication, usual GP care, cognitive-behaviour therapy (CBT), and as an adjunct to GP care (*i.e.* in combination with GP care). Findings suggest either that there is no difference between generic counselling and other treatment conditions, or that there are small advantages to counselling over usual GP care but only in the short-term with such differences disappearing at 1-year. Studies investigating the interpersonal therapies (IPT) have established that the content of such therapies differ in their content from behavioural and cognitive therapies despite the outcomes being broadly similar. Considerable research effort has focused on the process of change in IP therapies. Important factors include the level of prior commitment by the patient to psychological therapy and their confidence in the therapist. Patients with well assimilated problems tend to do better in CBT than psychodynamic-interpersonal therapy. Therapists need to be flexible and responsive to patient needs particularly concerning interpersonal and attachment issues. Future research in counselling needs to identify the effective components of generic counselling and relate these to a theoretical base. In the IP therapies, there needs to be a greater focus on the change outside the therapy session and on the effectiveness of such therapies in non-research settings.

Correspondence to:
Prof. Michael Barkham,
Psychological Therapies
Research Centre,
University of Leeds,
17 Blenheim Terrace,
Leeds LS2 9JT, UK

In this chapter, we review recent findings focusing on the efficacy and effectiveness of counselling and the interpersonal therapies in the treatment of depression. In contrast to cognitive therapy, there is considerably less research evidence derived from either counselling or the interpersonal therapies. Accordingly, the aim of this chapter is to provide an overview of the best available evidence that underpins the knowledge base for counselling and the interpersonal therapies as interventions for depression. For the purposes of this chapter, the commonality of approach lies in the centrality of the realm of the 'interpersonal'. Counselling is included with the psychological therapies in academic texts addressing the need for an evidence-based culture[1] as well as in Department of Health strategic documents[2]. However, each discipline has its own philosophy and tradition such that at the level of delivery, it is reasonable to consider each separately. Accordingly, the chapter is divided into two parts: the first presents the evidence for counselling and the second presents the evidence for the interpersonal therapies for depression.

Counselling as a treatment for depression

Definitions

Two important aspects of counselling require clarification. First, in terms of the approach itself, there are four components that define a generic counselling approach as set out by the British Association of Counselling and Psychotherapy (formally the British Association of Counselling)[3]. These are:

1　Counselling is the skilled and principled use of relationships that develop self-knowledge, emotional acceptance and growth, and personal resources.

2　The overall aim is to live more fully and satisfyingly.

3　Counselling may be concerned with addressing and resolving specific problems, making decisions, coping with crises, working through inner feelings and inner conflict, or improving relationships with others.

4　The counsellor's role is to facilitate the patient's work in ways that respect the patient's values, personal resources, and capacity for self-determination.

Second, counselling has recently been more appropriately defined in relation to a specific setting – in particular, that of primary care. Indeed, counselling in primary care is increasingly becoming recognised as a *bona fide* profession in its own right[4,5].

Overview to research in counselling

The research literature through the 1990s yielded discouraging results for counselling and presented challenges to its evidence-base. For example, reviews concluded that there was little evidence for the effectiveness of generic counselling over routine GP care[6] and urgently called for more research into the efficacy of counselling[7]. Set against this background, 4 studies have recently been carried out. The first study is a Cochrane Review that, although not specific to depression, sets a marker for establishing the amount of research on counselling that meets the criteria for inclusion in a Cochrane data base[8]. The second study is a partially randomised preference trial assessing the effectiveness of counselling versus antidepressant medication delivered by GPs for the treatment of depression in primary care[9,10]. The remaining two studies were carried out under the Health Technology Assessment (HTA) programme. One comprises a randomised controlled trial of non-directive counselling, cognitive-behaviour therapy and usual GP care in the management of depression as well as mixed anxiety and depression in primary care[11-13]. The other is a randomised controlled trial evaluating the effectiveness and cost-effectiveness of counselling patients with chronic depression[14]. All three primary studies used the Beck Depression Inventory (BDI) as a common outcome measure making comparisons across studies easier[15]. The remainder of this section on counselling will focus on these studies.

Cochrane Review of counselling

The Cochrane Review[8] considered the evidence for the effectiveness and cost-effectiveness of primary care counselling by assessing pragmatic trials of counselling. That is, trials that evaluated counselling as carried out under normal conditions. The review assessed randomised controlled trials and controlled patient preference trials of counselling in primary care completed prior to April 1998. Importantly in this review, counselling was defined as 'non-directive'. Hence, it excluded approaches that were labelled as cognitive, cognitive-behavioural, or behavioural, and included studies utilising counsellors who were accredited at British Association of Counselling (BAC) level or higher. The setting was defined as being provided in the GP's surgery. The outcome measures used were of psychological symptoms, recovery, social and occupational functioning, and patient satisfaction.

The search strategy revealed in excess of 2000 research articles of which 38 required detailed assessment for inclusion but only 4 articles met the inclusion criteria[16-19]. In terms of the overall findings, data from the 4 studies showed a between-group effect size advantage of 0.30 to counselling over standard GP care. Although a relatively small effect size, it is equivalent to stating that the average patient receiving counselling was better than approximately 62% of patients receiving standard GP care. The findings from this study confirm the paucity of research in counselling that meets the current 'gold standard'. However, where such studies do exist, they suggest that generic counselling for problems presented in primary care – of which a substantive proportion would be depressive symptoms – is at least as good as routine GP care, if not better.

Counselling versus antidepressants for depression in primary care

In the treatment of depression specifically, psychotropic medication is used as a front-line treatment method. Rather than comparing counselling with standard GP care, a more focused question would be to ask how counselling compares with the delivery of antidepressant medication. This question was addressed in a study carried out in the Trent Region and which also aimed to establish whether providing patients with a choice between these two treatment methods affected their outcome[9]. The randomised trial comprised 52 patients assigned to counselling and 51 to antidepressant treatment. In the preference group, 140 patients chose counselling compared with 80 choosing antidepressants. Patients in the randomised trial had a moderate-to-high level of depression as indicated by the BDI (mean = 27.0).

At 8 weeks after entry into the study, there was no significant difference in the BDI scores between the two groups: unadjusted BDI scores were 15.2 (counselling group) and 14.8 (antidepressant group). Using the Research Diagnostic Criteria for depression, there was no difference in the response rate for the two groups, each yielding 69% of patients having resolved their depression. However, if all non-responders were assumed to be treatment failures, then the rates became 48% (counselling) and 57% (anti-depressants), an odds-ratio of 1.42. At 12 month follow-up, there was no significant difference reported in the mean BDI scores between the two treatment groups in the randomised controlled trial[10]. There was also no evidence of a treatment by preference interaction. Hence, the randomised and patient preference groups were combined. Overall, the study reported similar outcomes (*i.e.* end state BDI) for counselled (BDI mean = 13.2) versus those receiving antidepressants (BDI mean = 12.8). The extent of pre-post treatment change can be represented by a within-group change effect size (ES; pre-treatment score minus post-treatment score divided by the pooled standard deviation of the pre-treatment scores for all groups). Figure 1 presents the change ESs at post-treatment and 12 month follow-up for this study. The difference in ESs at post-treatment approaches zero and at 12 months is small (*i.e.* 0.25).

Non-directive counselling in the management of depression in primary care

A logical extension to the comparison of counselling with psychotropic medication is to compare counselling with another brand of psychological therapy. A twin-site study carried out in London and Manchester addressed this issue by establishing the clinical and cost-effectiveness of two forms of intervention – NDC and CBT – compared with treatment-as-usual from the GP in the management of depression in primary care settings[11-13]. The study was a pragmatic RCT accompanied by two further allocation methods which took into account patient preference: (i) the option of treatment (*i.e.* preference allocation); and (ii) the option to be randomised to one of the psychological interventions only. The sample comprised 464 patients of whom 197 were randomised between the 3 treatments; 137 selected a specific treatment; and 130 were randomly allocated between one of the two psychological treatments. Follow-up assessments were at 4 and 12 months. The study comprised 24 GP practices in Greater Manchester and in London and comprised a total of 73 GPs.

Treatments comprised two brief psychological interventions delivered in 12 sessions or less. One was non-directive counselling (NDC) and was provided by counsellors were met accreditation for the British Association for Counselling (now the British Association for Counselling and Psychotherapy). The other was cognitive-behaviour therapy (CBT) and was provided by clinical psychologists who were qualified for accreditation by the British Association for Behavioural and Cognitive Psychotherapies (BABCP). Usual GP care comprised standard interactions with patients relating to their presenting symptoms and the prescription of medication. GPs were asked not to refer patients assigned to this condition for psychological interventions for a minimum period of 4 months.

The intake scores on the BDI for patients in the 3-way randomised group were 25.4 (NDC), 27.6 (CBT), and 26.5 (GP group). Outcomes included measures of depressive symptoms as well as general psychiatric symptoms, social functioning, and patient satisfaction. The outcomes, as represented

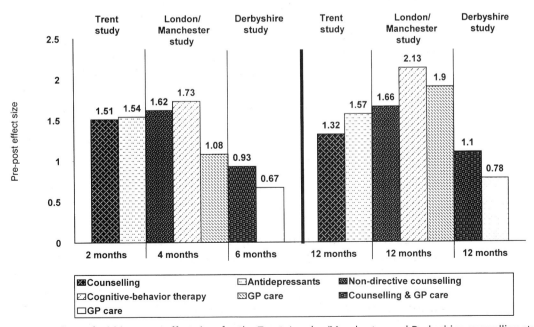

Fig. 1 Comparison of within-group effect sizes for the Trent, London/Manchester, and Derbyshire counselling studies at initial follow-up and 12-month follow-up.

by mean BDI scores, for patients randomised to one of the 3 treatment groups at 4 months and 12 months respectively were 11.5 and 11.1 (NDC), 12.7 and 9.3 (CBT), and 17.2 and 10.2 (GP care). The within-group change ESs are presented in Figure 1. At 4 months, there is a clear advantage to counselling (and CBT) over usual GP care represented by a medium ES advantage to counselling (and a slightly larger ES for CBT). Economic costs were calculated at both 4 months and 12 months and for direct, indirect, and societal (*i.e.* the sum of direct and indirect costs) costs. The results are summarised in Figure 2. Although this shows a consistent trend for NDC to have greater direct and indirect costs, the differences were not significant at either 4 months or 12 months between the randomised groups in total societal costs, total direct costs, or total indirect costs. The results of the efficacy data and the cost data can then be considered together. The significantly greater clinical effectiveness of both psychological interventions (CBT and NDC) at 4 months means that these treatments were more cost-effective approaches than standard GP care to reducing patients' depressive symptoms within this specific time frame.

Results suggested that the provision of brief psychological therapies in general practice is associated with greater short-term clinical benefit as compared with GP care. At 12 months, the psychological therapies yielded outcomes and costs broadly similar to standard GP care. Hence, it was concluded that service provision could be determined on other grounds (*e.g.* patient preferences).

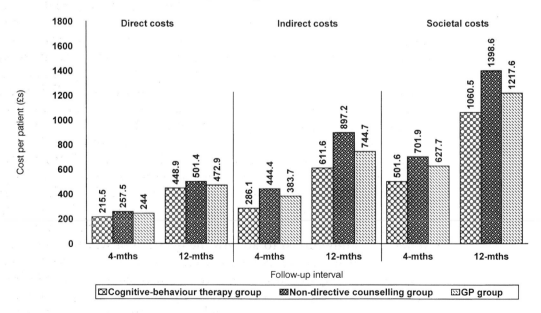

Fig. 2 Comparison of the average cost per patient (£s) in the London/Manchester study receiving CBT, counselling, and usual GP care at 4 month and 12 month follow-up.

Counselling patients with chronic depression

The previous two studies investigated counselling as a 'single' intervention compared with antidepressants, CBT, or usual GP care. A different question concerns the added value of providing counselling in combination with routine GP care. One study carried out in Derbyshire adopted this approach to evaluate the added value of counselling and routine GP care for patients presenting with chronic depression[14]. Hence, the two arms of the trial comprised counselling in combination with routine GP care versus routine GP care alone. This trial focused on patients presenting with mild-to-moderate symptoms of depression that they had experienced for the previous 6 months or more. However, no explicit or independent assessment of chronicity is reported. Patients presented with depression or anxiety as their main symptom and the severity level was operationalised in terms of a score of 14 or above on the BDI. Exclusion criteria included the following: severe depression or anxiety or anxiety only, 'hard-to-treat' patients (*i.e.* frequent attenders with unexplainable physical symptoms), and those who had received counselling in the past 6 months. There was no clinical assessment of presenting problems and all data are based on self-report schedules. Treatment was provided by 8 counsellors working across 9 GP settings and all were BAC accredited. Of the 8 counsellors, 6 took a broadly psychodynamic approach and 2 a mainly cognitive approach. Treatment was to be kept within 6–12 sessions (according to HA guidelines).

At intake, the mean BDI scores for the 'combination' and 'alone' groups were 21.5 and 19.9, respectively, a difference which approached statistical significance. More patients in the counselling group were prescribed medication at intake. At 6 months' follow-up, this difference disappeared. In addition, there were no statistically significant differences between groups in outcomes at 6 months (mean BDI = 16.0 for both groups) or at 12 months (mean BDI = 15.0 and 15.3 for combination and alone groups, respectively). However, as shown in Figure 1, the within-group ES was greater for counselling and GP care in combination although the difference in ES between the 2 groups was small. The authors acknowledge that one weakness of the trial design was that there were two different counselling approaches. Hence, they analysed the study only including PD-treated patients and similar results were obtained. Given the broad equivalence of the outcomes of the two groups, the study turned to address the question of which treatment is the more cost-effective? No significant cost differences were found between the groups at any time once the intervention costs had been excluded. However, receiving counselling increased the primary care costs during the interventions period – a cost that was not offset at a later stage via a reduction in service use.

Box 1 Summary of counselling research on depression	
Definitions	Counselling is the skilled and principled use of relationships which develop self knowledge, emotional acceptance and growth, and personal resources
Research findings	There are very few studies that meet criteria for inclusion in a Cochrane Review but those that do suggest counselling does as well as standard GP care
	Counselling performed as well as antidepressant medication
	Counselling performed as well as CBT at 4 months and better than usual GP care (a medium effect size difference) but there was no difference after 12 months
	There was no advantage to counselling in combination with GP care over GP care alone for patients presenting with chronic depression
	Counselling is not significantly different in costs (either direct or indirect) compared to other psychological interventions (*e.g.* CBT) or usual GP care
Recommendations	There is a need for 'process' studies to help identify the effective components of generic counselling and how they relate to its theoretical base
	There is a need for the adoption of a common outcome measurement to make possible direct comparisons across studies using patients presenting with more heterogeneous disorders

Summary of counselling and depression

In summary, there is now a developing evidence-base suggesting the efficacy of counselling for the treatment of depression. Key studies have been presented above and are summarised in Box 1. The counselling studies described have utilised sensitive and informative designs (*e.g.* patient preference trials) which go some way to being able to generalise results from efficacy trials to routine practice. However, a counter argument lies in the cost in research terms and their complexity. To provide a balance to the focus on outcomes, process studies of generic counselling need to be implemented to better specify the effective ingredients of generic counselling.

Interpersonal therapies

Forms of interpersonal therapies

Psychodynamic and interpersonal models and treatments of depression are based on the premise that depression occurs in a social and interpersonal context that needs to be understood for improvement to occur[20-24]. Psychoanalytic theorists, and more recently cognitive theorists[25] have described how early childhood experiences of interpersonal processes are important precursors of depression, in particular, the quality of the child–parent (usually mother) relationship.

In contrast, interpersonal theorists have tended to focus on the functional role of depression, looking at how problematic interpersonal interactions develop when a person becomes depressed.

There are three main forms of structured therapies used in research studies that have developed from interpersonal theories. These include interpersonal psychotherapy (IPT)[26], psychodynamic-interpersonal therapy (PDIPT)[27,28], and short-term psychodynamic psychotherapy (STPDT)[29–31]. IPT contrasts with the latter two forms of therapy in that it focuses on current rather than past relationships, and on the patient's social context rather than personality features that have their origin in early experiences. The distinctive feature of PDIP therapy is that patients are encouraged to focus on their here and now experiences, particularly emotional and relationship experiences. Both PDIPT and STPDT incorporate psychodynamic understandings of the early origins of depressive experiences. In this chapter when referring generally to these therapies we have used the term interpersonal therapy (IPT).

Content of interpersonal therapies

In a review of the distinctive features of IP therapies[32], seven types of interventions have been identified: (i) a focus on patients' emotions; (ii) an exploration of resistance or factors that inhibit the progress of therapy; (iii) discussion of patterns evident in patients' relationships and experiences; (iv) an emphasis on the past; (v) an emphasis on patients' interpersonal experiences; (vi) an exploration of the therapeutic relationship; and (vii) an exploration of patients' wishes and fantasies.

Confirmation of these distinctive features is found in studies that compare IP therapies with other (generally cognitive and behavioural [CB]) therapies. For example, a study was carried out of the therapeutic focus in PDIP and CB sessions from the Second Psychotherapy Project (SPP2)[33]. The study applied the five scales of the Coding System of Therapeutic Focus to two sessions of each SPP2 patient who had received 16 sessions of therapy. The authors found a large number of differences between the therapeutic focuses in the two treatment modes. In PDIP sessions, therapists were more likely to note how patients might be behaving in a way which could interfere with the process of therapy. There was a greater focus on the therapist and on the patient's parents and past life, including childhood, and on linking together different aspects of the patient's life, such as events that occurred at different times and with different individuals. Therapists in PDIP sessions were less likely to focus on external situations and the future than therapists in CB sessions. PDIP sessions were also characterised by a significantly greater focus on emotion than CB sessions.

In addition, therapist's session intentions for CB and PDIP therapies were investigated in the SPP2 study[34]. Results showed significant differences between the two therapy types, with less of the intentions of re-inforcing and encouraging change, patients' cognition's and behaviours, and getting information in PDIP, and more of the intentions of feelings-awareness, insight and patient–therapist relationship problems. Further examination of the differences between IP and other therapies has focused on the therapeutic relationship. For example, based on a self report alliance measure[35], patients who received CB therapy rated their relationship with their therapist as slightly more positive than patients who had PDIP therapy. They also reported a stronger partnership with, and greater confidence in, their therapist.

'Impact' refers to a session's immediate subjective effects, including patients' evaluations of the session, their assessment of the session's specific character, and their post-session affective state. Patients' reactions to sessions must logically intervene between session process and the final outcome of the treatment. PDIP and CB therapy of the Sheffield Projects were clearly experienced differently by patients and therapists. Patients reported that PDIP sessions were less smooth (*i.e.* less comfortable and more distressing) and less problem focused (*i.e.* both less emphasis in defining and working on the problem) than CB sessions. Patients also reported more negative impacts in PDIP compared to CB therapy[36]. Changes in impact for PDIP sessions were significantly greater than those for CB. For example, although initial patient ratings of session smoothness, positive mood and therapeutic relationship were less positive for PDIP than for CB therapy, this difference was not significant by the end of therapy. This may reflect difficult early sessions in PDIP, with an emotional focus, which became smoother, with a better patient–therapist relationship, over time. Problem solving also showed greater change in PDIP, indicating that this process was less evident in early sessions. In PDIP therapy, more severely depressed patients rated sessions as rougher and their post-session mood was less positive than those with more mild depression. This pattern was not found for CB patients.

Treatment efficacy

Studies focusing on the outcomes of IP therapies have been reviewed[37,38]. The conclusions of these reviews are still current: generally, trials have found IP therapies to be effective in the treatment of depression. Comparative studies have found the outcomes of different therapies to be similar, although in a minority of early studies found STPD therapies to be less effective than the comparison therapy[39,40]. The primary clinical trial of IPT is the NIMH Treatment of Depression Study[41,42]. This study compared the efficacy of IPT, cognitive therapy (CT), imipramine and a control condition of a placebo tablet plus clinical management, delivered across three different sites. All patients met criteria for major depressive disorder. Essentially all three active treatments produced similar reductions in depressive symptoms, overall functioning and social adjustment. Subsequent re-analysis of the data found that imipramine and IPT were more effective than CT for patients who were more severely depressed at the start of treatment.

The Second Sheffield Psychotherapy Project (SPP2)[28,43] compared PDIP therapy with a CB therapy delivered as either 8 or 16 weekly sessions in which patients were stratified for severity according to the BDI (low, moderate, severe). This study found that reductions in patients' depressive symptoms and improvements in their self-esteem and general well-being were substantial and broadly similar following either CB or PDIP psychotherapy. Figure 3 presents the change ESs at 3 month and 12 month follow-up for PDIP and CBT for 8 and 16 session treatments calculated by averaging the ESs for each of the three severity levels within each treatment condition. A related study from the Sheffield group investigated 3 sessions of PDIP *versus* CBT. Reported pre-post ESs after the 3 sessions were 0.83 for CBT and 0.92 for PDIP. At 12 months, these fell to 0.55 and 0.86, respectively[44].

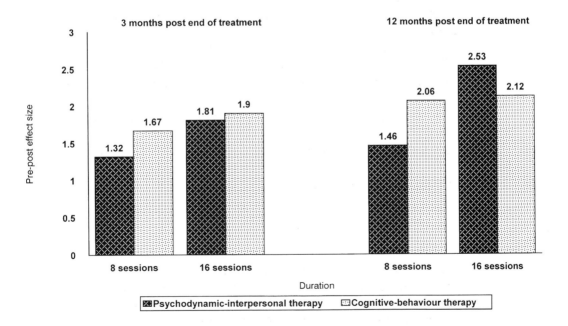

Fig. 3 Comparison of the average within-group effect size in the Second Sheffield Psychotherapy Project for each of the treatment modalities (CBT or PI therapy) x duration (8 or 16 sessions) at 3 month and 12 month follow-up.

Box 2 Summary of research on interpersonal therapies for depression

Definitions	Three main forms of interpersonal therapies (IP) have been studied:
	        Psychodynamic-interpersonal (PD)
	        Interpersonal psychotherapy (IPT)
	        Short-term psychodynamic psychotherapy (STPP)

Research findings	IP therapies differ in their content to the behavioural and cognitive therapies despite treatment outcomes for depression being broadly similar across therapies
	Psychodynamic-interpersonal therapy requires patients' commitment to psychological therapy prior to therapy commencing
	Patients with well assimilated problems tend to do better in CBT than PI therapy suggesting that patients should be socialised into the treatment process
	Therapists need to be flexible and responsive to patient needs, particularly interpersonal and attachment issues
	Patients do better in therapy if they are confident in their therapist
	Two important elements in therapy are: (i) using a language that captures patients' experiences; and (ii) the experiencing of feelings and events in the 'here-and-now'
Recommendations	Focus on change between rather than within sessions
	Extend evidence base to natural settings rather than research studies

In summary, the available evidence, although not large, comprises a select number of high quality trials that show IP therapies to perform broadly as well as CT, which is often viewed as the more researched treatment of depression. However, more studies are required in this area, particularly focusing on the psychodynamic therapies.

Individual differences in treatment outcome

Martial status significantly contributed to overall outcome differences in SPP2[28] and the NIMH study[41,42]: single patients were significantly more depressed (as indicated by their BDI scores), 3 months and 1 year after treatment, than were married, divorced or widowed patients. In SPP2, patients' ratings of their treatment's credibility was also predictive of treatment outcome[45]: the greater the patients' expectations of treatment, both immediately before and immediately after their first session, the greater their improvements in therapy. This latter finding was significant only for patients who received the shorter of the two therapy lengths, although it applied regardless of therapy type. For patients who received 16 sessions of therapy, their expectations of treatment did not predict outcome at either the end or in the middle of therapy.

Patient characteristics found to differentially predict outcome in SPP2 were patients' endorsement of treatment principles[45] and diagnosis of a

Cluster C personality disorder[46]. Cluster C personality disorders include dependent, avoidant and obsessive-compulsive disorders, which are the personality disorders most frequently associated with depression[47]. In CB therapy, neither patients' endorsements of any treatment principles nor a diagnosis of a personality disorder predicted treatment outcome. In contrast, patients who indicated lower endorsement of either CB or PDIP treatment principles, or patients who had a diagnosis of a personality disorder, did less well in PDIP therapy than those patients who highly endorsed CB or PDIP treatment principles, or who had no personality disorder diagnosis. The former findings suggest that maximum benefit from psychotherapy would not be achieved by simply offering patients the therapy they preferred. What appears to be more important, at least for PDIP therapy, is the extent of endorsement of the patient's psychological treatment. This aptitude or knowledge enables patients to make better use of PDIP therapy[45]. In the NIMH study, IPT was found to be more effective than CT for depressed patients with elevated levels of obsessive personality[48]. Single patients also improved more in IPT than in CT, leading these authors to suggest that patients did better in therapies that 'matched' their personality or interpersonal styles.

The possibility that therapists are responsive to the interpersonal style of patients was examined in a study using SPP2 data. It was hypothesised that patient interpersonal styles would 'pull' therapists to respond differentially even within theoretically pure, manualised therapies. SPP2 patients were divided according to their predominant interpersonal styles. Patients were classified as either overinvolved, underinvolved, or balanced in close interpersonal relationships. Therapists' responses to patients were then examined using the Therapist Session Intentions (TSI)[34] and independent ratings of therapist interventions (Sheffield Psychotherapy Rating Scale)[49]. These measures contain scales that tap CB and PDIP specific techniques and therapists tended to use more affective and relationship-oriented interventions with overinvolved patients, consistent with these patients' overriding concern about maintaining relationships. Therapists tended to use more cognitive treatment methods with underinvolved patients consistent with these patients' more distant, cognitive approaches to relationships. This finding was only significant for CB therapy[50]. This may be because therapists were able to use a greater range of interventions in CB than in PDIP therapy. PDIP procedures aimed at maintaining the therapeutic alliance and dealing with affect may be easily 'borrowed' by CB therapists as part of the collaborative approach, whereas addressing faulty cognitions and setting behavioural tasks are not easily woven into PDIP therapy.

A further study was conducted to help understand the process of responsiveness a qualitative study examining sections of therapy transcript was conducted. Transcripts that contained events that patients indicated had been the most helpful in the session were analysed. Patients' attachment style, attachment issues, and therapist response to the identified attachment issues were categorised[51]. Attachment issues tended to focus on three themes: (i) concerns about loss or rejection; (ii) conflict and danger; and (iii) the need for closeness or proximity. The authors hypothesised that therapists' responses to patients' attachment issues would be mediated by patients' attachment styles and indeed there is evidence for this: therapists responded to patients with preoccupied attachment styles with reflective interventions and to patients with dismissing styles with interpretative interventions[51].

Processes of change

Effective targeting of treatment depends, in part, on patients' presentation of their problems. The assimilation model[52] describes how patients present and may resolve their problems and how therapists' interventions assist in this process. The assimilation model argues that patients describe their problems in a way that reflects the degree to which they have assimilated a problematic experience into their own schemata. Schemata here represent cognitive structures that provide meaning and, therefore, link together a person's experiences. Several case studies have provided evidence that patients progress through the stages of assimilation during successful PDIP therapy[53,54].

The assimilation model also suggests that patients with poorly assimilated problems should do better in PDIP therapy. Therapists using PDIP therapies often consider the patient's presenting complaints as reflecting experiences that are not yet accessible or are avoided (low levels of assimilation). In these therapies, formulation of the problem and insight (moderate levels of assimilation) are often the therapeutic goals. Patients indicated that early sessions of PDIP therapy had lower levels of problem solving, were rougher, and had lower ratings of post-session positive mood than CB sessions[36]. CB therapies, in contrast, focus more on known problems, applying rational and practical solutions (high levels of assimilation). This suggests that patients with relatively clearly described problems will do better in CB therapies. This is consistent with the notion that therapists' begin work at lower levels of the assimilation model in PDIP therapy. Significant differences were found between the assimilation levels in good sessions of PDIP and CB sessions[55]. In PDIP sessions, therapy tended to focus on themes at lower assimilation levels, with a mean level between the stages of vague awareness and problem statement. In contrast, in CB sessions therapy focused on themes at higher assimilation levels, with a mean level between the stages of understanding and application. It was found that patients entering therapy with relatively well assimilated problems did better in CB than PDIP therapy[56]. However, patients with poorly assimilated problems did equally well in both CB and PDIP therapy.

Summary of IP therapies and depression

There are three main forms of IP that have been studied. These therapies have been found to differ in their content to the cognitive and behavioural therapies, although treatment outcomes for depression remain similar across therapies. Important factors influencing treatment outcome in IP therapies are engaging patients in the process of treatment; providing an appropriate focus to treatment; and recognising the impact of patients' interpersonal histories on the treatment process itself, and on the ability of patients to maintain the gains they make in treatment.

PDIP therapy appears to require patients' commitment to psychological therapy prior to therapy starting. So, for example, both patients' treatment preferences and degree of psychological orientation predicted outcome in PDIP therapy. In addition, patients with well assimilated problems did better in CB than PDIP therapy in SPP2. These findings suggest therapists should socialise patients into the treatment process, and carefully assess patients needs and formulate their problems, so that therapy can both clarify and be targeted at key patient problems.

Together the studies suggest that it is important for therapists to be flexible and responsive to patient needs, especially to the interpersonal or attachment issues that confront patients. Patients also did better in therapy if they were confident in their therapists, as attachment theory would predict. In particular, assimilation of problematic experiences seems to occur when therapists are firm, collaborative and challenging.

Finally, important and distinctive elements of PDIP therapy have been found to focus on two elements. First, finding the right language that captures the patients' experiences and is understood by both therapist and patient is a central component of PDIP therapy[27] and highlighted by a number of studies[51,57]. Second, studies have linked change in therapy to the experiential element of PDIP therapy, namely the experiencing of feelings and events in the here and now[55,58].

Conclusions

The above efficacy studies have made considerable headway in securing the evidence-base for counselling and the IP therapies. This meets the current need for evidence-based practice in the psychological therapies[59]. However, there now needs to be a concerted effort to support and carry out studies in routine settings (*i.e.* effectiveness studies) that will deliver to the complementary paradigm of practice-based evidence[60]. Although the studies reported here employed a common outcome measure (*i.e.* the BDI) – largely because of the focus on depression – studies of counselling and the IP therapies are likely to comprise more heterogeneous samples and there is need for the adoption of a pan-theoretical outcome measure[61]. The strength of the research in the IP therapies is in the focus on investigating what is happening and how this might account for change. In this respect, research in the IP therapies had yielded greater understanding of the models of change. A focus for future research would be on the inter-session change process as opposed to focusing on the session itself, and on broadening the evidence-base to non-research settings.

References

1   Rowland N, Goss S. (eds) *Evidence-Based Counselling and Psychological Therapies*. London: Routledge; 2000

2   Department of Health. *Treatment Choice in Psychological Therapies and Counselling: Evidence Based Clinical Practice Guidelines*. London: The Stationery Office; 2001

3   British Association of Counselling (BAC). *Code of Ethics and Practice for Counsellors*. Rugby: BAC; 1992

4   Mellor-Clark J, Simms-Ellis RE, Burton M. *National Survey of Counsellors Working in Primary Care: Evidence for Growing Professionalisation*. Occasional paper 79. London: Royal College of General Practitioners, 2001

5   Mellor-Clark J. (ed) Symposium: developing practice and evidence for counselling in primary care. *Br J Guidance Counselling* 2000; **28**: 157–266

6   Roth A, Fonagy P. *What Works for Whom? A Critical Review of Psychotherapy Research*. New York: Guilford, 1996

7   Godber E. *Is Counselling in Primary Care Growing too Fast? A Clinical, Economic and Strategic Assessment*. Southampton: Institute for Health Policy Studies, University of Southampton, 1996

8   Rowland N, Godfrey C, Bower P, Mellor-Clark J, Heywood P, Hardy R. Counselling in primary care: a systematic review of the research evidence. *Br J Guidance Counselling* 2000; **28**: 215–31

9   Bedi N, Chilvers C, Churchill R *et al*. Assessing effectiveness of treatment of depression in primary care. Partially randomised preference trial. *Br J Psychiatry* 2000; **177**: 312–8

10   Chilvers C, Dewey M, Fielding K *et al*. Antidepressant drugs and generic counselling for treatment of major depression in primary care: randomised trial with patient preference arm. *BMJ* 2001; **322**: 772–5

11   King M, Sibbald B, Ward E *et al*. Randomised controlled trial of non-directive counselling, cognitive-behaviour therapy and usual general practitioner care in the management of depression as well as mixed anxiety and depression in primary care. *Health Technol Assess* 2000; **4**: 19

12   Ward E, King M, Lloyd M *et al*. Randomised controlled trial of non-directive counselling, cognitive-behaviour therapy, and usual general practitioner care for patients with depression. I: Clinical effectiveness. *BMJ* 2000; **321**: 1383–8

13   Bower P, Byford S, Sibbald B *et al*. Randomised controlled trial of non-directive counselling, cognitive-behaviour therapy, and usual general practitioner care for patients with depression. II: Cost-effectiveness. *BMJ* 2000; **321**: 1389–92

14 Simpson S, Corney R, Fitzgerald P, Beecham J. A randomised controlled trial to evaluate the effectiveness and cost-effectiveness of counselling patients with chronic depression. *Health Technol Assess* 2000; **4**: 36

15 Beck AT, Ward CH, Mendelson M, Mock J, Erlbaugh J. An inventory for measuring depression. *Arch Gen Psychiatry* 1961; **4**: 561–71

16 Boot D, Gillies P, Fenelon J, Reubin R, Wilkins M, Gray P. Evaluation of the short term impact of counselling in general practice. *Patient Educ Counsel* 1984; **24**: 79–89

17 Friedli K, King M, Lloyd M, Horder J. Randomised controlled assessment of non-directive psychotherapy versus routine general-practice care. *Lancet* 1997; **350**: 1662–5

18 Harvey I, Nelson S, Llyons R, Unwin C, Monaghan S, Peters T. A randomised controlled trial and economic evaluation of counselling in primary care. *Br J Gen Pract* 1998; **48**: 1043–8

19 Hemmings A. Counselling in primary care: a randomised controlled trial. *Patient Educ Counsel* 1997; **32**: 219–30

20 Brown GW, Harris T. *Social Origins of Depression*. New York: Free Press, 1978

21 Cohen MB, Baker G, Cohen R, Fromm-Reichmann F, Weigert EV. An intensive study of 12 cases of manic-depressive psychosis. 1954. Reprinted in: Coyne JC (ed) *Essential Papers on Depression*. New York: New York University Press, 1985

22 Coyne JC. Depression and the response of others. *J Abnorm Psychol* 1976; **85**: 127–40

23 Freud S. Morning and melancholia (1917). Reprinted in: Coyne JC (ed) *Essential Papers on Depression*. New York: New York University Press, 1985

24 Mendelson M. *Psychoanalytic Concepts of Depression*. Springfield, IL: Thomas, 1960

25 Alloy LB. The developmental origins of cognitive vulnerability to depression: negative interpersonal context leads to personal vulnerability. *Cog Ther Res* 2001; **25**: 349–51

26 Klerman GL, Weismann NM, Rounsaville BJ, Chevron ES. *Interpersonal Psychotherapy of Depression*. New York: Basic Books, 1984

27 Hobson RF. *Forms of Feeling: The Heart of Psychotherapy*. New York: Basic Books, 1985

28 Shapiro DA, Barkham M, Rees A, Hardy GE, Reynolds S, Startup M. Effects of treatment duration and severity of depression on the effectiveness of cognitive-behavioral and psychodynamic-interpersonal psychotherapy. *J Consult Clin Psychol* 1994; **62**: 522–34

29 Malan DH. *The Frontier of Brief Psychotherapy*. New York: Plenum, 1976

30 Luborsky L. *Principles of Psychoanalytic Psychotherapy: A Manual for Supportive-Expressive Treatment*. New York: Basic Books, 1984

31 Strupp HH, Binder JL. *Psychotherapy in a New Key: A Guide to Time – Limited Dynamic Psychotherapy*. New York: Basic Books, 1984

32 Blagys MD, Hilsenroth MJ. Distinctive features of short-term psychodynamic-interpersonal psychotherapy: a review of the comparative psychotherapy literature. *Clin Psychol Sci Pract* 2000; **7**: 167–88

33 Goldfried MR, Castonguay LG, Hayes AM, Drozd JF, Shapiro DA. A comparative analysis of the therapeutic focus in cognitive-behavioral and psycho-dynamic-interpersonal sessions. *J Consult Clin Psychol* 1997; **65**: 740–8

34 Stiles WB, Startup M, Hardy GE *et al.* Therapist intentions in cognitive-behavioral and psychodynamic-interpersonal psychotherapy. *J Counsel Psychol* 1996; **43**: 402–14

35 Agnew-Davies R, Stiles WB, Hardy GE, Barkham M, Shapiro DA. Alliance structure assessed by the Agnew Relationship Measure (ARM). *Br J Clin Psychol* 1998; **37**: 155–72

36 Reynolds S, Stiles WB, Barkham B, Shapiro DA, Hardy GE, Rees A. Acceleration of changes in session impact during contrasting time-limited psychotherapies. *J Consult Clin Psychol* 1996; **64**: 577–86

37 Roth A, Fonagy P. *What Works for Whom: A Critical Review of Psychotherapy Research*. New York: Guilford, 1996

38 Shapiro DA. Efficacy of psychodynamic, interpersonal, and experiential therapies. In: Checkley S. (Ed) *The Management of Depression*. Oxford: Blackwell, 1998

39 MacLean PD, Hakstian AR. Clinical depression: comparative efficacy of outpatient treatments. *J Consult Clin Psychol* 1979; **47**: 818–36

40 Steuer JL, Mintz J, Hammen CL *et al.* Cognitive–behavioral and psychodynamic group psychotherapy in treatment of geriatric depression. *J Consult Clin Psychol* 1984; **52**: 180–9

41 Elkin I, Shea MT, Watkins JT *et al.* NIMH Treatment of Depression Collaborative Research Program: general effectiveness of treatments. *Arch Gen Psychiatry* 1989; **46**: 971–83

42 Elkin I. The NIMH Treatment of Depression Collaborative Research Program: where we began and where we are. In: Bergin AE, Garfield SL. (eds) *Handbook of Psychotherapy and Behavior Change*, 4th edn. New York: Wiley, 1994

43 Shapiro DA, Rees A, Barkham M, Hardy GE, Reynolds S, Startup M. Effects of treatment duration and severity of depression the maintenance of gains after cognitive-behavioral and psychodynamic-interpersonal psychotherapy. *J Consult Clin Psychol* 1995; **63**: 378–87

44 Barkham M, Shapiro DA, Rees A, Hardy GE. Psychotherapy in two-plus-one sessions: outcomes of a randomized controlled trial of cognitive-behavioral and psychodynamic-interpersonal therapy for subsyndromal depression. *J Consult Clin Psychol* 1999; **67**: 201–11

45 Hardy GE, Barkham M, Shapiro DA, Reynolds S, Rees A, Stiles WB. Credibility and outcome of cognitive-behavioural and psychodynamic-interpersonal psychotherapy. *Br J Clin Psychol* 1995; **34**: 555–69

46 Hardy GE, Barkham M, Shapiro DA, Stiles WB, Rees A, Reynolds S. Impact of cluster C personality disorders on outcomes of contrasting brief psychotherapies for depression. *J Consult Clin Psychol* 1995; **63**: 997–1004

47 Pilkonis PA, Frank E. Personality pathology in recurrent depression: Nature, prevalence, and relationship to treatment response. *Am J Psychiatry* 1988; **145**: 435–41

48 Barber J, Muenz P, Larry R. The role of avoidance and obsessiveness in matching patients for cognitive and interpersonal psychotherapy: empirical findings from the Treatment for Depression Collaborative Research Program. *J Consult Clin Psychol* 1996; **64**: 951–8

49 Startup M, Shapiro DA. Therapist treatment fidelity in prescriptive vs. exploratory therapy. *Br J Clin Psychol* 1993; **32**: 443–56

50 Hardy GE, Stiles WB, Barkham M, Startup M. Therapist responsiveness to client interpersonal styles during time-limited treatments for depression. *J Consult Clin Psychol* 1988; **66**: 304–12

51 Hardy GE, Aldridge J, Davidson C, Reilly S, Rowe C, Shapiro DA. Therapist responsiveness to client attachment styles and issues observed in client-identified significant events in psychodynamic-interpersonal psychotherapy. *Psychother Res* 1999; **9**: 36–53

52 Stiles WB, Elliott R, Llewelyn SP *et al*. Assimilation of problematic experiences by clients in psychotherapy. *Psychotherapy* 1990; **27**: 411–20

53 Field SD, Barkham M, Shapiro DA, Stiles WB. Assessment of assimilation in psychotherapy. A quantitative case study of problematic experiences with a significant other. *J Counsel Psychol* 1994; **41**: 397–406

54 Stiles WB, Morrison L, Haw S, Harper H, Shapiro DA, Firth-Cozens J. Longitudinal study of assimilation in exploratory psychotherapy. *Psychotherapy* 1991; **28**: 195–206

55 Mackay HE, Barkham M, Stiles WB. Staying with the feeling: an anger event in psychodynamic-interpersonal therapy. *J Counsel Psychol* 1998; **45**: 279–89

56 Stiles WB, Shankland M, Wright J, Field S. Aptitude-treatment interactions based on clients' assimilation of their presenting problems. *J Consult Clin Psychol* 1997; **65**: 889–93

57 Elliott R, Shapiro DA. Client and therapist as analysts of significant events. In: Toukmanian SG, Rennie DL. (eds) *Psychotherapeutic Change: Theory Guide and Descriptive Research Strategies*. Newbury Park, CA: Sage, 1992

58 Hardy GE, Rees A, Barkham M, Shapiro DA, Field SD, Elliott R. 'Whingeing versus working': Comprehensive Process Analysis of a vague awareness event. *Psychother Res* 1998; **8**: 334–53

59 Parry G. Evidence-based psychotherapy: an overview. In: Rowland N, Goss S. (eds) *Evidence-Based Counselling and Psychological Therapies*. London: Routledge, 2000

60 Barkham M, Mellor-Clark J. Rigour and relevance: practice-based evidence in the psychological therapies. In: Rowland N, Goss S. (eds) *Evidence-Based Counselling and Psychological Therapies*. London: Routledge, 2000

61 Barkham M, Margison F, Leach C *et al*. Service profiling and outcomes benchmarking using the CORE-OM: towards practice-based evidence in the psychological therapies. *J Consult Clin Psychol* 2001; **69**: 184–96

Written and computer-based self-help treatments for depression

Chris Williams and **Graeme Whitfield**

Department of Psychological Medicine, University of Glasgow, Glasgow, UK

Patients and health purchasers are demanding the provision of effective and accessible mental health treatments. Psychotherapeutic approaches are popular with patients, but access to specialist psychotherapy services is often limited. Other ways of offering treatment within the time and resources available to most practitioners need to be considered. One possible solution is the use of structured self-help materials that address common mental disorders such as depression. Self-help treatments are available in a variety of formats such as books, CD-ROMS, audio and videotapes. Evidence exists for their effectiveness; however, a relatively neglected area has been a discussion of the educational aspects of such materials. Self-help materials aim to improve patient knowledge and skills in self-management. They require very clear educational goals and a content and structure that is appropriate for those who use them. Such work will enhance the credibility, take-up, and effectiveness of self-help materials within clinical settings.

Depression is a common condition that is often poorly detected within both community and hospital settings[1]. It is associated with significant distress and has a marked social and economic impact. Patients with co-morbid psychiatric disorders have a greater use of non-psychiatric medical resources[2,3]. In addition, depression is associated with a significant risk of suicide[4]. For these reasons, the effective detection and management of depression have been identified as priority areas within the *National Service Framework for Mental Health*[5]. This aims to improve the detection and management of depression. However, both primary and secondary care mental health services are already very busy with existing patient workloads and many non-mental health specialists admit to a lack of time and the clinical skills required to manage depression effectively. For example, a study of newly qualified doctors found that less than 12% believed that they possessed the clinical skills required to offer treatment for depression[6].

Treatments for mental health problems include medication and psychosocial interventions such as counselling and the various psychotherapies. Psychological treatments are widely in demand, and have been shown to be effective[7]. The Department of Health has stated

Correspondence to:
Dr Chris Williams,
Department of
Psychological Medicine,
Academic Centre,
Gartnavel Royal Hospital,
1055 Great
Western Road,
Glasgow G12 0XH, UK

a preference for the delivery of psychological therapies over medication treatments where outcomes are shown to be equivalent[8]; however, access to specialised psychotherapy settings is often limited. The dilemma is how to offer such treatments effectively within the time and resources available within everyday clinical settings.

One possible solution is the use of structured self-help approaches.

Definitions of self-help

In the context of mental health treatment, 'self-help' as an approach has been used to describe very varied activities including patient self-help groups and organisations and also the concept of self-care where a person uses self-help resources to improve how they feel. Self-help books are often found in the top 20 best selling books and most large bookshops have a significantly sized self-help section. An internet search of the terms 'self+help' reveals about 2,110,000 internet web-sites. But what is self-help? Two definitions are:

1. The patient receives a standardised treatment method with which he can help himself without major help from the therapist. In (self-help) it is necessary that treatment be described in sufficient detail, so that the patient can work it through independently. Books, in which only information about depression is given to patients and their families cannot be used[9].

2. The use of written materials or computer programmes or the listening/viewing of audio/video tapes for the purpose of gaining understanding or solving problems relevant to a person's developmental or therapeutic needs. The goals of the (self-help approach) should be relevant to the fields of counselling and clinical psychology[10].

Although patient education and self-help approaches may have some overlap in content, the goals of self-help are different from pure patient education. The crucial difference is that while patient education aims to increase patient knowledge, self-help approaches aim to increase both patient knowledge **and** also lead to skill gain. In particular, self-help treatments aim to help patients to learn how to self-manage their condition better. Such materials may be delivered using a range of formats including books (so-called bibliotherapy), computers, audio and videotapes, and other formats such as interactive packages accessed via telephone.

Why use self-help?

There are a number of potential advantages to using self-help materials. Treatment is accessed with minimum delay and at low price. Self-help approaches are popular and acceptable to many patients. Such treatments respect patient privacy and can help avoid the stigma of formal psychotherapy. The patient can use the materials in their own time and at their own pace and this may be particularly helpful for patients who are working, or who live some distance from a practitioner. Importantly, the approach empowers the patient. The content can build upon sessions with the health care worker and can be used to re-inforce and consolidate learning. Finally, the materials allow patients to renew or update their treatment as often as they wish, and at no extra cost. It is also clear from outcome studies that self-help approaches can be effective treatments of depression.

It is not possible within this article to review all aspects of self-help treatment; therefore, we have chosen to focus upon the treatment of depression using paper based books/manuals or computer delivered self-help packages. Interestingly, almost all studies that have examined the effectiveness of self-help treatments have used the Cognitive Behaviour Therapy (CBT) model. This has a proven effectiveness for depression[11]. CBT is essentially a structured and educational form of psychotherapy that aims to teach patients effective strategies for the self-management of their problems. Therefore, it provides a structure that is easily delivered using self-help formats.

The effectiveness of written self-help materials for depression

Meta-analyses have drawn general conclusions about the usefulness and acceptability of the self-help approach in addressing a wide variety of clinical conditions and habitual behaviours[9,10,12,13]. Most of the studies incorporated into these meta-analyses used written self-help materials although one included audiotape materials[13], and another included written, audiotape, and videotape materials[12]. Only one of the meta-analyses looked solely at depression and this only used bibliotherapy studies[9]. Two of the meta-analyses observed that self-help was more effective with diagnosable problems including depression than with habitual behaviours[10,12]. Generally, studies comparing the outcomes of patients treated by self-help compared to face-to-face therapy have observed no significant difference in outcome[9,10,12,13]. Both forms of treatment had significantly better outcomes than a variety of control situations. Generally, those studies that analysed the effect of adding practitioner contact whilst the clients worked through the self-help materials did not appear to benefit from this addition[10,12,13]; although one meta-analysis concluded that anxious patients responded better when they had some therapist contact[10]. This general finding contrasts with the belief of many therapists and counsellors that supported self-help approaches are more likely to be effective than unsupported self-help treatments[14,15].

One of the major problems in many of the studies is that most of the above research has been carried out on US-based non-clinical populations. Many of the participants have been recruited by advertising in the media to the general public. Participants may have been much keener to comply with treatment as a result. Not surprisingly, these studies show much lower dropout rates than are experienced in UK-based studies of self-help where dropout rates approach 50%[16–18]. In one UK-based study, 51 patients with symptoms of anxiety with or without concomitant depression were given a self-help booklet and audiotape as well as receiving the treatments that they would otherwise have received from their GPs[16]. Another 50 patients only received the regular GP interventions without any self-help. The patients who used the self-help materials achieved significantly greater reductions in levels of depression and anxiety. The difference continued at 3 months' follow-up. A subsequent study, also based in a British primary care setting, recruited 106 patients diagnosed by their GPs as suffering from anxiety, depression or a combination of the two[17]. No significant advantage was observed by adding self-help to the regular treatments that the GPs normally gave. The authors believed that this might have been due in part to the high dropout rate reducing the power of the study.

The effectiveness of computer-administered self-help for depression

The use of computers to assist in the treatment of mental health problems has been recently reviewed[14]. This review emphasised that this is a rapidly advancing field and that, at present, computerised self-help is not widely distributed to the vast majority of clinicians.

A computerised self-help cognitive-behavioural therapy (CBT) package for depression has been compared to traditional therapist-led CBT in a randomised control trial (RCT)[19]. In this study 36 volunteer patients who met research diagnostic criteria for major or minor depressive disorder were randomised to three groups receiving either traditional therapist-led CBT, computerised self-help, or a control option. At the end of the 6 weeks of treatment and at 2 month follow-up, the patients from the two CBT groups had improved significantly more compared to the control group. The outcome of the two treatment groups did not differ from each other at either time. It is noteworthy that the self-help provided in this study incorporated some minimal therapist contact with input at the beginning and end of each session and also there was the option for users to ask the therapist questions throughout. A subsequent randomised controlled trial allocated 22 depressed in-patients into three treatment options of 2 weeks of daily sessions of traditional therapist-led CBT, computer-instructed cognitive therapy, or in-patient care as usual[20]. The therapy-led patients did significantly better than the computer-led group in terms of reduction in depression rating scale scores. This trial has been criticised in that the computer programme that was used only taught cognitive techniques rather than the cognitive and behavioural approach of the therapist. Thus it may not have been a fair comparison[14].

A recent method of computerised self-help has been described which uses touch-tone telephone calls to a computer-aided interactive voice response (IVR) system. One system known as 'COPE' is a CBT-based self-help regimen which uses an initial videotape, 9 booklets and 11 accompanying IVR telephone calls through to the IVR system that then makes recommendations to the patients based on the information they have entered[21]. An uncontrolled trial that tested COPE on 41 patients found that 28 (68%) completed the 12 week self-help programme with concomitant significant falls in depression rating scale scores and social adjustment scores. In common with studies that have used the IVR system for clients with obsessive compulsive disorder[22], most participants made the calls to the computer outside normal office hours. This illustrates one of the great benefits of self-help – that its participation is not dependent on the working hours of the practitioner. Hand-held (palmtop) computers have been incorporated into self-help treatments of a number of anxiety disorders particularly panic[23]. They are capable of providing advice at critical moments as well as recording information such as symptoms or behaviours. As yet, they have found less of a niche in the treatment of depression although they could have a role in the recording of mood, thoughts and behaviours in real-time.

As with written self-help interventions, there is some controversy about the need for some face-to-face therapist input in computerised treatments. Certainly some patients find it very difficult to follow self-help regimens without some encouragement and guidance from a practitioner[25]. Perhaps the most important ingredient that remains largely absent from computerised self-help systems presently available is an ability to respond to the patient's non-verbal cues, misinterpreting their natural language, and, therefore, not being able to place a patient's communication into an appropriate context[25]. It appears that it is still extremely difficult to design a computer system that is broad-based enough to respond to all the complex needs of a patient throughout the therapy process without some assistance from a therapist[14]. Most packages have, therefore, opted to provide a more educational and informative input that aims to increase the patients' knowledge about depression, and teach specific skills that can be used to improve how they feel. In spite of the promising results of reported studies, computerised self-help treatment packages have failed to be adopted in everyday clinical settings and we are currently engaged in research examining the reasons for this.

Who benefits from self-help treatments?

Self-help appears to benefit some patients, but not all. Some depressed patients by the very nature of the condition will not be capable of concentrating on the material[15], while the experience of failing when set the task of working through the self-help could result in increased despondency. Personality factors have also been found to predict outcome in self-help treatments for patients diagnosed with depression or dysthymia[26-28]. Furthermore, because of poor-eyesight or poor reading skills, some patients will not be able to use self-help unless they use a computer-based voice recogniser. The stepped care model suggests that patients will respond differently to varying types and intensities of psychosocial interventions, and that it is, therefore, sensible to provide a range of interventions perhaps ranging from self-help to long-term individual treatments[29]. The model has been described as a means of maximising the efficiency of resource allocation.

Using self-help treatment in practice

Within health service settings, self-help materials can be offered to: (i) patients on waiting lists as they wait to be seen by secondary care based services; (ii) individual patients to support work with a health care practitioner either within primary or secondary care settings; and (iii) groups of patients to support group-based interventions.

We have looked at different ways of using self-help effectively within our own clinical setting and developed a specific self-help room to support the treatments offered within an acute adult psychiatric day hospital. This provides a centralised resource for use by staff and out-patients (including waiting list patients). Two sets of written materials are provided in the room – *Mind over Mood*[30] and *Overcoming Depression: A Five Areas Approach*[31]; both are structured self-help materials that use a CBT model of treatment. This ensures that all staff are familiar with the content of the self-help materials used. One person uses the room at a time and books into the room for up to 1 h. Patients are encouraged to use the room once or twice a week, and to keep all their completed workbooks and worksheets so as to create their own personalised treatment pack. The room is kept neat and tidy, and has an open aspect with plants, rugs and pictures to encourage a relaxed atmosphere.

The effectiveness of a CBT self-help room in a UK setting

We have evaluated the effectiveness of various aspects of the self-help room. The following briefly describes an open study evaluating the effectiveness of the CBT book *Mind over Mood*[30]. This was offered to consecutive routine referrals with symptoms of depression and/or anxiety. Patients were all routine referrals aged 16–65 years referred from primary care to a psychiatric sector team based in inner city Leeds. The only exclusions were urgent referrals, or patients at risk of suicide or homicide, and those patients with illiteracy or marked visual impairment as identified on a standard referral form. All 42 patients referred between 19 April and 19 July 1999 who fulfilled these criteria were written to and offered a one-off brief (20 min) introduction on how to use the self-help room, and then were encouraged to attend the room to work through *Mind over Mood* on a weekly basis during their 6 week wait for a routine assessment interview by a team member. Baseline assessments were made of psychological distress, dysfunctional attitudes and degree of hopelessness during the period of use of the self-help manual, as well as patient satisfaction with the room and the book. Twenty-two of 42 consecutive referrals attended the room (mean 3.55 sessions, SD 1.71). The Beck Hopelessness Scale (BHS)[32], the General Health Questionnaire (GHQ)[33], and Dysfunctional Attitudes Scale (DAS)[34], as well as measures of patient participation and satisfaction were completed at the beginning and end of the 6 week period in those patients who attended the room. Scores on all three scales fell clinically and statistically significantly over the study period. The patients generally judged that the self-help intervention was acceptable and effective, and that their knowledge in a number of key areas had been improved. Conclusions regarding effectiveness are limited by the absence of control group data; nonetheless, this study does suggest that the provision of a structured CBT self-help manual is useful for patients with low mood and anxiety on a waiting list for a psychiatric outpatient assessment. A full description of this study has been published[18].

Self-help as health technology

It seems clear that self-help treatment using written CBT materials can be effective; however, the study also found that the patient's experience of using the materials is also crucial. Self-help approaches are not for everyone – 48% of patients in our study chose not to take up the offer of the self-help material and the mean number of sessions attended by the 22 patients who attended their initial introductory session to the self-help room was 3.55. The concept of non take-up and dropout from treatment is not new to the health service and a significant literature has examined this. It does raise, however, the issue of how to offer self-help interventions that engage patients in treatment so that they receive the right materials, delivered using the right format and at the right pace for them[35].

One interesting viewpoint on the role of self-help materials has been suggested by Dr David Richards of the University of Manchester. This sees self-help as a form of health technology – a means of delivering health care. The NHS R&D Health Technology Assessment Programme summarises health technology as covering 'any method used by those working in health services to promote health, prevent and treat disease and improve rehabilitation and long-term care. Technologies in this context are not confined to new drugs or pieces of sophisticated equipment' (www.hta.nhsweb.nhs.uk). Using this definition, all forms of self-help can be termed a health technology. The problem with technology, however, is how best to offer this effectively within a health care setting. Technologies can be used ineffectively without effective staff training. In addition, technology alone does not necessarily equate with user-acceptability; we need, therefore, to consider the structure and content of self-help materials to ensure that they are user-friendly and beneficial for patients.

A number of quality assessment resources can be used to ensure that self-help materials meet the patient's needs including the Help for Health Trust web-site (www.hfht.org) and the PoPPi guide[36] (www.kingsfund.org.uk). Bringing together their recommendations, effective patient materials should provide:

1. *Accessibility*: materials that are provided in an appropriate format for the target audience. The design and layout must also be simple to use and understand.

2. *Appropriateness*: materials should be relevant to and designed for a specific target audience that is defined clearly at outset.

3. *Availability*: materials must be made available to a wide audience. This means that materials should be delivered using different formats (*e.g.* CD-ROM, the internet and as books/leaflets) and include electronic versions of the information. Dissemination via a national databases such as NHS Direct on-line (www.nhsdirect.nhs.uk) is preferable to increase availability.

4. *Legibility*: so that text/content is clearly presented. For example, in depression concentration is often impaired. Providing an appropriate font size and line spacing, clear chunking of text into sections and the use of shading can aid the user's ability to use the materials effectively. Legibility tools can be used. In addition, the words and sentences used in materials

should be kept short and medical/psychological jargon minimised. Readability tests such as the Flesch or that of the Plain English campaign (www.plainenglish.co.uk/freepub.html) can be helpful.

5. *User involvement*: in order to meet patient needs, the target audience for the materials should be involved in the production of the content.

The Overcoming Depression Course

This course of 10 structured CBT workbooks was initially funded for development by a NHS Health Authority. It aims to offer ready access to the evidence-based CBT treatment for depression and to provide this in an accessible, jargon-free form. Each workbook has been tested within a collaborative group of GPs, psychologists, practice nurses, CPNs, and others who have used the workbook with patients and have offered feedback that has then been used to improve their content. The reading age of each workbook is 11–14 years (most aged 11–12 years). The development of the materials meet the criteria for producing effective patient materials as described above, and provide a structured step-by-step approach that supports 1:1 work with the practitioner. The structure of the *Overcoming Depression Course* is summarised in Figure 1.

The course workbooks include a single entry workbook that helps the patient self-assess current problems (situation, relationship and practical problems, altered thinking, mood, physical symptoms and behaviour). This then helps the patient and their health care practitioner to decide which of workbooks 2–9 should be chosen for use. Finally, a single exit workbook teaches effective strategies for relapse prevention. The materials are designed to support work by the health care practitioner and as many or as few of the materials as are relevant to the patient or practitioner may be used. Patients are seen once every 1–3 weeks for monitoring.

Users are encouraged to take time reading and responding to questions in the workbooks. They are invited to answer all the questions asked and to *Stop, Think and Reflect* on their answers. The materials are aimed at patients with mild-to-moderate depression in primary or secondary care, who have a reading age of 12 years or over. They provide very clear targets for change and aim to help improve:

- extreme/unhelpful thinking
- poor problem solving/lack of assertiveness skills
- problems of reduced activity
- unhelpful behaviours (such as drinking excessively)
- problems such as poor sleep/insomnia
- the patient's ability to take antidepressants (if prescribed)

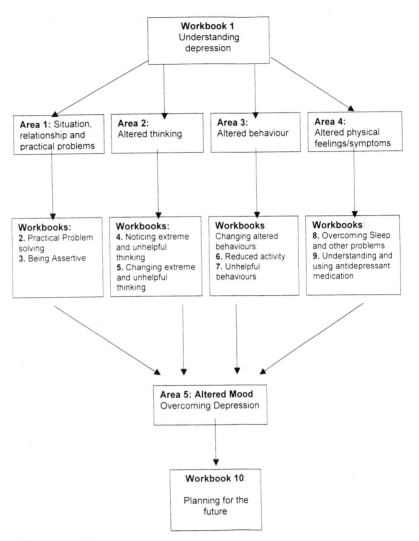

Fig. 1 The
Overcoming
Depression Course.

The materials are available in a range of delivery formats including as a book[31], via the web[37] and as an interactive CD-ROM for use by patients[38]. Together, the different formats of delivery offer patients access to the same materials in ways that address the different personal preferences and skills of patients/practitioners. In addition, a range of accompanying written and CD training materials for practitioners provide staff training in using the approach. Several health authorities have set up training courses in the approach and a trainer's manual will shortly be available to support such training. This is seen as crucial in supporting the use of the materials, so that they can be used effectively by practitioners who are familiar with their content.

In order to provide ready access to materials, a license for unlimited photocopying for use with patients and in training is provided with the book, and six of the ten workbooks are available free of charge from the web-site www.calipso.co.uk

Key points for clinical practice

- Self-help approaches offer a potentially important and useful way of providing ready access to effective psychosocial interventions
- Most self-help approaches use the Cognitive Behaviour Therapy approach and a strong evidence base supports the effectiveness of this form of psychotherapy, and its effectiveness as a structured self-help approach
- Delivery may be by more traditional book or tape-based formats, or by more modern approaches such as by interactive CD-ROMs or via the Internet
- Patients are all very different and providing materials that meet these different needs is important
- With the increasing focus on the use of technology to deliver self-help treatments, there is a need to re-visit the basics of patient engagement to ensure that computer-based and written self-help materials provide materials that are developed with the patient in mind and that such materials are delivered by trained practitioners who are able to use them effectively and appropriately with the patients they treat[35]

Acknowledgement

Figure 1 is reproduced with permission of Dr CJ Williams and University of Leeds Innovations.

References

1   Goldberg D. Identifying psychiatric illness among general medical patients [editorial]. *BMJ* 1985; **291**: 161–2
2   Levenson JL, Hamer RM, Silverman JJ, Rossiter LF. Psychopathology in medical in-patients and its relationship to length of hospital stay: a pilot study. *Int J Psychiatry Med* 1986; **16**: 231–6
3   Fulop G, Strain JJ, Vita J, Lyons JS, Hammer JS. Impact of psychiatric co-morbidity on length of hospital stay for medical/surgical patients: a preliminary report. *Am J Psychiatry* 1987; **144**: 878–82
4   Blair-West GW, Cantor CH, Mellsop GW, Eyeson-Annan ML. Lifetime suicide risk in major depression: sex and age determinants. *J Affect Disord* 1999; **55**: 171–8
5   Department of Health. *National Service Framework for Mental Health: Modern Standards and Service models*. London: Department of Health, 1999
6   Williams CJ, Milton J, Strickland P *et al.* The impact of medical school teaching on pre-registration house officers' knowledge of psychiatry – a three centre intervention study. *BMJ* 1997; **7113**: 917–8
7   Roth A, Fonagy P. *What Works for Whom? A Critical Review of Psychotherapy Research*. London: Guilford, 1996
8   Department of Health. *Health of the Nation*. London: HMSO, 1991
9   Cuijpers P. Bibliotherapy in unipolar depression: a meta-analysis. *J Behav Ther Exp Psychiatry* 1997; **28**: 139–47

10   Marrs R. A meta-analysis of bibliotherapy studies. *Am J Community Psychol* 1995; **23**: 843-70
11   Andrews G. Talk that works: the rise of cognitive behaviour therapy. *BMJ* 1996; **313**: 1501–2
12   Gould RA, Clum AA. Meta-analysis of self-help treatment approaches. *Clin Psychol Rev* 1993; **13**: 169–86
13   Scogin F, Bynum J, Stephens G, Calhoon S. Efficacy of self-administered programs: meta-analytic review. *Prof Psychol Res Pract* 1990; **21**: 42–7
14   Marks I, Shaw S, Parkin R. Computer-aided treatments of mental health problems. *Clin Psychol Sci Pract* 1998; **5**: 151–70
15   Scogin F, Jamison C, Gochneaur K. Comparative efficacy of cognitive and behavioral bibliotherapy for mildly and moderately depressed older adults. *J Consult Clin Psychol* 1989; **57**: 403–7
16   Donnan P, Hutchinson A, Paxton R, Grant B, Firth M. Self-help materials for anxiety: a randomized control trial in general practice. *Br J Gen Pract* 1990; **40**: 498–501
17   Holdsworth N, Paxton R, Seidel S, Thomson D, Shrubb S. Parallel evaluations of new guidance materials for anxiety and depression in primary care. *J Mental Health* 1996; **5**:195–207.
18   Whitfield G, Williams CJ, Shapiro D. An evaluation of a self-help room in a general adult psychiatry service. *Behav Cog Psychother* 2001; **29**: 333–343
19   Selmi PM, Klein MH, Greist JH, Sorrell SP, Erdman HP. Computer-administered cognitive-behavioural therapy for depression. *Am J Psychiatry* 1990; **147**: 51–6
20   Bowers W, Scott S, MacFarlane R, Gorman L. Use of computer-administered cognitive-behavior therapy with depressed inpatients. *Depress* 1993; **1**: 294–9
21   Osgood-Hynes DJ, Greist JH, Marks IM *et al*. Self-administered psychotherapy for depression using a telephone-accessed computer system plus booklets: An open US-UK study. *J Clin Psychiatry* 1998; **59**: 358–65
22   Marks IM, Baer L, Greist J *et al*. Home self-assessment of obsessive-compulsive disorder: use of a manual and a computer-conducted telephone interview: two US-UK studies. *Br J Psychiatry* 1998; **172**: 406–12
23   Newman MG, Kenardy J, Herman S, Barr Taylor C. The use of hand-held computers as an adjunct to Cognitive-Behavior Therapy. *Comput Hum Behav* 1995; **12**: 135–43
24   Ghosh A, Greist JH. Computer treatment in psychiatry. *Psychiatr Ann* 1988; **18**: 246–50
25   Stuart S, LaRue S. Computerized cognitive therapy: The interface between man and machine. *J Cog Psychother* 1996; **10**: 181–91
26   Beutler LE, Engle D, Mohr D *et al*. Predictors of differential response to cognitive, experiential, and self-directed psychotherapeutic procedures. *J Consult Clin Psychol* 1991; **59**: 333–40
27   Mahalik JR, Kivlighan DM. Self help treatment for depression: who succeeds? *J Counsell Psychol* 1988; **35**: 237–42
28   Tyrer P, Seivewright N, Ferguson B, Murphy S, Johnson AL. The Nottingham study of neurotic disorder: effect of personality status on response to drug treatment, cognitive therapy and self-help over two years. *Br J Psychiatry* 1993; **162**: 219–26
29   Haaga DAF. Introduction to the special section on stepped care models in psychotherapy. *J Consult Clin Psychol* 2000; **68**: 547–8
30   Greenberger D, Padesky CA. *Mind over Mood: Change how you feel by changing the way you think*. New York: Guilford, 1995
31   Williams CJ. *Overcoming Depression: a Five Areas Approach*. London: Arnold, 2001
32   Beck AT, Weissman A. Lester D, Trexler L. The measurement of pessimism: The Hopelessness Scale. *J Consult Clin Psychol* 1974; **42**: 861–5
33   Goldberg DP, Hillier VF. A scaled version of the GHQ. *Psychol Med* 1974; **9**: 139–45
34   Weissman AN. The dysfunctional attitude scale: a validation study. Dissertation, University of Pennsylvania. *Dissertation Abstr Int* 1979; **40**: 1389B–90B
35   Williams CJ. Ready access to proven psychosocial interventions? The use of written CBT self-help materials to treat depression. *Adv Psychiatr Treat* 2001; **7**: 233–40
36   Duman M, Farrell C. *The PoPPi Guide – Practicalities of Producing Patient Information*. London: Kings Fund, 2000
37   www.calipso.co.uk
38   *Overcoming Depression* Training CD-ROM. Available from Stephen Taylor-Parker, Leeds Innovations, 175 Woodhouse Lane, Leeds LS2 3AR, UK. Tel: +44 (0)113 233 3444. E-mail: s.taylor-parker@ulis.co.uk

Continuation and maintenance therapy in depression

E S Paykel

Department of Psychiatry, University of Cambridge, Cambridge, UK

This paper reviews longer term treatment for unipolar depression. Anti-depressant continuation for prevention of early relapse has been routine for many years. Recent evidence supports a longer period of 9 months to 1 year after remission. Antidepressants are also effective in maintenance treatment for recurrent depression, and are indicated where there is clear risk of further episodes. Antidepressant withdrawal after continuation and maintenance should always be gradual, over a minimum of 3 months and longer after longer maintenance periods, to avoid withdrawal symptoms or rebound relapse. Trials of interpersonal therapy in the prevention of recurrence show some benefit, but effects are weaker than those of drug and additional benefit in combination is limited. There is better evidence for effects of cognitive therapy in preventing relapse and an emerging indication for its addition to antidepressants, particularly where residual symptoms are present.

Longer term outcome in depression

This paper will review the use of medication, principally anti-depressants, and of psychological treatments in the longer term treatment of unipolar depression.

Most modern treatments for depression are comparatively recent in development. Tricyclic and MAO inhibitor antidepressants were introduced at the end of the 1950s, other medications, and modern specific psychological and psychotherapeutic treatments tailored to depression, later. Prior to the modern antidepressant era many follow-up studies of depression were published. Robins and Guze[1], in reviewing these, found a wide range of outcomes in different studies. There was some consistency in the proportion of deaths due to suicide, which spanned a narrow range of 13–17%. Scott[2] obtained a reasonably consistent proportion of 15% for chronic depression in earlier studies.

The advent of antidepressants produced optimism regarding the treatment of depression, but in fact relatively few long-term follow-up studies of depression were published in the 1960s and 1970s. There was also a tendency to label depression with poor outcome as 'characterological depression' or

Correspondence to:
Prof. E S Paykel,
Department of Psychiatry,
University of Cambridge,
Douglas House,
18E Trumpington Road,
Cambridge CB2 2QQ, UK

'depressive personality', implying a disturbance of personality rather than an illness. More recent studies have made it clear that, although the immediate outcome of depression following treatment is good in terms of improvement, there are continuing problems in the longer term.

When the first antidepressants were introduced, it was assumed that only short-term treatment of about 3 months was usually required. By the mid 1960s, it was becoming apparent that this was often too short and by the early 1970s antidepressants were usually continued longer. Problems in spite of this pattern of treatment became evident with follow-up studies reported by Keller and colleagues from the US[3-6]. Although most patients reached remission moderately rapidly, 30% of those who had remitted relapsed within a year. Later extension of the study[7] showed that over 15 years 85% of recovered subjects experienced a recurrence, although only 58% of those who remained well for at least 5 years did so. Two 16 year British and Australian follow-up studies of patients admitted to university hospitals during the late 1960s[8,9] showed that approximately 60% of patients had been re-admitted at least once, reducing to 50% in those for whom the index episode was the first admission. Only 20% had recovered fully with no further episodes, while just under 20% were incapacitated throughout or died of suicide. The remainder had courses characterised by recovery and recurrences.

More recent studies have found similar outcomes[10,11]. A further problem which has become increasingly clear is occurrence of residual symptoms after partial remission[12], which occurs in up to one-third of depressed patients, and is associated with very high risk of relapse.

Data are still lacking on depression treated in primary care, the common setting for treatment of depression in most countries, and on patients presenting with index episodes requiring psychiatric out-patient rather than in-patient treatment. These groups, more mildly ill than hospitalised subjects, might have better outcome.

The renewed attention to longer term outcome has led to a more precise terminology[13]. The term remission is now used to describe the earlier part of the time when symptoms have subsided. It may be complete or incomplete with residual symptoms and it may be followed by subsequent problems. The term recovery is used by contrast to describe a state of freedom from symptoms which is both complete and persistent. The word relapse has been reserved for an early return of symptoms which can be regarded as return of the original episode, and the term recurrence for a later occurrence of symptoms which can be regarded as a new episode. There is no precise separation between these two, but there is evidence that rates of symptom return are highest in the first 6–12 months after remission and then diminish[11].

In parallel, a new terminology has developed in relation to drug treatment. The term continuation therapy has been applied to the continuation of antidepressants following acute treatment which ought to be routine for some months, with the purpose of preventing relapse. The term maintenance treatment is applied to longer treatment aimed at preventing recurrence in those at high risk.

Continuation therapy with antidepressants

Since the 1970s, good evidence has accumulated regarding the efficacy of longer term antidepressant treatment[14,15]. The earliest studies were of tricyclic antidepressants and MAO inhibitors, but there are now increasing studies of SSRIs and newer drugs. It would appear that all drugs which have substantial acute antidepressant effects have some effects in prevention of relapse and recurrence.

Table 1 shows results of randomised controlled trials (RCTs) of continuation in relapse prevention. These have usually been withdrawal studies comparing effects of treatment for 6–9 months in responders to acute treatment, with withdrawal to placebo after 2–3 months.

All the studies showed considerable benefit from continuation, with relapse rates at least halved. The absolute rates vary among studies because of sample characteristics. Relapse rates were particularly high

Table 1 Controlled trials of antidepressant continuation in prevention of relapse

	Relapse rate	
	Placebo %	Active drug %
Tricyclics		
Mindham et al 1973[22]	50	22
Klerman et al 1974[61], Paykel et al 1975[63]	29	12
Coppen et al 1978[77]	31	0
Stein et al 1980[78]	69	28
Prien et al 1973[40]	73	32
Prien & Kupfer 1986[23]	38	5
MAO inhibitors		
Davidson & Raft 1984[79]	100	14
Harrison et al 1986[80]	100	20
SSRIs		
Montgomery et al 1993[81]	31	11
Robert & Montgomery 1995[82]	24	13
Reimherr et al 1998[19]		
12 weeks	49	26
26 weeks	23	9
50 weeks	16	11
Nefazodone		
Feiger et al 1999[83]	33	17

after discontinuation of MAO inhibitors, although it is unclear whether this indicates a particular effect of the drugs, or something about the kinds of patients likely to respond to them. Two further studies, not shown in the table, examined effects of administering antidepressants or placebo after ECT[16,17]. Both found relapse rates lowered on antidepressants. A controlled trial of antidepressant augmentation by lithium found significantly higher relapse rates after early lithium withdrawal than continuation[18].

A recent study[19] employed a staged randomised design, with withdrawal to placebo after 3 months, 6 months or one year. Relapse rates in the next 3 months on fluoxetine or after withdrawal to placebo were 26% *versus* 49%, 9% *versus* 23%, and 11% *versus* 16%, respectively.

It is recommended that where response to acute antidepressant treatment has occurred, there should routinely be a following continuation period. Recommendations for its length have been for approximately 6 months after response[20] or for 4 months after complete remission with no residual symptoms[21]. In view of the Reimherr study, a longer period of 9–12 months after complete remission would now appear more prudent. Withdrawal should always be slow over at least 3 months. Relapse is particularly likely to follow drug withdrawal in patients with residual symptoms[22,23].

In some patients, withdrawal will be followed by return of depressive symptoms. Where withdrawal has been slow, this may occur while the patient is still on a low dose. Clinical experience indicates that this phenomenon usually reflects impending relapse, and if the symptoms persist, full dose should be resumed followed by continuation for a further 9–12 months. Some of these patients relapse again on later drug withdrawal and a period of maintenance treatment then becomes appropriate.

ECT continuation after acute treatment has not been tested in controlled trials but one is now under way in the US. Occasionally patients are encountered clinically who respond to ECT but relapse repeatedly when it is stopped, in spite of vigorous treatment with antidepressants and lithium. There may be a limited place for continuing it with a reduced frequency of 1–4 per month for up to 6 months. In the author's view, longer continuation or maintenance is best avoided, in view of effects on memory and anaesthetic risks in out-patients.

Maintenance therapy

There have also been many controlled trials of antidepressants *versus* placebo in longer term maintenance of 2 years or more in prevention of recurrences. These are summarised in Table 2. The most common design is

Table 2 Controlled trials of antidepressant maintenance in prevention of recurrence in unipolar depression

	Recurrence rate	
	Placebo %	Active drug %
Tricyclics		
Prien et al 1973[40,a]	85	29
Kane et al 1982[43]	83	100[b]
Prien et al 1984[41,a]	71	41
Glen et al 1984[44,a]	89	51
Rouillon et al 1989[84,a]	35	16
Georgotas et al 1989[85]	63	54[b]
Frank et al 1990[26]	78	22
Old Age Depression Interest Group 1993[86,a]	61	40
Kocsis et al 1996[87,c]	52	15
Reynolds et al 1999[64]	87	32
MAO inhibitors		
Georgotas & McCue 1989[85]	63	13
Robinson et al 1991[88]	81	20
Stewart et al 1997[89]	87	23
SSRIs		
Bjork 1983[90]	84	32
Montgomery et al 1988[91]	57	26
Doogan & Caillard 1992[92,a]	46	13
Montgomery & Dunbar 1993[93,a]	43	6
Franchini et al 1998[94,d]	52	24
Terra & Montgomery 1998[95]	35	12
Milnacipran		
Rouillon et al 2000[96,a]	24	16

[a]Mixed continuation/maintenance design.
[b]No benefit.
[c]Dysthymia.
[d]Partial reduction from 40 mg to 20 mg daily.

again a withdrawal one, after acute treatment of recurrent depression, and response. The more recent studies have also required a symptom-free continuation period before randomised assignment to the maintenance phase has commenced. A few studies have started maintenance treatment *de novo*, following acute treatment with a variety of antidepressants or ECT.

Maintenance studies also show benefit from long-term antidepressants although differences between drug and placebo treated groups are not as marked as for continuation therapy, and a few studies have been negative.

The US Agency for Health Care Policy and Research clinical guidelines for unipolar depression[24] recommended maintenance treatment very strongly if there had been three or more episodes of major depression prior to the inception episode and recommended it strongly if there had been two episodes of major depression in the past, or one or more in addition to the index episode in the last 2 years, together with recurrence within 1 year of previous medication discontinuation, family history of bipolar disorder, onset before 20 years of age, or a severe, sudden or life threatening episode in the past 3 years. The last three indications are not well established.

Treatment length required for maintenance is not yet fully determined. Kupfer et al[25], in an extension of the study of Frank et al[26] found that even after 3 years' maintenance in recurrent depressives who remained well on imipramine, there was a high rate of recurrence (67%) in the next 2 years on imipramine withdrawal, compared with 5 years' maintenance (9%). Regarding dose, a comparison of full dose and half dose maintenance found a substantially higher recurrence rate on the latter[27].

Clinically, it is reasonable to employ a combination of indications for maintenance, and for its length. Three years maintenance is appropriate almost as a routine for recurrent patients, particularly where an episode prior to the present one has occurred in the last 5 years or where remission has been difficult to achieve. Maintenance for 5 years or more is appropriate for those at greater risk, and indefinite or life-long maintenance where two or three attempts to withdraw medication have been followed by another episode within a year.

Generally, as in continuation therapy, the antidepressant used will be that to which the patient has already responded in acute treatment. If side effects are a problem, including the weight gain that can develop on tricyclics[28], change to an antidepressant with fewer side effects is indicated. Unnecessary change should be avoided since the patient may be unresponsive to the new drug. Doses may be lowered slightly from acute treatment, but only to a limited degree.

Reliable predictors of relapse and recurrence would be of value in focusing treatment. Relapse has been found related to occurrence of stressful life events and absence of social support in the follow-up period[29], to expressed emotion, particularly hostility, in key relatives[30,31], to older age of onset and more previous episodes[11,32]. The social factors appear more important in milder depression and earlier episodes and relatively unimportant in severe recurrent disorder[33-35]. Residual symptoms consistently predict higher relapse rates[12]. In longer follow-up studies, higher recurrence rates have been found where there have been more previous episodes, and less consistently with endogenous or psychotic depression[36].

There are not yet biological markers of incomplete recovery and risk of relapse which are useful in practice. Persistent dexamethasone non-suppression after antidepressant treatment predicts a greater risk of early relapse[37], but no more than 50% of depressives overall show non-suppression even when depressed.

Lithium in maintenance treatment of unipolar depression

The place of lithium in bipolar disorder is discussed elsewhere in this issue. There is also evidence from controlled trials that lithium is effective in the long-term prevention of unipolar recurrent depression[38-44]. Coppen et al[45] also found it superior to placebo after ECT in a one year study which was intermediate between continuation and maintenance. In direct comparisons, lithium has sometimes been found superior to antidepressant[43,46-48], sometimes equal[40,44], sometimes inferior[41,49]. Two studies have also found lithium-tricyclic combinations superior to either drug alone[41,43], although a third study failed to do so[50].

This might seem to render choice of maintenance treatment in unipolar depression equivocal. In practice, many more unipolar patients are managed long-term on antidepressants alone than on lithium alone, reflecting continuing use of the regimen successful in acute treatment. Also the trials of lithium in long-term treatment of unipolars have predominantly been in severe and recurrent disorder, and some of them have been in subjects who have already had long periods on lithium and may be prone to recurrence on its withdrawal.

There is little long-term evidence regarding anticonvulsant mood stabilisers in unipolars. Use of lithium and other mood stabilisers in bipolar disorder is outside the scope of this paper.

There have only been a small number of controlled trials of anti-depressants in long treatment of bipolars. They suggest that tricyclics are not of benefit alone, and may precipitate mania[40,41,43]. There is some evidence for the value of antidepressant-lithium combinations[43,51], but also evidence of risk of mania[52]. In practice, most clinicians do have some patients who remain well on antidepressant alone. Tricyclics appear more likely to precipitate rapid cycling and are preferably avoided. Evidence is not clear for SSRIs. Clinically, I have found MAO inhibitors easier than re-uptake inhibitors for stabilisation of bipolars.

Mode of withdrawal

Findings of controlled trials show good benefit from continuation and maintenance treatment, but findings of naturalistic follow-up studies show high rates of relapse and recurrence. There are several possible explanations for this discrepancy[53].

First, some key published follow-up studies have been based on samples treated in special university centres, which tend to have referred to them the more severe, resistant and recurrent patients with poorer outcome.

Secondly, modern maintenance studies require subjects to be recurrent on inclusion, to respond well to the study antidepressant, and to remain well during continuation treatment, before being included in the randomised maintenance phase. Such samples, with poor spontaneous long-term outcome without maintenance, and good response to the particular study antidepressant, may get much greater long-term benefit from it than the average patient.

Thirdly, treatment delivered in practice may fail to conform to recommendations. This is known to occur in acute depression. A British study of hospitalised depressives did not find major deficiencies in long-term medication treatment or compliance in the 18 months after discharge, and recurrences did not appear to be related primarily to deficient treatment[53]. However American studies have suggested some deficiencies and that these may be associated with worse outcome[54-56].

An important possibility concerns mode of withdrawal. In long-term trials withdrawal has often been rapid, over 2–4 weeks. Rapid drug withdrawal might increase relapse and recurrence rates. There is accumulating evidence pointing to the need for slow withdrawal of psychotropic drugs. A naturalistic study of lithium in bipolars found high and rapid rates of recurrence of mania after stopping[57]. A further report found lower recurrence rates when withdrawal was slow rather than abrupt[58].

Three phenomena need to be distinguished: relapse (return of the original symptoms), rebound (return of original symptoms but with greater intensity or more likelihood), withdrawal (development of different symptoms related to drug stoppage). There is clear evidence of withdrawal symptoms on abrupt stoppage, particularly from high dose or longer treatment, both after tricyclics[59], and SSRIs[60]. Symptoms are particularly gastrointestinal and influenza-like. This is a true withdrawal phenomenon, easily avoided by slower withdrawal over a month or so. It now appears probable that there is also rebound relapse if withdrawal is too rapid, even if slow enough to avoid withdrawal symptoms.

In clinical practice, antidepressants should always be withdrawn slowly after continuation or maintenance therapy, over a minimum of 3 months in gradual steps. If treatment has been over several years, dose reduction and stopping should take longer.

Interpersonal therapy

Although psychotherapy has been widely used in depression for many years, most approaches have been little evaluated in controlled trials. However, the last 20 years has seen the advent of more specific therapies, tailored to specific disorders, often with detailed treatment manuals, and evaluation in controlled trials.

Among psychotherapies for depression, interpersonal therapy (IPT) has been the best studied and the only one to be evaluated in longer term designs. One controlled trial, carried out in the late 1960s and early 1970s, examined relapse prevention in a factorial design with continuation antidepressant[61–63]. Patients responding to amitriptyline were randomised to six groups: drug continuation for a further 8 months, withdrawal to placebo double blind after 2 months continuation, withdrawal openly to no medication; in each drug group either with or without what later became codified as IPT. As shown in Table 1, antidepressant continuation halved the relapse rate compared to early withdrawal; results were the same, whether this was double blind or open. IPT had no effect on relapse rates or symptoms, although it was superior to low contact in effects on measures of social adjustment and interpersonal relationships.

Two more recent studies have examined effects of IPT on recurrence, again in factorial designs. Frank et al[26] treated recurrent major depressives with both imipramine and IPT to remission and for 4 months continuation followed by randomisation to a maintenance design for 3 years. Recurrence rates on placebo alone were very high (around 90%), on imipramine around 20%, with no further benefit from combination with IPT; on IPT without imipramine, recurrence was reduced but only by a small amount. The preferred treatment from this study was antidepressant.

Reynolds et al[64] treated elderly patients with recurrent non-psychotic major depression acutely with nortriptyline plus weekly IPT. After a 16 week continuation phase, responders were randomised to maintenance treatment for the next 3 years. Recurrence rates were: placebo and medication clinic 90%, placebo plus IPT 64%, nortriptyline plus medication clinic 43%, nortriptyline and IPT 20%. Thus there were stronger effects for nortriptyline than for IPT, but an additive effect of combination with a further worthwhile benefit.

Unfortunately, the recurrence studies have not reported on social adjustment, where there might be improvement due to IPT not achieved by medication. At present, it is still difficult to make a strong argument that IPT offers sufficient advantage for relapse and recurrence prevention in clinical practice to outweigh its additional cost, compared with medication alone, but further studies are under way.

Cognitive behavioural therapy

The second well-evaluated psychological therapy specifically tailored to depression is cognitive-behavioural therapy (CBT). The first evidence suggesting relapse prevention emerged in follow-up studies from acute controlled trials of antidepressants against cognitive therapy in depression. Three studies showed significantly lower relapse rates after cognitive therapy[65-67], with non-significant trends in the same direction were found in three other studies[68-70]. However, naturalistic follow-up studies of acute trials cannot be definitive. Different kinds of patients with different prognoses for relapse may respond initially to cognitive therapy and to antidepressant acute treatment. Also, antidepressant continuation was not always undertaken or well controlled in the follow-up studies. In one study in which it was[67], a relapse rate of 52% after antidepressant withdrawal was reduced to 32% with one year's continuation, not significantly different from the 21% relapse after cognitive therapy, although still suggestive.

Fava and colleagues[71-73] undertook a small trial of 40 patients with residual depressive symptoms after acute antidepressants, who were randomised to a modified form of cognitive therapy or clinical management. Relapse and recurrence were significantly reduced at 4 years. In a second 40 patient trial in recurrent depression, there was significant prevention of recurrence[74]. In both these studies, the cognitive therapy was much modified from standard, and antidepressants were withdrawn, rendering patients highly at risk of symptom return and maximising the possible effects of the cognitive therapy. Usually these patients will be continued on antidepressants, and the relevant question is what cognitive therapy adds to the drug therapy.

More recently, a larger controlled trial of cognitive therapy has been carried out in 158 patients with residual symptoms after major depression[75,76]. Antidepressants were continued in moderately high dose throughout the 17 months of the treatment trial and controlled follow-up. Subjects were randomised to receive clinical management alone or clinical management with 5 months' cognitive therapy. Cognitive therapy significantly reduced relapse rates from 47% in the clinical management group to 29% in the cognitive therapy group[75]. There were also significant differences in the proportions reaching full remission, but only a relatively small proportion of subjects in either group remitted fully. Symptom ratings showed limited significant effects particularly on ratings of worthlessness and hopelessness, key targets for cognitive therapy[76]. Cognitive therapy also produced some significant benefit in social adjustment. Relapse prevention appeared to be the principal effect of cognitive therapy in this study.

This study showed major benefit by adding cognitive therapy to drug treatment which had produced only partial improvement, in a group of subjects highly at risk of relapse. CBT, like IPT, is costly, but prevention of further episodes in patients at higher risk of these is emerging as a specific indication for it, particularly in combination with medication. Further studies of psychological therapies used in this way are needed. Conventional cognitive therapy requires the presence of negative cognitions, at least at residual symptom level, to be feasible, but modifications for recovered previously depressed subjects are currently being evaluated, as are cognitive approaches in bipolar disorder.

Key points for clinical practice

- Antidepressant continuation following acute treatment and response should be routine. Doses should be the same or only a little lower than for acute treatment. Recent evidence suggests duration of 9–12 months after remission, rather than shorter periods. Where symptoms return during or after withdrawal, full dose continuation for a further similar period should be initiated

- For depressives with already recurrent histories, particularly with recent recurrences, longer term maintenance is indicated. Duration may vary from 3 years to life-time, but in general the more adverse the prognosis, the longer the maintenance treatment

- Adverse prognostic indicators for relapse and recurrence, strengthening treatment indications, include residual symptoms at remission, longer episode, more previous episodes, previous chronicity, more severe episodes, previous episode in the last year, relapse after medication withdrawal, onset early in life

- Withdrawal of antidepressants and lithium after longer term use should always be gradual, with dose reductions over at least 3 months. Probably the longer the duration of treatment the slower the reduction. Abrupt cessation of antidepressants after longer term use can lead to withdrawal syndromes; rapid although not abrupt withdrawal to rebound relapse and recurrence

- The indications for psychological therapies in relapse and recurrence are less well established, but cognitive therapy appears to have a specific indication when added to medication where there is high risk of relapse and recurrence, particularly in presence of residual symptoms

References

1 Robins E, Guze S. Classification of affective disorders – the primary-secondary, the endogenous-reactive and the neurotic-psychotic dichotomies. In: Williams TA, Katz MM, Shield JA. (eds) *Recent Advances in Psychobiology of the Depressive Illnesses*. Washington: US Printing Office, 1972; 283–93
2 Scott J. Chronic depression. *Br J Psychiatry* 1988; **153**: 287–97
3 Keller MB, Shapiro RW, Lavori PW, Wolfe N. Recovery in major depressive disorder: analysis with the life table and regression models. *Arch Gen Psychiatry* 1982; **39**: 905–10
4 Keller MB, Shapiro RW, Lavori PW, Wolfe N. Relapse in major depressive disorder: analysis with the life event table. *Arch Gen Psychiatry* 1982; **39**: 911–5
5 Keller MB, Klerman GL, Lavori PW, Coryell W, Endicott J, Taylor J. Long-term outcome of episodes of major depression: clinical and public health significance. *JAMA* 1984; **252**: 788–92

6   Coryell W, Endicott J, Keller M. Outcome of patients with chronic affective disorder: a five-year follow up. *Am J Psychiatry* 1990; **147**: 1627–33

7   Mueller TI, Leon AC, Keller MB *et al*. Recurrence after recovery from major depressive disorder during 15 years of observational follow-up. *Am J Psychiatry* 1999; **156**: 1000–6

8   Kiloh LG, Andrews GA, Neilson M. The long-term outcome of depressive illness. *Br J Psychiatry* 1988; **153**: 752–7

9   Lee AS, Murray RM. The long-term outcome of Maudsley depressives. *Br J Psychiatry* 1988; **153**: 741–51

10   Surtees PG, Barkley C. Future imperfect: the long-term outcome of depression. *Br J Psychiatry* 1994; **164**: 327–41

11   Ramana R, Paykel ES, Cooper Z, Hayhurst H, Saxty M, Surtees PG. Remission and relapse in major depression: a two-year prospective follow up study. *Psychol Med* 1995; **25**: 1161–70

12   Paykel ES, Ramana R, Cooper Z, Hayhurst H, Kerr J, Barocka A. Residual symptoms after partial remission: an important outcome in depression. *Psychol Med* 1995; **25**: 1171–80

13   Frank E, Prien F, Jarrett RB *et al*. Conceptualisation and rationale for consensus definitions of terms in major depressive disorder. Remission, recovery, relapse and recurrence *Arch Gen Psychiatry* 1991; **48**: 851–5

14   Paykel ES. The place of antidepressants in long-term treatment. In: Montgomery SA, Corn TH. (eds) *Psychopharmacology of Depression*. British Association for Psychopharmacology monograph 1994; **13**: 218–39

15   Paykel ES. Tertiary prevention: longer-term drug treatment in depression. In: Kendrick T, Tylee A, Freeling P. (eds) *The Prevention of Mental Illness in Primary Care*. Cambridge: Cambridge University Press, 1996; 281–93

16   Seager CP, Bird RL. Imipramine with electrical treatment in depression. *J Ment Sci* 1962; **108**: 704–7

17   Imlah NW, Ryan E, Harrington HA. The influence of antidepressant drugs on the response to ECT and on subsequent relapse rates. *Neuropsychopharmacology* 1965; **4**: 438–42

18   Bschor T, Kunz D, Bauer M *et al*. Successful lithium augmentation: how long should lithium be continued? *Paper presented at XI World Congress of Psychiatry, Hamburg, Germany, 6–11 August 1999*

19   Reimherr FW, Amsterdam JD, Quitkin FM *et al*. Optimal length of continuation therapy in depression: a prospective assessment during long-term fluoxetine treatment. *Am J Psychiatry* 1998; **155**: 1247–53

20   Paykel ES, Priest RG. Recognition and management of depression in general practice: consensus statement. *BMJ* 1992; **305**: 1198–202

21   Prien RF. Maintenance treatment. In: Paykel ES. (ed) *Handbook of Affective Disorders*, 2nd edn. Edinburgh: Churchill Livingstone, 1992; 419–35

22   Mindham RH, Howland C, Shepherd M. An evaluation of continuation therapy with tricyclic antidepressants in depressive illness. *Psychol Med* 1973; **3**: 5–17

23   Prien RF, Kupfer DJ. Continuous drug therapy for major depressive episodes: how long should it be maintained? *Am J Psychiatry* 1986; **143**: 18–23

24   Depression Guideline Panel. *Clinical Practice Guideline No 5: Depression in Primary Care, vol 2 – Treatment of Major Depression*. US Department of Health and Human Services, Rockville MD: AHCPR Publications, 1993; 71–123

25   Kupfer DJ, Frank E, Perel JM *et al*. Five year outcome for maintenance therapies in recurrent depression. *Arch Gen Psychiatry* 1992; **49**: 769–73

26   Frank E, Kupfer DJ, Perel JM *et al*. Three year outcomes for maintenance therapies of recurrent depression. *Arch Gen Psychiatry* 1990; **47**: 1093–9

27   Frank E, Kupfer DJ, Perel JM *et al*. Comparison of full-dose versus half-dose pharmacotherapy in the maintenance treatment of recurrent depression. *J Affect Disord* 1993; **27**: 139–45

28   Paykel ES, Mueller PS, de la Vergne PM. Amitriptyline, weight gain and carbohydrate craving: a side effect. *Br J Psychiatry* 1973; **123**: 501–7

29   Paykel ES, Cooper Z. Life events and social stress. In: Paykel ES. (ed) *Handbook of Affective Disorders*, 2nd edn. Edinburgh: Churchill Livingstone, 1992; 149–70

30   Vaughn CE, Leff JP. The measurement of expressed emotion in the families of psychiatric patients. *Br J Soc Clin Psychol* 1976; **15**: 157–65

31 Hooley JM, Orley J, Teasdale JD. Levels of expressed emotion and relapse in depressed patients. *Br J Psychiatry* 1986; **148**: 642–7

32 Keller M, Lavori BP, Lewis CE, Klerman GL. Predictors of relapse in major depression. *JAMA* 1983; **250**: 3299–304

33 Andrew B, Hawton K, Fagg J, Westbrook D. Do psychosocial factors influence outcome in severely depressed female psychiatric outpatients? *Br J Psychiatry* 1993; **163**: 747–54

34 Paykel ES, Cooper Z, Ramana R, Hayhurst H. Life events, social support and marital relationships in the outcome of severe depression. *Psychol Med* 1996; **26**: 121–33

35 Hayhurst H, Cooper Z, Paykel ES, Vearnals S, Ramana R. Expressed emotion and depression: a longitudinal study. *Br J Psychiatry* 1997; **171**: 439–43

36 Coryell W, Winokur G. Course and outcome. In: Paykel ES. (ed) *Handbook of Affective Disorders*, 2nd edn. Edinburgh: Churchill Livingstone, 1992; 89–108

37 Nemeroff CB, Evans DL. Correlation between the dexamethasone suppression test in depressed patients and clinical response. *Am J Psychiatry* 1988; **141**: 247–9

38 Baastrup PC, Poulsen JC, Schou M, Thomsen K, Amdisen A. Prophylactic lithium: double blind discontinuation in manic-depressive and recurrent-depressive disorders. *Lancet* 1970; **ii**: 326–30

39 Coppen A, Noguera R, Baily J *et al*. Prophylactic lithium in affective disorders. *Lancet* 1971; **ii**: 275–9

40 Prien RF, Klett CH, Caffey EM. Lithium carbonate and imipramine in prevention of affective episodes. *Arch Gen Psychiatry* 1973; **29**: 420–5

41 Prien RF, Kupfer DJ, Mansky PA *et al* Drug therapy in the prevention of recurrences in unipolar and bipolar affective disorders. *Arch Gen Psychiatry* 1984; **41**: 1096–104

42 Fieve RR, Kumbaraci T, Dunner DL. Lithium prophylaxis of depression in bipolar I, bipolar II and unipolar patients. *Am J Psychiatry* 1976; **133**: 925–9

43 Kane JM, Quitkin FM, Rifkin A, Ramos-Lorenzi JR, Nayak DP, Howard A. Lithium carbonate and imipramine in the prophylaxis of unipolar and bipolar II illness. *Arch Gen Psychiatry* 1982; **39**: 1065–9

44 Glen AIM, Johnson AL, Shepherd M. Continuation therapy with lithium and amitriptyline in unipolar depressive illness: a randomised double-blind controlled trial. *Psychol Med* 1984; **14**: 37–50

45 Coppen A, Abou-Saleh MT, Milln P *et al*. Lithium continuation therapy following electroconvulsive therapy. *Br J Psychiatry* 1981; **139**: 284–7

46 Coppen A, Montgomery S, Gupta RK, Bailey JE. A double-blind comparison of lithium carbonate and maprotiline in the prophylaxis of the affective disorders. *Br J Psychiatry* 1976; **118**: 479–85

47 Coppen A, Ghose K, Rao V, Bailey J, Peet M. Mianserin and lithium in the prophylaxis of depression. *Br J Psychiatry* 1978; **133**: 206–10

48 Greil W, Ludwig-Mayerhofer W, Erazo N *et al*. Comparative efficacy of lithium and amitriptyline in the maintenance treatment of recurrent unipolar depression: a randomised study. *J Affect Disord* 1996; **40**: 179–90

49 Franchini L, Gasperini Smeraldi E. A 24 month study of unipolar subjects: a comparison between lilthium and fluvoxamine. *J Affect Disord* 1994; **32**: 225–31

50 Johnstone EC, Owens DGC, Lambert MT, Crow TJ, Frith CD, Done DJ. Combination tricyclic antidepressant and lithium maintenance medication in unipolar and bipolar depressed patients. *J Affect Disord* 1990; **20**: 225–33

51 Shapiro DR, Quitkin FM, Fleiss JL. Response to maintenance therapy in bipolar illness: effect of index episode. *Arch Gen Psychiatry* 1989; **46**: 401–5

52 Quitkin FM, Kane J, Rifkin A, Ramos-Lorenzi JR, Nayak DV. Prophylactic lithium carbonate with and without imipramine for bipolar 1 patients. *Arch Gen Psychiatry* 1981; **38**: 902–7

53 Ramana R, Paykel ES, Surtees PG, Melzer D, Mehta M. Medication received by patients with depression following the acute episode: adequacy and relation to outcome. *Br J Psychiatry* 1999; **174**: 128–34

54 Dawson R, Lavori PW, Coryell WH *et al*. Maintenance strategies for unipolar depression – an observational study of levels of treatment and recurrences. *J Affect Disord* 1998; **49**: 31–44

55 Fennig S, Craig TJ, Tanenberg-Karant M *et al*. Medication treatment in first admission patients with psychotic affective disorders: preliminary findings on research facility diagnostic

agreement and rehospitalisation. *Ann Clin Psychiatry* 1995; **7**: 87–90

56 Glick ID, Burti L, Suzuki K *et al.* Effectiveness in psychiatric care. 1: a cross-national study of the process of treatment and outcomes of major depressive disorder. *J Nerv Ment Dis* 1991; **48**: 851–5

57 Suppes T, Baldessarini RJ, Faedda GL, Tohen M. Risk of recurrence following discontinuation of lithium treatment in bipolar disorder. *Arch Gen Psychiatry* 1991; **48**: 1082–8

58 Faedda GL, Tondon L, Baldessarini RJ, Suppes T, Tohen M. Outcome after rapid vs gradual discontinuation of lithium treatment in bipolar disorders. *Arch Gen Psychiatry* 1993; **50**: 448–55

59 Dilsaver SC, Greden JF. Antidepressant withdrawal phenomena. *Biol Psychiatry* 1984; **13**: 237–56

60 Schatzberg AF, Haddad P, Kaplan EM *et al.* Serotonin reuptake inhibitor discontinuation syndrome: a hypothetical definition. Discontinuation Consensus Panel. *J Clin Psychiatry* 1997; **58 (Suppl 7)**: 5–10

61 Klerman GL, DiMascio A, Weissman MM, Prusoff BA, Paykel ES. Treatment of depression by drugs and psychotherapy *Am J Psychiatry* 1974; **131**: 186–91

62 Weissman MM, Klerman GL, Paykel ES, Prusoff BA, Hanson B, Treatment effects on the social adjustment of depressed outpatients. *Arch Gen Psychiatry* 1974; **30**: 771–8

63 Paykel ES, DiMascio A, Haskell D, Prusoff BA. Effects of maintenance amitriptyline and psychotherapy on symptoms of depression. *Psychol Med* 1975; **5**: 67–77

64 Reynolds CF, Frank E, Perel JM *et al.* Nortriptyline and interpersonal psychotherapy as maintenance therapies for recurrent major depression: a randomised controlled trial in patients older than 59 years. *JAMA* 1999; **281**: 39–45

65 Simons AD, Murphy GE, Levine JL, Wetzel RD. Cognitive therapy and pharmacotherapy of depression: sustained improvement over one year. *Arch Gen Psychiatry* 1986; **43**: 43–50

66 Blackburn IM, Eunson KM, Bishop S. A two year naturalistic follow up of depressed patients treated with cognitive therapy, pharmacotherapy and a combination of both. *J Affect Disord* 1986; **10**: 67–75

67 Evans MD, Hollon SD, De Rubeis RJ *et al.* Differential relapse following cognitive therapy and pharmacotherapy for depression. *Arch Gen Psychiatry* 1992; **49**: 802–8

68 Kovacs M, Rush AJ, Beck AT, Hollon SD. Depressed outpatients treated with cognitive therapy or pharmacotherapy. *Arch Gen Psychiatry* 1981; **38**: 33–41

69 Miller IW, Norman WG, Keitner GI. Cognitive-behavioural treatment of depressed inpatients: six- and twelve-month follow-up. *Am J Psychiatry* 1989; **146**: 1274–9

70 Shea MT, Elkin I, Linber S *et al.* Course of depressive symptoms over follow-up. *Arch Gen Psychiatry* 1992; **49**: 782–7

71 Fava GA, Grandi S, Zielezny M, Canestrari R, Morphy MA. Cognitive behavioural treatment of residual symptoms in primary major depressive disorder. *Am J Psychiatry* 1994; **151**: 1295–9

72 Fava GA, Grandi S, Zielezny M, Rafanelli C, Canestrari R. Four-year outcome for cognitive behavioural treatment of residual symptoms in major depression. *Am J Psychiatry* 1996; **153**: 945–7

73 Fava GA, Rafanelli C, Grandi S, Canestrari R, Morphy MA. Six year outcome for cognitive behavioural treatment of residual symptoms in major depression. *Am J Psychiatry* 1998; **155**: 1443–5

74 Fava GA, Rafanelli C, Grandi S, Conti S, Belluardo P. Prevention of recurrent depression with cognitive behavioural therapy: preliminary findings. *Arch Gen Psychiatry* 1998; **55**: 816–20

75 Paykel ES, Scott J, Teasdale JD *et al.* Prevention of relapse by cognitive therapy in residual depression: a controlled trial. *Arch Gen Psychiatry* 1999; **56**: 829–35

76 Scott J, Teasdale JD, Paykel ES *et al.* Effects of cognitive therapy on psychosocial symptoms and social functioning in residual depression. *Br J Psychiatry* 2000; **177**: 440–6

77 Coppen A, Ghose K, Montgomery S, Rao VAR, Bailey J, Jorgensen A. Continuation therapy with amitriptyline in depression. *Br J Psychiatry* 1978; **133**: 28–33

78 Stein MK, Rickels K, Weisse CC. Maintenance therapy with amitriptyline: a controlled trial. *Am J Psychiatry* 1980 **137**: 370–1

79 Davidson J, Raft D. Use of phenelzine in continuation therapy. *Neuropsychobiology* 1984; **11**: 191–4

80 Harrison W, Rabkin J, Stewart JW, McGrath PJ, Tricamo E, Quitkin F. Phenelzine for chronic depression: a study of continuation treatment. *J Clin Psychiatry* 1986; **47**: 346–9

81 Montgomery SA, Rasmussen JGC, Tanghøj P. A 24-week study of 20 mg citalopram, 40 mg citalopram, and placebo in the prevention of relapse of major depression. *Int Clin Psychopharmacol* 1993; **8**: 181–8

82 Robert P, Montgomery SA. Citalopram in doses of 20–60 mg is effective in depression relapse prevention: a placebo-controlled 6 month study. *Int Clin Psychopharmacol* 1995; **10 (Suppl 1)**: 29–35

83 Feiger AD, Bielski RJ, Bremner J *et al*. Double-blind, placebo-substitution study of nefazodone in the prevention of relapse during continuation treatment of outpatients with major depression. *Int Clin Psychopharmacol* 1999; **14**: 19–28

84 Rouillon F, Phillips R, Serrurier D, Ansart E, Gérard MJ. Rechutes de dépression unipolaire et efficacité de la maprotilinne. *L'Encéphale* 1989; **15**: 527–34

85 Georgotas A, McCue RE, Cooper TB. A placebo-controlled comparison of nortriptyline and phenelzine in maintenance therapy of elderly depressed patients. *Arch Gen Psychiatry* 1989; **46**: 783–6

86 Old Age Depression Interest Group. How long should the elderly take antidepressants? A double blind placebo-controlled study of continuation/prophylaxis therapy with dothiepin. *Br J Psychiatry* 1993; **162**: 175–82

87 Kocsis JH, Friedman RA, Markowitz JC *et al*. Maintenance therapy for chronic depression: a controlled clinical trial of desipramine. *Arch Gen Psychiatry* 1996; **53**: 769–74

88 Robinson DS, Lerfald SC, Bennet B *et al*. Continuation and maintenance treatment of major depression with monoamine oxidase inhibitor phenelzine: a double-blind placeob-controlled discontinuation study. *Psychopharmacol Bull* 1991; **27**: 31–9

89 Stewart JW, Tricamo E, McGrath PJ, Quitkin FM. Prophylactic efficacy of phenelzine and imipramine in chronic atypical depression: likelihood of recurrence on discontinuation after 6 months' remission. *Am J Psychiatry* 1997; **154**: 31–6

90 Bjork K. The efficacy of zimeldine in preventing depressive episodes in recurrent major depressive disorders – a double blind placebo-controlled study. *Acta Psychiatr Scand* 1983; **68**: 182–9

91 Montgomery SA, Dufour H, Brion S *et al*. The prophylactic efficacy of fluoxetine in unipolar depression. *Br J Psychiatry* 1988; **153 (Suppl 3)**: 69–76

92 Doogan DP, Caillard V. Sertraline in the prevention of depression. *Br J Psychiatry* 1992; **160**: 217–22

93 Montgomery SA, Dunbar G. Paroxetine is better than placebo in relapse prevention and the prophylaxis of recurrent depression. *Int Clin Psychopharmacol* 1993; **8**: 189–95

94 Franchini L, Gasperini M, Perez J *et al*. Dose efficacy of paroxetine in preventing depressive recurrences: a randomised, double-blind study. *J Clin Psychiatry* 1998; **59**: 229–32

95 Terra JL, Montgomery SA. Fluvoxamine prevents recurrence of depression: results of a long-term, double-blind, placebo-controlled study. *Int Clin Psychopharmacol* 1998; **13**: 55–62

96 Rouillon F, Berdeaux G, Bisserbe JC *et al*. Prevention of recurrent depressive episodes with milnacipran: consequences on quality of life. *J Affect Disord* 2000; **58**: 171–80

Meta-analytical studies on new antidepressants

Ian M Anderson

Neuroscience and Psychiatry Unit, School of Psychiatry and Behavioural Sciences, University of Manchester, Manchester, UK

A systematic search found 108 meta-analyses of the use of antidepressants in depressive disorders. Defining newer antidepressants as those introduced since the early 1980s, 18 meta-analyses were selected as being informative about their relative efficacy and tolerability in comparative randomised controlled studies (RCTs).

Findings with higher confidence include: little difference in efficacy between most new and old antidepressants; superior efficacy of serotonin and noradrenaline re-uptake inhibitors (SNRIs) over selective serotonin re-uptake inhibitors (SSRIs); a slower onset of therapeutic action of fluoxetine over other SSRIs; a different side effect profile of SSRIs to TCAs with superior general tolerability of SSRIs over TCAs; poorer tolerability of fluvoxamine than other SSRIs in a within group comparison; no increased the risk of suicidal acts or ideation in fluoxetine compared with TCAs (or placebo) in low-risk patients.

Findings with a lower level of confidence include: greater efficacy of TCAs than SSRIs in in-patients; greater efficacy of amitriptyline than SSRIs; better tolerability of moclobemide than TCAs; no demonstrable difference in tolerability between SSRIs and TCAs in the elderly; no better tolerability of fluvoxamine than TCAs; better tolerability of dothiepin (dosulepin) than SSRIs; better tolerability of sertraline and greater frequency of agitation on fluoxetine than other SSRIs in a within group comparison.

In general, the meta-analyses were of uneven quality, as were the studies included, which limits the confidence in many of the results. Generalising from mostly short-term randomised controlled studies to clinical practice requires caution.

Methodological considerations

Correspondence to:
Dr Ian M Anderson,
Neuroscience and
Psychiatry Unit, Room
G809, Stopford Building,
University of Manchester,
Oxford Road,
Manchester M13 9PT, UK

Randomised controlled trials (RCTs) are the 'gold standard' for treatment trials[1] but may still be prone to bias[2] and are often too small to have adequate power to show a difference between treatments (type II statistical error). False positive results can also occur by chance (type I statistical error), particularly if subgroup or secondary analysis is used, a common feature of most antidepressant studies.

Meta-analysis aims to overcome some of these problems and provide an overview and quantification of treatment effects. To be meaningful,

Table 1 Summary measures and terms commonly used in meta-analysis

Measure	Definition
Effect size (ES)	Change score in a continuous rating scale measure ÷ standard deviation of final score in control condition
Relative effect size	Difference in change or final rating scale scores between experimental and control conditions ÷ pooled standard deviation of experimental and control final scores A relative effect size of 0 indicates no difference between conditions
Odds	Number with outcome ÷ number without outcome
Odds ratio (OR)	Ratio of odds in experimental condition to odds in control condition An odds ratio of 1 indicates no difference between conditions
Risk (event/response rate)	Number with outcome ÷ total number This is sometimes expressed as a percentage
Risk ratio (relative risk/ event/response rate) (RR)	Ratio of risk in experimental condition to risk in control condition A risk ratio of 1 indicates no difference between conditions
Risk difference (RD)	Difference between risk in experimental condition and risk in control condition This is often reported as a percentage
Number needed to treat (NNT) or harm (NNH)	1 ÷ absolute risk difference This is the number of patients who need to be given the experimental treatment for one more patient to experience the outcome than with the control treatment. It is rounded up to a whole number by convention
Heterogeneity	Significant difference between the results from individual studies being pooled suggesting that they are not measuring a common population effect
Sensitivity analysis	Pooling studies in different ways/combinations to assess the robustness of the overall result

it must to be applied with the correct methodology in the context of a systematic review (see Henry & Wilson[3] and Wilson & Henry[4] for non-technical reviews). Unfortunately, the quality of meta-analyses and their interpretation remains problematic with limited standardisation of methods and analysis[5]. A proposal for improving the quality of meta-analyses of RCTs has been published with a useful checklist for their assessment[6]. Meta-analyses published as part of the Cochrane Collaboration have rigorous methodology and standardised reporting methods[7].

Making sense of meta-analyses

Combining results requires summary measure from each study in a form that allows statistical pooling. Different summary measures are used in the literature; the commonest are defined in Table 1 and briefly discussed here. The analysis of continuous data (such as rating scale scores) can be carried out using raw scores, but more commonly uses standardised differences or effect sizes (ES). These provide more statistical information than dichotomised data, but can be difficult to interpret. Effect sizes of 0.2, 0.5 and 0.8 have been suggested to indicate small, moderate and large effects, respectively[8], and more recently it has been suggested that the number needed to treat (NNT) can be estimated from the ES and control event rate[9]. For dichotomous data, such as responder/non-responder or dropout/continuation, the different analyses give different information. The risk ratio (relative risk, RR) is arguably more easily understood than the odds ratio (OR)[10] and the reciprocal of the absolute risk difference (RD), known as the number needed to treat (NNT) has become a popular way of interpreting the clinical significance of a finding. The 95% confidence interval (95% CI) provides information about the likely range within which the actual value lies.

Combining (pooling) summary outcome measures in meta-analysis traditionally weights studies by the inverse of the variance in each study which tends to give greater weight to larger studies in which the estimate is more precise. The issue of statistical heterogeneity between individual studies is beyond the scope of this article but a 'random effects' model is often employed to take account of this (as opposed to a traditional 'fixed effects' model). Increasingly, an approach using Bayesian techniques is being employed as it does not require large sample assumptions and allows the effect of predictive variables to be examined (meta-regression).

Scope and methodology

This article is an overview of meta-analyses examining the use of newer antidepressants in the treatment of depression. 'Newer' antidepressants are taken to mean currently available antidepressants marketed since the early 1980s. The review is confined to meta-analyses of comparative studies of antidepressants as it is the relative advantages and dis-advantages of antidepressants that is of most interest. Studies simply comparing a drug against placebo and single arm meta-analyses of non-comparative studies are not included.

Meta-analysis were identified from a computerised search to March 2001 of MEDLINE, EMBASE, PSYCHInfo and the Cochrane Library using the terms 'meta-analysis' OR 'systematic review' combined with 'anti-depressant' OR 'anti-depressant' OR 'antidepressive' OR 'anti-depressive'. This was supplemented by hand searching the references for other reviews. A total of 108 meta-analyses were identified, but many were of older antidepressants only, considered the same comparisons, were of subgroups of studies or have been superseded. Only the most recent or informative are discussed (Table 2) with some others mentioned briefly for comparison purposes. A list of the other meta-analyses is available on request.

Meta-analyses of individual antidepressant/class comparisons

The potential number of comparisons is large although in practice most newer drugs have been compared with tricyclic antidepressants (TCAs) or

Table 2 Summary of meta-analyses considered in detail in this article

Study	Drug comparisons (no. of studies)	Methodology	Main findings in drug versus drug comparisons	Comments
Anderson 2000[11]	SSRIs *versus* TCAs and maprotiline (102)	Medline search to 1997, references/reviews/articles. RCTs of unipolar depressive disorders. Primary outcomes: efficacy relative effect size, relative risk of total, side effect and failure dropouts. Publication bias, heterogeneity and sensitivity analyses considered	Efficacy: SSRIs = TCAs overall; SSRIs < amitriptyline (publication bias possible); SSRIs < TCAs in in-patients. Tolerability: *total and side effect dropouts* SSRIs as a group > TCAs; fluvoxamine = TCAs. *Side effect dropouts* dothiepin > SSRIs	Data extraction only by author. Effect sizes calculated from change scores. Individual drugs and subgroup analyses; however, these may result in chance findings
Anderson 2001[12]	SNRIs *versus* SSRIs (22) Mirtazapine *versus* SSRIs (3)	Medline and Embase searches to 2000, references/reviews/articles, contacting drug companies. RCTs depressive disorders. Primary outcome: response relative risk. Publication bias, heterogeneity and sensitivity analysis considered	Efficacy: SNRIs > SSRIs, mirtazapine = SSRIs	Small number of studies available for milnacipran and mirtazapine. No tolerability data
Barbui & Hotopf 2001[13]	Amitriptyline *versus* other AD (186) Amitriptyline *versus* SSRIs (40) Amitriptyline *versus* TCAs + heterocyclic AD	Comprehensive database search to 1998, references/reviews/articles, contacting drug companies. RCTs of depression. Primary outcomes: efficacy relative effect size, odds ratio and risk difference for response (modified ITT), total dropouts and emergent side-effects. Publication bias, heterogeneity and sensitivity analyses considered	Efficacy: amitriptyline > other AD; amitriptyline > TCAs + heterocyclics and SSRIs considered separately. Tolerability: *total dropouts* amitriptyline = other AD, TCAs + heterocyclics, SSRIs. *Side effects* amitriptyline < other AD, TCAs + heterocyclics, SSRIs	Effect sizes calculated from final scores
Barbui et al. 2001[14]	SSRIs *versus* OA and lofepramine grouped into amitriptyline + imipramine, other TCAs and heterocyclics (136)	Comprehensive database search to 1999, references/reviews/articles, contacting drug companies. RCTs of depressive disorders. Primary outcomes: odds ratios for total, side-effect and failure dropouts. Heterogeneity and sensitivity analyses considered	Tolerability: *total and side effect dropouts* SSRIs > comparators; SSRIs > amitriptyline + imipramine and other TCAs considered separately; SSRIs = heterocyclics. *Side effects dropouts* SSRIs < dothiepin; *failure dropouts* SSRIs = comparators; SSRIs < amitriptyline + imipramine	Cochrane review. NNTs not calculated. Group and individual drug analyses. Publication bias not considered
Beasley et al. 1991[15]	Fluoxetine *versus* placebo (7) Fluoxetine *versus* TCAs (12)	Drug company database to 1989. RCTs of depression. Primary outcomes: risk difference of suicidal acts, worsening, emergence and improvement of ideation. Heterogeneity considered	Fluoxetine = TCAs	Patients at high risk of suicide excluded from trials
Davis et al. 1993[16]	General comparison of AD *versus* placebo (112) and AD *versus* imipramine and amitriptyline (127)	Unspecified systematic review. RCTs of affective disease. Primary outcome: response difference	Efficacy: individual AD = amitriptyline and imipramine	No confidence intervals or significance values for drug comparisons. Methodology obscure. No tolerability data reported

*(**Table 2** continued on next page. See p. 167 for abbreviations etc.)*

Table 2 (*continued*) Summary of meta-analyses considered in detail in this article

Study	Drug comparisons (no. of studies)	Methodology	Main findings in drug versus drug comparisons	Comments
Edwards & Anderson 1999[17]	SSRIs versus SSRIs (20)	Medline search to 1997, references/reviews/articles, contacting drug companies RCTs of major depression Primary outcomes: Efficacy effect size, relative risk of total, side effect, failure dropouts and emergent side-effects Heterogeneity and sensitivity analysis considered	Efficacy: individual SSRIs = other SSRIs. Fluoxetine slower onset of action than other SSRIs Tolerability: *total and side effect dropouts* fluvoxamine < other SSRIs. *Side effect dropouts* sertraline > other SSRIs. *Emergent side-effects* individual SSRIs = other SSRIs except agitation fluoxetine < other SSRIs	Effect sizes calculated from change scores. Only a few studies provided data to compare individual emergent side-effects
Freemantle et al 2000[18]	SSRIs versus other ADs (105)	Medline and Embase searches to 1997, references/reviews/articles RCTs of depression Primary outcome: predictive value of pharmacological and structural factors on efficacy effect size	No predictive value of dual action (serotonin + noradrenaline re-uptake inhibition), triple action (dual action + serotonin2 antagonism), study setting, patient age, comparator dose, funding	Effect sizes calculated from final scores. Important limitations in the determination of pharmacology of individual drugs
Geddes et al 2001[19]	SSRIs, venlafaxine and nefazodone versus other ADs (mostly TCAs) (98)	Comprehensive database search to 1999, references/reviews/articles, contacting drug companies RCTs of depressive disorders Primary outcome: efficacy relative effect size Heterogeneity and sensitivity analyses considered	Efficacy: SSRIs and associated AD = other antidepressants. No subgroup differences	Cochrane review. Effect sizes calculated from final scores. Includes mixed group of drugs. Individual drugs and some subgroup analyses. Unclear if publication bias considered
Kerihuel & Dreyfus 1991[20]	Lofepramine versus TCA1 and maprotiline (29)	Medline search, drug company data RCTs of depressive illness Primary outcomes: response odds ratio (ITT), side-effect odds ratio, total dropout percentages	Efficacy: lofepramine > TCA1 (but = amitriptyline and imipramine individually) Tolerability: *total dropouts* lofepramine = TCA1. *Side effects* lofepramine > TCA1 (and > amitriptyline and imipramine individually)	Original data re-analysed. Most studies before 1980, many unpublished and quality uneven. Diagnosis and outcomes ratings not standardised. Side-effects and dropouts not reported. Heterogeneity considered, no sensitivity or publication bias analysis
Lotufo-Neto et al 1999[21]	RIMAs versus placebo (11) RIMAs versus comparators, mostly OA (53)	Medline, Psychological Abstracts search to 1996 RCTs > 2 weeks duration of depressive disorders Primary outcome: response difference (modified ITT)	Efficacy: brofaromine = OA, moclobemide = comparators and TCA, SSRIs and MAOIs separately but > mixed group of maprotiline + mianserin, moclobemide = comparators in out-patients and in-patients	Many studies not peer reviewed. No significance values; standard deviations not 95% confidence intervals reported. No tolerability meta-analysis. No examination of publication bias or explicit sensitivity analysis
Mittmann et al 1997[22]	Comparisons of SSRIs, RIMAs, TCAs, AD2 with each other (28) (Also single arm analyses carried out and placebo comparisons)	Medline and Embase database searches to 1996, references/reviews/articles RCTs major/unipolar depression in subjects ≥ 60 years Primary outcomes: response, total dropout and emergent side-effect risk difference Heterogeneity and sensitivity analysis considered	Efficacy: SSRIs > AD2 otherwise no differences found Tolerability: no differences found	Very small numbers available for comparisons. Side-effects and dropouts not analysed

(**Table 2** *continued on next page. See p. 167 for abbreviations etc.*)

Table 2 *(continued)* Summary of meta-analyses considered in detail in this article

Study	Drug comparisons (no. of studies)	Methodology	Main findings in drug versus drug comparisons	Comments
Mulrow et al 2000[23]	NA vs placebo and NA versus TCAs (28)	Comprehensive data base search 1980–98 RCTs > 5 weeks duration of major and non-major depression Primary outcomes: response risk ratio (modified ITT), total, side-effect dropout differences Publication bias, heterogeneity and sensitivity analyses considered	Efficacy: NA = TCAs Tolerability: *side-effect dropouts NA > TCAs*	Part of Williams *et al*[27] analysis
Puech et al 1997[24]	Milnacipran *versus* placebo (3) Milnacipran *versus* imipramine (6) Milnacipran *versus* SSRIs (2)	Drug company data RCTs of major depression Primary outcome: efficacy weighted mean difference (ITT); response and remission differences also presented	Efficacy: milnacipran = imipramine. milnacipran > SSRIs Tolerability: *side effect dropouts milnacipran = SSRIs; milnacipran > TCAs*	Small numbers. Drug company studies with selection of studies for TCA and SSRI comparison. Tolerability data inadequately presented
Thase et al 2001[25]	Venlafaxine *versus* SSRIs (8) and placebo (4)	Drug company data RCTs major depression Primary outcome: remission odds ratio (LOCF). Heterogeneity and sensitivity analysis considered	Efficacy: venlafaxine > SSRIs Tolerability: *side effect dropouts venlafaxine = SSRIs.* *Failure dropouts venlafaxine > SSRIs*	Remission defined as 17-item Hamilton Depression Rating Scale score < 8. Only subgroup of possible studies included. Tolerability assessed from simple sum of numbers
Trindade & Menon 1997[26]	SSRIs *versus* placebo (48) SSRIs *versus* SSRIs (10) SSRIs *versus* other AD (118) SSRIs *versus* amitriptyline + imipramine + clomipramine (46)	Comprehensive database search to 1996, references/reviews/articles RCTs of major depression Primary outcomes: relative effect size, risk difference for response, total, side effect and failure dropouts and side-effects Publication bias, heterogeneity and sensitivity analyses considered	Efficacy: SSRIs > placebo SSRIs = TCAs and other AD Tolerability: *total, side effect and failure dropouts SSRIs = TCAs and other AD Nausea, anorexia, diarrhoea, anxiety, agitation, insomnia, nervousness SSRIs < TCAs Dry mouth, constipation, blurred vision, sweating, dizziness SSRIs > TCAs*	Comprehensive review. Effect sizes calculated from change scores. Individual side effect rates from subgroups of studies, some relatively small
Williams et al 2000[27]	NA *versus* placebo (114) NA *versus* OA (206) NA *versus* NA (37) St John's wort *versus* placebo (14) St John's wort *versus* OA (6)	Comprehensive data base search 1980–98 RCTs > 5 weeks' duration of major and non-major depression analysed separately Primary outcomes: response risk ratio (modified ITT), total, side-effect dropout differences Publication bias, heterogeneity and sensitivity analyses considered	Efficacy: NA = OA except SNRIs > trazodone; fluoxetine < other SSRIs Tolerability: *total dropouts NA = OA.* *Side-effect dropouts RIMAs, SSRIs > TCA; SSRIs = maprotiline*	Comprehensive systematic review funded by the US AHRQ[a]. Also considers special situations such as the elderly, co-existing disorders, children and primary care Pooling method not fully explained but available in full report
Zivkov et al 1995[28]	Mirtazapine *versus* amitriptyline (5)	Drug company database Selected RCTs of DSMIII major depression Primary outcomes: efficacy weighted mean difference (ITT), relative response rate (ITT) Heterogeneity considered	Efficacy: mirtazapine = amitriptyline Tolerability: not formally analysed but percentages of dropouts mirtazapine = amitriptyline	Two amitriptyline studies excluded and other TCAs not included No sensitivity analysis

(Table 2 *continued on next page. See p. 167 for abbreviations etc.)*

Footnote to **Table 2 pp 164–166**

AD, antidepressant; AD2, 2nd generation ADs – trazodone, mianserin, nomifensine, viloxazine, maprotiline; SSRI, selective serotonin re-uptake inhibitor; SNRI, serotonin and noradrenaline re-uptake inhibitor; RIMA, reversible inhibitor of monoamine oxidase A; MAOI, monoamine oxidase inhibitor, TCA, tricyclic antidepressant; OA, older antidepressants including tricyclic antidepressants (except lofepramine), trazodone, mianserin, maprotiline, irreversible monoamine oxidase inhibitors; NA, newer antidepressants introduced after 1980 including lofepramine, amoxapine, selective serotonin re-uptake inhibitors, reversible inhibitors of monoamine oxidase A, venlafaxine, milnacipran, mirtazapine, nefazodone, reboxetine; TCA1, 1st generation TCAs – amitriptyline, clomipramine, doxepin, imipramine, trimipramine; TCA2, 2nd generation TCAs – desipramine, nortryptiline; RCT, randomised controlled trial; NNT, number needed to treat; ITT, intention to treat; modified ITT, responders ÷ number randomised (patients lost to follow-up assumed to be treatment failures); LOCF, last observation carried forward after specified number of weeks; AT, adequate treatment/completers.
> efficacy – more effective than; tolerability – better tolerated than.
≥ efficacy – trend to be more effective than; tolerability – trend to be better tolerated than
= no significant difference in efficacy; no significant difference in tolerability.
< efficacy – less effective than; tolerability – less well tolerated than.
≤ efficacy – trend to be less effective than; tolerability – trend to be less well tolerated than.
[a]Agency for Healthcare Research and Quality: Treatment of Depression – Newer Pharmacotherapies (AHRQ Publication No. 99-E014) http:/www.ahcpr.gov/

more recently with selective serotonin re-uptake inhibitors (SSRIs). Many meta-analyses consider a variety of drugs, often grouped differently so the results are considered by drug/drug class drawing on the results of the meta-analyses summarised in Table 2.

Lofepramine

Lofepramine is a tricyclic antidepressant which inhibits the re-uptake of noradrenaline, differing from the older tricyclics in being safer in overdose. Kerihuel and Dreyfus[20] used drug company data to obtain evaluable data from a reasonable number of studies. Interpretation is mainly limited by the quality of the studies which were small, a third were very short by current standards (3–4 weeks) and many were pre-1980 with a lack of information on important quality issues. The authors addressed the latter point by checking 34% of the 2040 original case report forms and found no major deviation from the published data. Evaluation of efficacy was based on global improvement and 24 studies (1714 patients) provided data, 16 against amitriptyline or imipramine. More patients improved on lofepramine compared with other TCAs (64% *versus* 56%; OR 1.4, 95% CI 1.2–1.8). Doses of the comparator TCAs were within the range 75–150 mg. The advantage was less marked and non-significant against amitriptyline and imipramine. Tolerability in terms of total number of dropouts was only given as percentages which were numerically similar for lofepramine and comparators. However, using data available from 14 studies, significantly fewer patients on lofepramine experienced side-effects (53% *versus* 64%; OR 0.6, 95% CI 0.5–0.7) with individual studies tending to report less dry mouth, dizziness and sedation.

No other meta-analyses provide useful information about lofepramine as Davis et al[16] (Table 2) only included 4 studies (160 patients). Within the limits of the data available, meta-analysis supports at least equal efficacy for lofepramine compared with standard TCAs but with better tolerability. Comparison with other newer antidepressants is extremely limited, only 2 studies are available comparing lofepramine with SSRIs[14] which does not allow conclusions to be drawn.

Amoxapine

Amoxapine is a cyclic antidepressant which inhibits the re-uptake of noradrenaline as well as having antagonist actions at dopamine and serotonin receptors. There are no good quality meta-analyses available but Davis et al[16] (Table 2) report a non-significant efficacy advantage to amoxapine over older TCAs (79% responders versus 73%) in 19 studies (784 patients). It is difficult to draw any conclusions from this.

Reversible inhibitors of monoamine oxidase A (RIMAs)

This class includes moclobemide and brofaromine but only the former has been marketed. Lotufo-Neto et al[21] (Table 2) pooled results from 6 brofaromine studies (659 patients) compared with tranylcypromine or imipramine in all but one case, with a high proportion of in-patients and TCA-resistant patients. With 58.6% of brofaromine patients responding, it was non-significantly favoured over comparators (RD 4.8%, 95% CI –5.9 to 15.2). In 28 studies (3220 patients) comparing moclobemide with TCAs (mostly imipramine, clomipramine and amitriptyline), 54.5% responded to moclobemide with no difference between drugs (RD 1.8%, 95% CI –2.7 to 6.3). Compared with traditional MAOIs (4 studies, 357 patients), 68.1% of moclobemide patients responded, non-significantly fewer than on MAOIs (RD –5.8%, to –22.5 to 10.9). In 7 studies (561 patients) against SSRIs, moclobemide had a response rate of 58.1% and a non-significant efficacy advantage (RD 6.5%, –1.3 to 14.3). Finally, moclobemide had a response rate of 64.7% and was more effective than a group of 7 studies (655 patients) in which it was compared with mianserin, maprotiline or amineptine (RD 10.6%, 0.8 to 20.4, NNT 10). Tolerability was not directly analysed but other reviews were cited that reported the most common side-effects (both around 20%) were insomnia and gastrointestinal symptoms such as nausea and diarrhoea with less drowsiness, anti-muscarinic and sexual side-effects than TCAs. Williams et al[27] (Table 2) also found no difference efficacy comparing RIMAs with TCAs in a smaller sample of 12 studies (1967 patients) but reported fewer side effect dropouts than older TCAs (5% *versus* 11%, RD –6%, –7 to –3, NNT 17) although total dropouts did not differ (26% *versus* 27%, RD –1%, –5 to 2).

There appears to be fairly good evidence that moclobemide has comparable efficacy to older TCAs and SSRIs and is probably better tolerated than TCAs.

Selective serotonin re-uptake inhibitors (SSRIs)

The SSRIs (citalopram, fluoxetine, fluvoxamine, paroxetine and sertraline) are the first antidepressants since the TCAs to make a major impact on prescribing practice. There are a considerable number of meta-analyses available so I will only present representative results and highlight areas of uncertainty.

SSRIs compared with other antidepressants

Anderson[11] (Table 2) found no difference in efficacy between SSRIs and TCAs in 102 studies (10,553 patients). The effect size was –0.03 (–0.09 to 0.03, negative value favouring TCAs) in agreement with Geddes *et al*[19] (ES 0.030, –0.018 to 0.092, positive value favouring TCAs) in an analysis of 67 studies (Table 2). Geddes *et al*[19] also grouped SSRIs and what they termed 'related drugs', venlafaxine and nefazodone, and compared them with all comparators in 98 studies (9554 patients) finding a very similar result (ES 0.035, –0.006 to 0.076). Comparisons between individual SSRIs and TCAs/comparators revealed no differences in efficacy apart from an advantage to amitriptyline found by Anderson[11] (ES –0.14, –0.25 to –0.03) but not Geddes *et al*[19] (ES 0.057, –0.027 to 0.14). This difference is likely to be accounted for both by the different method of analysis (change scores *versus* final score) as well as the different number of studies included (30 in the former *versus* 23 in the latter). A further complication is that publication bias cannot be ruled out[11], although other explanations such as study setting are also possible (see below) which may also explain the statistical heterogeneity that was found between studies. In support of the finding by Anderson[11], Barbui and Hotopf[13] (Table 2) examined the efficacy of amitriptyline compared with other antidepressants in 99 studies (6745 patients) and concluded that amitriptyline was slightly more effective than comparators (RR 1.12, 95% CI 1.01–1.24, NNT 40) with no evidence of publication bias. Compared with SSRIs, amitriptyline was more effective in the pooled effect size (21 studies; 0.106, 0.02 to 0.19) but the pooled odds ratio, although favouring amitriptyline, was not significant (17 studies; 1.14, 0.94 to 1.38).

Anderson[11] also examined lower (75–100 mg) and higher (150 mg and above) TCA dose studies separately. While higher dose studies showed a slightly, but non-significantly, greater advantage to TCAs (ES −0.08, −0.21 to 0.05) compared with those using lower doses (ES 0.025, −0.04 to 0.09) there appears little support for the contention that TCAs at doses between 75–100 mg are ineffective.

There is consistent evidence that SSRIs as a group are better tolerated than TCAs and possibly second generation antidepressants. Anderson[11] reported results from 95 studies (10,553 patients) and found that 27% of patients discontinued treatment on SSRIs compared with 31.4% on TCAs (RD −3.9%, −5.6 to −2.2, NNT 26). Dropouts due to side-effects appeared to account for this difference (12.5% *versus* 17.3%, RD −3.1%, −4.7 to −1.5, NNT 33) with no difference in dropouts due to inefficacy (6.3% *versus* 6%). Geddes *et al*[19], Williams *et al*[27] and Barbui *et al*[14] (Table 2) found the same results. The last study also compared SSRIs with second generation antidepressants (*e.g.* maprotiline, mianserin, trazodone; 25 studies, 2246 patients) and divided TCAs into old (amitriptyline and imipramine; 77 studies, 9197 patients) and new (other TCAs; 33 studies, 4782 patients). With an odds ratio > 1 indicating an advantage to SSRIs, essentially similar results were found for each comparison for dropouts overall (old TCAs: OR 1.22, 1.11 to 1.34, new TCAs: OR 1.20, 1.05 to 1.38, second generation: OR 1.17, 0.95 to 1.43) and due to side-effects (old TCAs: OR 1.61, 1.40 to 1.86, new TCAs: OR 1.28, 1.02 to 1.59, second generation: OR 1.30, 0.91 to 1.85). The results for second generation antidepressants were very similar in size to those for the TCAs although non-significant, and an advantage to SSRIs cannot be ruled out. Of interest, there were fewer dropouts due to inefficacy on TCAs than SSRIs, only significant for old TCAs (OR 0.82, 0.67 to 1.00).

Comparison involving individual drugs largely follow the same pattern with two exceptions. Anderson[11] found that fluvoxamine (25 studies) did not have fewer dropouts compared with TCAs either overall (RR 1.10, 0.86 to 1.19) or due to side-effects (RR 0.94, 0.72 to 1.22: an RR < 1 indicates an advantage to SSRIs). Dothiepin (dosulepin, 8 studies), alone of the TCAs, resulted in fewer dropouts than SSRIs (total: RR 1.24, 0.95 to 1.62, side effect: RR 2.64, 1.50 to 4.63, NNH 12), a result also found by Barbui *et al*[14].

The earlier meta-analysis by the Canadian Co-ordinating Office for Health Technology Assessment[26,29] did not find any difference in dropout rates between SSRIs and TCAs, presumably because many fewer studies were analysed. Of interest are the results for specific side-effects. Compared with TCAs, SSRIs caused significantly more nausea (48 studies: RD 10.3%, 7.3 to 13.3, NNT 10), diarrhoea (15 studies: RD 9%, 4 to 14, NNT 12), agitation (11 studies: RD 6%, 1 to 10, NNT 17), anorexia (11 studies: RD 5%, 0.6 to 9, NNT 20), insomnia (32 studies: RD 4%, 1 to 6, NNT 25), nervousness (14 studies: RD 4%, 0.6 to 7.4, NNT 25) and anxiety (17 studies: RD 3%, 0.8 to 5.5, NNT 34). On the other hand,

TCAs caused more dry mouth (56 studies: RD -28.1%, −34.9 to −24.8, NNT 4), constipation (49 studies: RD −11%, −14 to −8, NNT 10), dizziness (37 studies: RD −9%, −12 to −6, NNT 12), sweating (27 studies: RD −3.6%, −6.7 to −0.4, NNT 28) and blurred vision (19 studies: RD −2.8%, −5.4 to −0.02, NNT 36). Williams et al[27] also mention more headache on SSRIs compared with TCAs (15% versus 11%) and more tremors (11% versus 7%) and urinary disturbance (8% versus 3%) on TCAs compared with SSRIs.

SSRI are increasingly replacing TCAs as the standard comparators for newer antidepressants and these are considered separately below. In summary, SSRIs have proven to be generally as effective as older antidepressants apart from in comparison with amitriptyline against which they may be marginally less effective. Tolerability is better than with TCAs and probably second generation antidepressants although the magnitude is modest in short-term studies. The profile of SSRIs is significantly different from TCAs with less antimuscarinic but more gastrointestinal and stimulatory side-effects.

SSRIs compared with each other

Edwards and Anderson[17] (Table 2) identified 20 studies (3283 patients) comparing two SSRIs and determined the efficacy of individual SSRIs against the rest; 15 of the studies (2542 patients) were against fluoxetine. The efficacy at the end of study was non-significantly less for fluoxetine (ES −0.06, −0.14 to 0.01) but significantly so at 2–3 weeks (ES −0.11, −0.18 to −0.03), suggesting a slower onset of action compared with other SSRIs. No other efficacy differences were found between other SSRIs. Of interest, Williams et al[27] reported that slightly fewer patients on fluoxetine responded than on other SSRIs (RR 0.9, 0.8 to −1.0) but only 8 studies were included in the analysis. Trindade and Menon[26] found no difference between SSRIs based on an analysis of 10 studies.

The comparative tolerability of SSRIs was examined in 19 studies (2999 patients)[17]. The overall discontinuation rate was 25.6% with 10.8% attributed to side-effects. Fluvoxamine (5 studies, 594 patients) had significantly poorer tolerability than other SSRIs with more overall (RD 7.6%, 0.7 to 14.5, NNH 14) and side-effect dropouts (RD 6.5%, −1.5 to 14.6, NNH 16). In contrast, sertraline had slightly fewer dropouts due to side-effects than other SSRIs (RD −5.5, −10.9 to −0.01, NNT 19). Most individual side-effects were reported in only a minority of studies. An exception was nausea which occurred in 21.3% of 2706 patients in 17 studies with no difference between SSRIs. Agitation occurred more often with fluoxetine than other SSRIs (RD 3.3%, 0.4 to 6.3, NNT 30) but was reported in only 6 studies (1001 patients) so publication bias cannot be excluded, particularly as most studies were sponsored by its competitors.

In summary, it appears likely that fluoxetine has a slower onset of action than other SSRIs in the dosing schedules used in these studies (20 mg for the first week) and that fluvoxamine is less well tolerated (compatible with the results of comparisons with TCAs).

Serotonin and noradrenaline re-uptake inhibitors (SNRIs)

Venlafaxine and milnacipran inhibit the re-uptake of both serotonin and noradrenaline but, unlike TCAs, lack significant affinity for other receptors. Venlafaxine is widely marketed and there have been claims for its superior efficacy over SSRIs.

Williams et al[27] grouped together SNRIs and mirtazapine (see below) and reported no difference in efficacy in 6 studies (1400 patients) against TCAs. However, in 3 studies (449 patients) against trazodone they were more effective (RR 1.2, 1 to 1.4). Puech et al[24] examined the efficacy of milnacipran compared with imipramine in 6 studies (726 patients) and found equal efficacy (RD −1%, −8.1 to 6). Anderson[12] pooled 22 studies (3925 patients) and found that more patients on SNRIs responded compared with those on SSRIs (66% versus 60%, RR 1.09, 1.02 to 1.17, NNT 18) with similar results for the 17 venlafaxine studies (3021 patients, RR 1.09, 1.02 to 1.17) and the 5 milnacipran studies (904 patients, RR 1.09, 0.90 to 1.33). In a study examining remission, Thase et al[25] pooled data from 8 studies (1599 patients), 5 against fluoxetine, and found that 45% of venlafaxine-treated patients remitted compared with 35% of SSRI-treated patients (OR 1.5, 1.3 to 1.9). The numbers of patients dropping out due to side-effects were numerically, but non-significantly, greater on venlafaxine (9% versus 7%) but slightly more patients on SSRIs dropped out due to inefficacy (6% versus 4%, $P < 0.05$).

These results provide some support that dual re-uptake inhibition confers greater efficacy than inhibition of serotonin re-uptake alone.

Mirtazapine

Mirtazapine is related to mianserin and enhances both serotonin and noradrenaline function through antagonism of presynaptic receptors. Zivkov et al[28] reported on 5 studies (814 patients) comparing mirtazapine with amitriptyline. The weighted mean difference in 17-item Hamilton Depression Rating Scale points was 0.58 (−0.57 to 1.73) with 63.9% of amitriptyline patients responding compared with 61.3% of mirtazapine patients (RR 0.95, 0.85 to 1.05). This suggests little difference in efficacy but judgement needs to be reserved over publication bias given that only half of available TCA studies are included in this analysis. A meta-analysis of 3 studies (653 patients) comparing mirtazapine with SSRIs[12] found response rates of 69.9% versus 65.4% (RR 1.11, 0.87 to 1.42) which, although not significant, is very similar in size to that seen with the SNRIs. Mirtazapine may have a more rapid onset of action than SSRIs as significantly more patients had responded at 2 weeks (34% *versus* 24%, RR 1.38, 1.08 to 1.76, NNT 11). However, a faster onset of action was not apparent in the studies against amitriptyline[28] and the small numbers make the results vulnerable to chance.

Few data on tolerability are available from meta-analysis. Zivkov *et al*[28] found that about equal numbers dropped out on mirtazapine and amitriptyline due to lack of efficacy/adverse events or both (13.3% *versus* 13%). However, this might hide a difference in reasons for dropouts as Stahl *et al*[30], in a smaller meta-analysis of 4 placebo controlled studies (580 patients), found that non-significantly fewer patients dropped out due to side-effects on mirtazapine (10.1% *versus* 17.2%) but significantly more due to inefficacy (15.1% *versus* 7.4%, $P < 0.05$). The pattern of side-effects confirmed a lack of antimuscarinic and stimulant effects but dry mouth, sedation and weight gain occurred significantly more than with placebo.

Meta-analyses and other aspects

Clinical variables

Study setting
In-patients may be a group with more severe depression in which differences between antidepressants might be more pronounced. Anderson[11] found that TCAs were more effective than SSRIs in the 25 studies (1377 patients) in in-patients (ES −0.23, −0.40 to −0.05) whereas no advantage was seen in out-patients or primary care. However, Geddes *et al*[19] in 23 studies (1347 patients) found the advantage to be smaller and non-significant (0.1, −0.07 to 0.27) using slightly different methodology and Trindade and Menon[26] noted a similar finding. In comparisons between SNRIs and SSRIs, Anderson[12] found a greater advantage to SNRIs in in-patients (5 studies, 1.24, 1.08 to 1.41, NNT 8) than out-patients (13 studies, RR 1.08, 0.99 to 1.18) and no difference in general practice patients (2 studies, 0.97, 0.88 to 1.08). However, the general practice result may have been explained by the low dose of venlafaxine (75 mg).

Most treatment of depression occurs in primary care but there are relative few studies available in this setting. Mulrow *et al*[23] (Table 2) examined 28 primary care studies (5940 patients) and concluded that newer agents had equal efficacy to TCAs in this setting (RR 1.0, 0.9 to 1.1) but dropouts due to side-effects were fewer (8% *versus* 13%, RD −4, −7 to 0). Anderson[11], comparing SSRIs with TCAs in primary care studies, found fewer total (9 studies, RR 0.78, 0.68 to 0.90) and side-effect dropouts (8 studies, 0.75, 0.61 to 0.85).

The available meta-analyses do not give consistent findings but differences in efficacy may be more important in in-patient than community settings.

Elderly patients

Two studies which considered the elderly in a subgroup analysis concluded that there were no differences in efficacy between older and newer antidepressants in 16 studies[27] or between SSRIs and TCAs in 11 studies (1207 patients)[11], similar to the overall analysis. In contrast tolerability, which was better on SSRIs than TCAs in the whole group analysis, did not differ between the two groups of drugs. The dropout rate was high in the elderly with 36.5% of patients stopping treatment, 21.8% due to side-effects, in comparative SSRI-TCAs studies and there was a very small non-significant difference in side-effect dropouts (21.3% *versus* 22.4%, RR 0.91, 0.74 to 1.11)[11]. A number of meta-analyses have examined studies in elderly patients alone, that by Mittmann *et al*[22] being probably the most informative. Efficacy comparisons showed SSRIs to be more effective than second generation antidepressants (2 studies, 66 patients; RD –36.9%, –65.4 to –8.4) and non-significantly favoured over TCAs (4 studies, 423 patients; RD 3.3%, –6.3 to 12.8). Occurrence of side-effects was non-significantly less frequent on second generation antidepressants compared with RIMAs (2 studies, 105 patients; –11.8%, –30.5 to 6.8) and on SSRIs compared with second generation antidepressants (3 studies, 134 patients; –7.5%, –34.3 to 19.3) and TCAs (4 studies, 418 patients; –9.6%, –18.7 to 1.5) with a similar picture for total dropouts. Menting[31], in contrast, concluded that SSRIs were better tolerated than TCAs if the analysis was limited to the 4 better quality studies. However, the sensitivity of results to differences in study inclusion makes interpretation difficult. Therefore, in the elderly the evidence suggests that antidepressants are more poorly tolerated in general than in younger patients with no confidence that any one group of drugs is superior.

Antidepressants and suicide

There has been concern that SSRIs may increase the risk of suicidal actions in depressed patients, possibly as a consequence of agitation which occurs more often than with TCAs[26]. In order to address this, Beasley *et al*[15] (Table 2) analysed studies of fluoxetine compared with TCAs (12 studies, 1451 patients). They found non-significantly more patients on fluoxetine made suicidal acts (0.7% *versus* 0.4%, RD 0.3%, –0.4 to 1.1) but fewer experienced the emergence of suicidal ideas (1.7% *versus* 3.6%, RD –1.8, –4.0 to 0.4). Separate comparisons with placebo showed no increased risk for either group of antidepressants and a greater improvement in suicidal ideation on fluoxetine compared with placebo, presumably due to greater alleviation of depression. This study is important evidence against fluoxetine causing a general increase in suicidal risk, but does not exclude a role in individual cases or in patients at high risk of suicide.

Pharmacology in relation to efficacy

There is a lack of empirical evidence to link the acute pharmacology of antidepressants and efficacy. In an attempt to explore this using meta-regression analysis, Freemantle et al[18] (Table 2) explored the possible contribution of combinations of pharmacological actions to efficacy compared with serotonin re-uptake inhibition alone but were unable to demonstrate an effect. This probably partly reflects limitations in our understanding of the *in vivo* pharmacology of many older antidepressants

Table 3 Summary of findings from meta-analyses of new antidepressants

Higher confidence

Lofepramine at least as effective as TCAs
Moclobemide as effective as TCAs and SSRIs
SSRIs generally as effective as TCAs
Fluoxetine slower onset of therapeutic action than other SSRIs
Venlafaxine more effective than SSRIs

SSRIs better tolerated than TCAs
SSRIs cause more gastrointestinal and stimulatory side-effects than TCAs
TCAs cause more anti-muscarinic side-effects and dizziness than SSRIs
Fluoxetine no more generally likely to promote suicide than TCAs in low suicide risk patients
Fluvoxamine less well tolerated than other SSRIs

Lower confidence

Lofepramine better tolerated than older TCAs
RIMAs more effective than second generation antidepressants
RIMAs as effective as older MAOIs
TCAs more effective than SSRIs in in-patients
Amitriptyline more effective than SSRIs
SNRIs more effective than trazodone
Mirtazapine as effective as amitriptyline

RIMAs better tolerated than TCAs
Dothiepin better tolerated than SSRIs
Fluvoxamine no better tolerated than TCAs
Fluoxetine causes more agitation than other SSRIs

Uncertainty

SSRIs better tolerated than second generation antidepressants
Sertraline better tolerated than other SSRIs
Mirtazapine faster onset than SSRIs
SSRIs no better tolerated than TCAs in elderly patients

SNRIs, serotonin and noradrenaline re-uptake inhibitors; SSRIs, selective serotonin re-uptake inhibitors; RIMAs, reversible inhibitors of monoamine oxidase A; TCAs, tricyclic antidepressants.

in humans. The results with SNRIs compared with SSRIs (see above) are at present the best evidence that dual action at serotonin and noradrenaline transporters is better than a single action on serotonin.

Conclusions

The available meta-analyses provide the best summary of a bewildering variety of studies comparing antidepressants; the main findings are given in Table 3. They are, however, beset with limitations related to the number and quality of individual RCTs as well as variations in grouping and inclusion criteria. These factors limit the confidence with which many of the findings can be viewed. In addition, the results are from short-term RCTs and caution is required in extrapolating them to clinical practice in which longer term treatment is recommended[32]; however, the first 6–8 weeks is a crucial time and necessary step in treatment. These analyses do provide a counterbalance to promotional claims for individual antidepressants although the loss of detail necessary for meta-analysis necessarily excludes potentially important factors in the treatment of individual patients. In the future, effectiveness studies will hopefully provide additional guidance, but for the present these results are a starting point in weighing the evidence as to choice of antidepressant. The need to tailor treatment for individual patients, however, cautions against dogmatism.

Acknowledgements

Wyeth Laboratories provided additional details on venlafaxine studies and financial support for the venlafaxine analyses.

Declaration of interest: the author has received research funding, honoraria for speaking and advice and support for attending scientific meetings from a number of pharmaceutical companies producing antidepressants discussed in this article.

References

1   Barton S. Which clinical studies provide the best evidence? The best RCT still trumps the best observational study. *BMJ* 2000; **321**: 255–6
2   Stewart LA, Parmar MKB. Bias in the analysis and reporting of randomized controlled trials. *Int J Technol Assess Health Care* 1996; **12**: 264–75
3   Henry DA, Wilson A. Meta-analysis. Part 1: an assessment of its aims, validity and reliability. *Med J Aust* 1992; **156**: 31–8

4   Wilson A, Henry DA. Meta-analysis. Part 2: assessing the quality of published meta-analyses. *Med J Aust* 1992; **156**: 173–87

5   Walker A. Meta-style and expert review. *Lancet* 1999; **354**: 1834–5

6   Moher D, Cook DJ, Eastwood S, Olkin I, Rennie D, Stroup DF. Improving the quality of reports of meta-analyses of randomised controlled trials: the QUORUM statement. *Lancet* 1999; **354**: 1896–900

7   Bero L, Rennie D. The Cochrane Collaboration: preparing, maintaining and disseminating systematic reviews of the effects of health care. *JAMA* 1995; **274**: 1935–8

8   Cohen J. *Statistical Power Analysis for the Behavioral Sciences*. Orlando, FL: Academic Press, 1977

9   Furukawa TA. From effect size to number needed to treat. *Lancet* 1999; **353**: 1680

10 Sinclair JC, Bracken MB. Clinically useful measures of effect in binary analyses of randomized trials. *J Clin Epidemiol* 1994; **47**: 881–9

11 Anderson IM. Selective serotonin re-uptake inhibitors versus tricyclic antidepressants: a meta-analysis of efficacy and tolerability. *J Affect Dis* 2000; **58**: 19–36

12 Anderson IM. Meta-analyses of antidepressant drugs: selectivity versus multiplicity. In: den Boer JA, Westenberg HGM. (eds) *Focus on Psychiatry; Antidepressants: Selectivity or Multiplicity?* Amsterdam: Syn-Thesis, 2001; In press

13 Barbui C, Hotopf M. Amitriptyline v. the rest: still the leading antidepressant after 40 years of randomised controlled trials. *Br J Psychiatry* 2001; **178**: 129–44

14 Barbui C, Hotopf M, Freemantle N *et al*. Selective serotonin re-uptake inhibitors versus tricyclic and heterocyclic antidepressants: comparison of drug adherence (Cochrane Review). *The Cochrane Library*. 1. Oxford, Update Software. 2001

15 Beasley CM, Dornseif BE, Bosomworth JC *et al*. Fluoxetine and suicide: a meta-analysis of controlled trials of treatment for depression. *BMJ* 1991; **303**: 685–92

16 Davis JM, Wang Z, Janicak PG. A quantitative analysis of clinical drug trials for the treatment of affective disorders. *Psychopharmacol Bull* 1993; **29**: 175–81

17 Edwards JG, Anderson I. Systematic review and guide to selection of selective serotonin re-uptake inhibitors. *Drugs* 1999; **57**: 507–33

18 Freemantle N, Anderson IM, Young P. Predictive value of pharmacological activity for the relative efficacy of antidepressant drugs. Meta-regression analysis. *Br J Psychiatry* 2000; **177**: 292–302

19 Geddes JR, Freemantle N, Mason J, Eccles MP, Boynton J. SSRIs versus other antidepressants for depressive disorder (Cochrane Review). *The Cochrane Library* 1. Oxford, Update Publishers. 2001.

20 Kerihuel JC, Dreyfus JF. Meta-analyses of the efficacy and tolerability of the tricyclic antidepressant lofepramine. *J Int Med Res* 1991; **19**: 183–201

21 Lotufo-Neto F, Trivedi M, Thase ME. Meta-analysis of the reversible inhibitors of monoamine oxidase type A moclobemide and brofaromine for the treatment of depression. *Neuropsychopharmacology* 1999; **20**: 226–47

22 Mittmann N, Herrmann N, Einarson TR *et al*. The efficacy, safety and tolerability of antidepressants in late life depression: a meta-analysis. *J Affect Dis* 1997; **46**: 191–217

23 Mulrow CD, Williams JWJ, Chiquette E *et al*. Efficacy of newer medications for treating depression in primary care patients. *Am J Med* 2000; **108**: 54–64

24 Puech A, Montgomery SA, Prost JF, Solles A, Briley M. Milnacipran, a new serotonin and noradrenaline re-uptake inhibitor: an overview of its antidepressant activity and clinical tolerability. *Int Clin Psychopharmacol* 1997; **12**: 99–108

25 Thase ME, Entsuah AR, Rudolph RL. Remission rates during treatment with venlafaxine or selective serotonin re-uptake inhibitors. *Br J Psychiatry* 2001; **178**: 234–41

26 Trindade E, Menon D. *Selective serotonin re-uptake inhibitors (SSRIs) for major depression. Part 1. Evaluation of the clinical literature*. Ottawa: Canadian Coordinating Office for Health Technology Assessment, 1997

27 Williams JWJ, Mulrow CD, Chiquette E, Noel PH, Aguilar C, Cornell J. A systematic review of newer pharmacotherapies for depression in adults: evidence report summary. *Ann Intern Med* 2000; **132**: 743–56

28 Zivkov M, Roes KCB, Pols AG. Efficacy of Org 3770 (mirtazapine) vs amitriptyline in patients with major depressive disorder: a meta-analysis. *Hum Psychopharmacol* 1995; **10**: S135–S145

29   Trindade E, Menon D, Topfer L-A, Coloma C. Adverse effects associated with selective serotonin re-uptake inhibitors and tricyclic antidepressants: A meta-analysis. *Can Med Assoc J* 1998; **159**: 1245–52

30   Stahl S, Zivkov M, Reimitz PE, Panagides J, Hoff W. Meta-analysis of randomized, double-blind, placebo-controlled, efficacy and safety studies of mirtazapine versus amitriptyline in major depression. *Acta Psychiatr Scand* 1997; **96** (**Suppl 391**): 22–30

31   Menting JE, Honig A, Verhey FR *et al.* Selective serotonin re-uptake inhibitors (SSRIs) in the treatment of elderly depressed patients: a qualitative analysis of the literature on their efficacy and side-effects. *Int Clin Psychopharmacol* 1996; **11**: 165–75

32   Anderson IM, Nutt DJ, Deakin JFW. Evidence-based guidelines for treating depressive disorders with antidepressants: a revision of the 1993 British Association for Psychopharmacology guidelines. *J Psychopharmacol* 2000; **14**: 3–20

Developments in mood stabilisers

I Nicol Ferrier

Department of Psychiatry, University of Newcastle upon Tyne, Newcastle upon Tyne, UK

Bipolar affective disorder is a life-long condition with profound effects on sufferers' social and occupational life. Despite efficacy in clinical trials and in some groups of patients, lithium's effectiveness in clinical practice is hampered by its side effect profile and limited concordance. Alternative and adjunctive treatments to lithium in bipolar disorder have been sought and the anticonvulsants carbamazepine and valproate show promise. Despite these advances, treatment resistance persists. Lamotrigine, a new anticonvulsant, is increasingly used in treatment-resistant cases under specialist supervision. Further pharmacological and non-pharmacological strategies for bipolar prophylaxis are currently under investigation. These developments are the focus of this review.

Classically, bipolar disorder takes the form of repeated periods of mania, hypomania or depression with full inter-episode recovery. However, in practice, approximately one-third of patients suffer chronic symptoms[1] and persistent psychosocial difficulties are common[2]. Amongst mental illnesses, bipolar disorder is ranked second only to unipolar depression as a cause of world-wide disability[3]. Over the past decade, there have been many advances in the pharmacological and psychological treatment of this disorder which are the subject of this article.

The lifetime risk of bipolar disorder is 1.2%, increasing to 10% in first-degree relatives. Prevalence does not differ with sex, but is higher in urban areas[4]. Of the 1845 patients on the average general practitioner's list in the UK[5], 22 will develop bipolar disorder at some point in their lives. Bipolar disorder may go unrecognised in a substantial number of patients.

Mania is characterised by elated mood accompanied by over-activity, pressure of speech and disturbed sleep. There is increased speed of thought and activity until efficiency is compromised by poor concentration. Irritability may occur rather than elation. Patients may experience hallucinations and mood-congruent delusions. Disinhibition, impractical and extravagant plans and grandiose ideas may result in grave consequences for an individual's professional life, social functioning and financial stability. In hypomania, these symptoms are less severe and there are no psychotic symptoms. Depressive episodes are manifest in low mood, loss of interest and enjoyment, diminished

Correspondence to:
Prof. I Nicol Ferrier,
Department of Psychiatry,
University of Newcastle
upon Tyne, Newcastle
upon Tyne NE1 4LP, UK

energy, poor concentration, disturbed sleep and appetite. Self-esteem and confidence are low and ideas of guilt, hopelessness and suicide may occur. Psychotic symptoms may feature in severe episodes. Episodes of mania and depression may happen in isolation or follow in quick succession. Poor prognostic indicators in bipolar disorder include the development of rapid-cycling disorder, where four or more episodes occur within a year, and mixed states, where manic and depressive symptoms are experienced together.

Mood stabilisers have become the cornerstone of pharmacological treatment of bipolar disorder. An ideal mood stabiliser should both treat episodes of mania and depression and be effective in prophylaxis. It should not precipitate mania or depression, nor should it induce rapid cycling disorder.

Lithium

Lithium has been used in the treatment of bipolar disorder for the past 50 years Although it continues as a first-line treatment, approximately one-third of bipolar patients do not respond satisfactorily to this treatment[6], especially those with rapid cycling disorder and mixed episodes. Because of its narrow therapeutic window, frequent blood monitoring is required. Lithium is often associated with side effects, even at therapeutic levels. Fine tremor can be troublesome and is hard to manage – dose reduction is generally ineffective and β blockade only partially effective. Despite controversy, it now seems clear that chronic use of lithium even with adequate blood level control can be associated with loss of renal glomerular function. Persistent polyuria is also troublesome and can worsen the risk of dehydration which, alone or in association with other causes, can lead to neurotoxicity which may be irreversible. Goitre and transient hypothyroidism occur commonly at the onset of treatment and a significant percentage of patients (2–3%) – predominantly female (90%) – will develop hypothyroidism on treatment. It is recognised that neurotoxicity can occur at therapeutic levels leading to the maxim that one should watch and listen to the patient, not just the blood level. For a fuller review of the current use and side-effect burden of lithium readers are referred elsewhere.[7]

In addition to (and probably because of) these difficulties, compliance is often poor: the median length of continuous use of lithium in one naturalistic study of a sub-group of patients with bipolar disorder was only 65 days[8]. Non-compliance is particularly problematic because lithium discontinuation may precipitate manic recurrence[9,10]. Women planning pregnancy face the possibility of developing mania on stopping this potentially teratogenic medication. The risk of lithium 'rebound mania' is lessened by its gradual withdrawal over a 15–30 day period[11]. Concerns that lithium withdrawal may result in subsequent resistance to its prophylactic effect have not been substantiated[12]. In summary, of all the agents used as mood stabilisers currently, lithium has the strongest evidence base. However, its effectiveness is limited by adverse effects, a narrow therapeutic window and non-compliance.

Newer mood stabilisers – the anticonvulsants

Over the past 10 years, better mood stabilising treatments have been sought. The anticonvulsants valproate and carbamazepine are now established as alternative and adjunctive treatments to lithium. Carbamazepine is the only anticonvulsant licensed for use in bipolar disorder in the UK. However, valproate is the most frequently prescribed mood stabiliser in the US and is used increasingly in Europe. In January, 2001, 'Depakote' (valproate semi-sodium) was licensed for the treatment of acute mania in the UK.

Despite these developments, treatment resistance persists. In particular, bipolar depression remains a therapeutic problem: lithium, valproate and carbamazepine are more effective in treating and preventing mania than depression. Rapid-cycling disorder and mixed mania still challenge the clinician. Recently, the new anticonvulsants have been studied as potential mood stabilisers in the hope of finding more effective treatments. Of these, lamotrigine appears to have the largest evidence base in the form of randomised controlled trials (RCTs). Aspects of carbamazepine, valproate and lamotrigine treatment are now considered in detail, and brief accounts of some other emerging treatments are included.

Carbamazepine

Although carbamazepine has efficacy in treating mania, demonstrated in RCTs, the evidence for its antidepressive and prophylactic efficacy is not strong. Comparator trials against lithium have produced conflicting results[13]. Some authors have suggested that the efficacy of carbamazepine may fade with longer term treatment[14]. Most authorities suggest that carbamazepine is best used in combination with lithium[15].

Side effects of carbamazepine include blurred vision, dizziness, ataxia and gastrointestinal disturbance. These effects are reversible and dose-related but often occur at doses used in bipolar disorder. Rash commonly occurs and treatment should be withdrawn if it persists or worsens. Carbamazepine can precipitate Stevens-Johnson syndrome and toxic epidermal necrolysis, and therapy should be stopped immediately if a patient develops mucocutaneous blisters or epidermal erosions with unexplained fever. Urgent dermatological advice should be sought and renal, hepatic and clotting function should be monitored[16].

Carbamazepine is metabolised through the liver enzyme cytochrome P450. Carbamazepine induces the 3A4 isoform of this enzyme, thus enhancing its own metabolism. Its use may reduce the effectiveness of other drugs metabolised through the same system including other anticonvulsants, hormonal contraceptives and neuroleptics. The teratogenic effects of carbamazepine are discussed below. It is, therefore, particularly important that effective contraceptive measures are taken, and higher doses of hormonal contraceptives or alternative methods of birth control should be used. Some SSRIs and nefazodone may slow the metabolism of carbamazepine through inhibition of cytochrome P450 3A4, potentially precipitating toxic effects[17].

Because of doubts regarding its efficacy, problems relating to its side effect profile and its interactions with other medications, carbamazepine is falling out of favour with most specialists prescribing for bipolar disorder.

Valproate

The efficacy of valproate in the treatment of mania has been established through RCTs and it has particular efficacy in dysphoric or mixed mania[18]. However, there are no such trials examining its efficacy in bipolar depression. Despite its widespread use, particularly in the US, its use in prophylaxis is based on open studies. The only RCT[19] with bipolar patients reported valproate's prophylactic efficacy on some measures over a 12-month period. However, the significance of this result is questionable because of methodological limitations, and there is a need for further studies. Currently, a large randomised controlled study, the Balance Trial, is being planned aiming to recruit up to 2000 bipolar patients throughout the UK. This study will compare the prophylactic efficacy of lithium with that of valproate and combination treatment. It is hoped that this, one of the first trials of its size in psychiatry, will provide reliable evidence on which to base decisions on prophylactic treatment.

Valproate is generally well-tolerated. The commonest side effects are gastric irritation, nausea, ataxia and tremor. Increased appetite and weight gain can be problematic. The development of curly scalp hair and hair loss are rare occurrences. Most serious side effects can be avoided by a slow increase in dose. Rarely, non-dose-related severe hepatic damage can occur within the first six months of treatment. Valproate treatment is contra-indicated in those with active liver disease or a family history of hepatic dysfunction. Liver function should be monitored as described below. Rarely, valproate has been associated with acute pancreatitis. The polycystic ovarian syndrome has been reported in epileptic patients, but this has not been replicated in bipolar patients[20].

Valproate competes with some anticonvulsants such as carbamazepine and lamotrigine for hepatic drug-metabolising enzymes, raising their plasma levels. It may enhance the anticoagulant effects of warfarin.

In summary, valproate is increasingly frequently prescribed for bipolar disorder and is the leading mood stabiliser in the US. Its effects against mania are established, but its antidepressant and prophylactic effects remain unproven. It has fewer problematic drug interactions than carbamazepine.

Lamotrigine

Lamotrigine is licensed as an adjunctive therapy for complex partial and generalised tonic-clonic seizures. Recently, controlled trials have been conducted on its use in mania[21], bipolar depression[22,23] and rapid-cycling disorder[24]. Although this research supports its efficacy in bipolar disorder (at doses of 50 mg and 200 mg), it remains unlicensed for this purpose. It should be reserved for cases of treatment resistance or for those intolerant to more conventional treatments.

The commonest adverse effects associated with the use of lamotrigine are headache, nausea, diplopia, dizziness and ataxia; sedation occurs occasionally. However, the main concern is a skin rash which occurs in 5% of patients, usually early in treatment: risk factors are polypharmacy, particularly with valproate and rapid dose increments. Children are particularly at risk. Usually, the rash is mild and abates independent of treatment withdrawal. However, occasionally serious generalised illnesses such as erythema multiforme, angio-oedema and Stevens-Johnson syndrome occur and fatalities have been reported. Renal, hepatic and clotting function should be monitored if a rash or influenza-type symptoms develop and treatment should be withdrawn immediately unless the rash is clearly not drug related. In epilepsy, lamotrigine has been safely re-introduced at a very slow rate in patients who have had a mild rash on first introduction[25].

Lamotrigine does not induce cytochrome P450 enzymes and has no effects on other psychotropic medications. Carbamazepine induces lamotrigine metabolism. This combination has been reported to have neurotoxic effects through a pharmacodynamic interaction[26]. As discussed above, valproate potentially enhances the toxic effects of lamotrigine by impairing its elimination.

There is growing evidence supporting the mood stabilising effects of lamotrigine. Its efficacy in areas of treatment resistance such as bipolar depression and rapid-cycling disorder make it a welcome addition to the pharmacological armoury. However, it remains unlicensed for bipolar disorder and should be prescribed for treatment resistant cases under specialist supervision.

Gabapentin

Gabapentin is an anti-epileptic agent structurally related to γ-aminobutyric acid (GABA) with an unknown mechanism of action. It is in current use as augmentation therapy in patients with partial seizures resistant to conventional therapies. Gabapentin is not metabolised in humans. It is not protein bound. It has no known pharmacokinetic interactions with valproic acid, carbamazepine, other anticonvulsants or oral contraceptives and is excreted unchanged. Gabapentin has a high therapeutic index and a relatively benign side effect profile. Side effects reported with gabapentin are transient and minor, the most common being somnolence, dizziness, ataxia and fatigue[27]. It is not associated with hepatic or haematological problems. It has a wide dose range 900–3000 mg/day. Gabapentin's use in rapid cycling bipolar disorder, mania and bipolar depression is supported by open trials[28–30]. These findings have not been replicated in RCTs, two of which have been negative[23,31].

Topiramate

Topiramate is a new anti-epileptic drug which is used as adjunctive therapy for partial seizures. It enhances GABA activity and blocks glutamate at non N-methyl D-aspartate (NMDA) receptors. Preliminary open observations of adjunctive topiramate treatment suggest that it may have antimanic or anticycling effects in some patients with bipolar disorder including those who are treatment resistant and it may be associated with appetite suppression and weight loss[32–34]. There is one case report of topiramate monotherapy in maintenance treatment of bipolar disorder[35]. RCTs are underway.

Tiagabine

There has been recent interest in the novel anticonvulsant, tiagabine, which reduces the re-uptake of GABA into neuronal and glial cells. Preliminary case reports have yielded conflicting results. The most promising reports use doses much lower than those typical for the treatment of seizures[36–38].

Issues related to prescribing anticonvulsants as mood stabilisers

Mechanisms of anticonvulsant action in bipolar affective disorder

The mechanisms underlying the mood stabilising properties of anticonvulsants are poorly understood. It is unclear whether their mood-stabilising and anticonvulsant properties result from the same pharmacological effects. The GABA-mediated inhibitory effects of carbamazepine and valproate may play a central role in their therapeutic effect. Lamotrigine may act through the reduction of glutamate-stimulated excitatory processes and the modulation of signal transduction through its effects on membrane cation conductance. Clinical effects may also be mediated by a direct effect on central monoamines and through second messenger systems linked to the central actions of catecholamines[39].

Combination treatments

Combination treatments may be more effective than monotherapy, but they require further study in the form of RCTs. Combination treatments may increase the likelihood of side effects and toxicity.

Blood monitoring

The therapeutic serum levels for anticonvulsants in bipolar disorder have not been firmly established. There is little evidence for a direct relationship between anticonvulsant blood levels and efficacy in treatment of acute episodes or in the prophylactic treatment of bipolar affective disorder. One study of 65 manic patients using valproate suggested that levels above 45 mg/l were necessary for its antimanic effect[40]. From retrospective open studies, the optimum blood level for prophylaxis appears to be 60–90 mg/l, with 100–120 mg/l in difficult-to-treat cases and a high side effect burden is likely at > 125 mg/l[41].

Blood disorders can occur with carbamazepine, and so regular full blood count monitoring is required during therapy. Liver function should be monitored prior to commencing valproate treatment and regularly thereafter, especially in the first 6 months of treatment. Mild elevation of hepatic enzymes requires further monitoring. Valproate should be withdrawn immediately if there is evidence of hepatic failure or severe oedema. Lamotrigine does not require regular monitoring, though a baseline full blood count, renal function and liver function tests should be undertaken.

Teratogenesis

Teratogenicity is a major concern when considering the use of any medication in long-term prophylactics. There is an increased risk of teratogenicity associated with the use of anticonvulsant medication. Much of the data available on teratogenicity are on patients with epilepsy, a condition which itself has an increased incidence of developmental disorders. The risk of teratogenicity in non-epileptic patients remains unclear.

Neural tube defects are associated with the first trimester use of the folate antagonists carbamazepine and valproate. One study reported a reduction in the incidence of first occurrence and recurrence of neural tube defects in women with epilepsy receiving carbamazepine or valproate with folic acid supplementation prior to conception[42]. Maternal carbamazepine treatment may result in bleeding disorders in the new-born. Valproate has been reported to cause congenital anomalies, digit anomalies, oral clefts and orofacial dysmorphic features[16]. Lamotrigine is a weak folate antagonist with theoretical teratogenic potential. The Glaxo-Wellcome prospective pregnancy registry reported an unspecified birth defect rate of 8 among 149 patients exposed to lamotrigine (in combination therapy). All occurred with first trimester exposure; there were no reports of defects in pregnancies with exposure in the second and third trimesters of pregnancy[43].

Given the teratogenic risks of anticonvulsant treatment particularly during the period of neural tube formation in the first trimester, pregnancy should be planned. The risks and benefits of on-going treatment should be carefully weighed. Withdrawal of treatment should be undertaken prior to conception. If anticonvulsant treatment is continued into pregnancy, then folate supplementation should be prescribed in the first trimester although its benefits are not firmly established.

Rebound phenomena

In contrast to lithium, there is little evidence regarding the existence of rebound mania on withdrawal of anticonvulsants. One case series examining the effects of carbamazepine withdrawal in bipolar patients did not support a rebound effect[44]. Anticonvulsant mood stabilisers may be a better choice for patients who are poorly compliant with medication but, as yet, there is insufficient evidence to recommend a change to prescribing practice.

Effects on suicide rate

It is estimated that 25–50% of bipolar patients attempt suicide at least once[45]. The recognised life-time risk of completed suicide is 15%, but this may be an over-estimate. Young men, early in the course of their illness, are at highest risk, especially those with a history of suicide attempts or alcohol misuse, and those recently discharged from hospital[46]. Lithium is thought to have direct anti-suicidal effects[46]; there is little information on the effects of anticonvulsants in reducing suicide rates.

Bipolar depression

The depressive phase of bipolar disorder is associated with considerable morbidity and mortality. Some treatments may precipitate mania and increase cycle frequency[47]. In general terms, the best strategies are to optimise mood stabiliser medication[48] and to use antidepressants less likely to induce hypomania[49] (*e.g.* SSRIs rather than tricyclics) and to avoid prolonged and high dose use. It is not yet clear if the anticonvulsants are more or less efficacious than lithium in the management of bipolar depression.

Other pharmacological and non-pharmacological developments in the management of bipolar disorder

Antipsychotics

Although typical antipsychotics are used frequently in the treatment of mania, they may worsen postmanic depression. Their prophylactic use risks the induction of tardive dyskinesia. Recently, the role of atypical antipsychotic medications has been investigated in bipolar disorder. Olanzapine is newly licensed in the US for the treatment of acute mania, and other atypical antipsychotics such as risperidone have also shown anti-manic efficacy in randomised controlled trials. Further research on atypical antipsychotic medication in bipolar depression and in prophylaxis is underway[50].

Electroconvulsive therapy (ECT)

ECT is an effective treatment of bipolar disorder[51]. A 50-year review suggests that 66% of manic patients respond to ECT[52]. Furthermore, there is a good response to ECT in manic patients who have failed to respond to an antipsychotic or lithium[53]. Analysis of sequential therapeutic trials conducted over a 16-year period suggests that ECT followed by lithium maintenance is superior in efficacy to treatment with lithium or antipsychotics in hospitalised manic patients[54]. Maintenance or continuation ECT has been shown to reduce the incidence of relapse in patients with previously refractory depressive episodes[55].

Transcranial magnetic stimulation (TMS)

There is preliminary open evidence of therapeutic efficacy of TMS in bipolar disorder[56,57]. However, there are also reports of hypomania induced by TMS[58,59].

Thyroid hormones

The role of thyroid hormones in bipolar disorder continues to be investigated. Low levels of thyroxine (T_4) have been associated with more affective episodes during maintenance treatment with lithium[60]. Whether this mood instability is causally related to low free T4 levels and whether it can be attenuated with thyroxine replacement remain to be studied in a controlled setting. Open trials suggest efficacy for thyroxine as an augmenting agent in resistant bipolar depression and rapid cycling disorder[61,62].

Psycho-education and psychological treatments

Psycho-education and psychological treatments may be used to encourage healthy life-styles, to enhance coping strategies, to target early warning symptoms, to enhance compliance with medication and to address the psychosocial difficulties associated with the illness[2]. A recent RCT[63] examined the efficacy of bipolar patients' learning to identify early symptoms of recurrence and to seek help. These patients experienced delays in the onset of manic, but not depressive, episodes. Improvements in social functioning and employment were also reported. Patients with bipolar disorder in remission have higher levels of cognitive vulnerability to depression than healthy subjects, a possible target for psychological treatments[64]. Preliminary results of controlled trials of cognitive therapy for established bipolar depression are encouraging[65].

Conclusions

Bipolar affective disorder is a life-long condition with profound effects on sufferers' social and occupational life. Carbamazepine and valproate have become established as alternative and adjunctive treatments to lithium therapy. Despite these advances, treatment resistance in bipolar disorder persists. Of the newer anticonvulsants, lamotrigine has the largest evidence base for its mood stabilising effects. In particular, it appears to be efficacious in bipolar depression and rapid-cycling disorder, two areas in which treatment has proved difficult in the past. Further pharmacological and non-pharmacological developments are currently under investigation and hopes are high that this increased research activity will not only identify effective treatments but also lead to the development of early and specific predictors of response to individual treatments.

Key points for clinical practice

For prophylaxis of bipolar disorder:

- Lithium is best reserved for those with the classical form of the illness who are likely to be compliant. Non-compliance with lithium is a common and significant clinical problem

- The efficacy of carbamazepine in prophylaxis is not well established and its pharmacology leads to the need for careful vigilance for side effects and interactions with other drugs

- Valproate is the drug of choice in practice but the evidence base for its use is low. Monitoring for non-efficacy and side effects is necessary

- A variety of other drugs are in the process of evaluation and are best reserved for specialist use until further information is to hand

- All bipolar patients would benefit from psychosocial support and psycho-education. Specific forms of psychotherapy may be very helpful for selected cases

References

1   Goodwin GK, Jamieson KR. Manic-depressive illness. In: *Epidemiology*. Oxford: Oxford University Press, 1990; Chapter 7
2   Scott J. Psychotherapy for bipolar disorder. *Br J Psychiatry* 1995; **167**: 581–8
3   Murray CJ, Lopez AD. Global mortality, disability and the contribution of risk factors: global burden of disease study. *Lancet* 1997; **349**: 1436–42
4   Gelder M, Gath D, Mayou R, Cowen P. The epidemiology of mood disorders. In: *Oxford Textbook of Psychiatry*, 3rd edn. Oxford: Oxford University Press, 1996; 210–3
5   Department of Health. *Statistics for General Medical Practitioners in England: 1989–1999*. Department of Health Statistical Bulletin Number 2000/8. London, Department of Health, 2000
6   Post RM. Non-lithium treatment of bipolar disorder. *J Clin Psychiatry* 1990; **51**: 9–16
7   Ferrier IN, Tyrer SP, Bell AJ. Lithium therapy. *Adv Psychiatr Treat* 1995; **1**: 102–10
8   Johnson RE, McFarland BH. Lithium use and discontinuation in a health maintenance organisation. *Am J Psychiatry* 1996; **153**: 993–1000

9   Dickson WE, Kendell RE. Does maintenance lithium therapy prevent recurrence of mania under ordinary clinical conditions? *Psychol Med* 1986; **16**: 521–30

10   Goodwin G. Recurrence of mania after lithium withdrawal. Implications for the use of lithium in the treatment of bipolar affective disorder. *Br J Psychiatry* 1994; **164**: 149–52

11   Baldessarini RJ, Tondo L, Floris G, Rudas N. Reduced morbidity after gradual discontinuation of lithium treatment for bipolar I and II disorders: a replication study. *Am J Psychiatry* 1997; **154**: 551–3

12   Tondo L, Baldessarini RJ, Florence G, Rudas N. Effectiveness of restarting lithium treatment after its discontinuation in bipolar I and bipolar II disorders. *Am J Psychiatry* 1997; **154**: 548–50

13   Keck PE, Mendlwicz J, Calabrese JR *et al*. A review of randomized, controlled clinical trials in acute mania. *J Affect Disord* 2000; **59 (Suppl 1)**: S31–7

14   Sachs GS, Thase ME. Bipolar disorder therapeutics: maintenance treatment. *Biol Psychiatry* 2000; **48**: 573–81

15   Freeman MP, Stoll AL. Mood stabilizer combinations: a review of safety and efficacy. *Am J Psychiatry* 1998; **155**: 12–21

16   Battino, Dukes M, Perucca. Anticonvulsants. In: Dukes MNG & Aronson JK, eds. *Meyler's Side Effects of Drugs. An Encyclopaedia of Adverse Reactions and Interactions*, 14th edn. Amsterdam: Elsevier, 1996; 172–80

17   Nemeroff C, DeVane C, Pollock B. Newer antidepressants and the cytochrome P450 system. *Am J Psychiatry* 1996; **153**: 311–20

18   Swann AC, Bowden CL, Morris D *et al*. Depression during mania. Treatment response to lithium or divalproex. *Arch Gen Psychiatry* 1997; **54**: 37–42

19   Bowden CL, Calabrese JR, McElroy SL *et al*. A randomised placebo-controlled 12-month trial of divalproex and lithium in the treatment of outpatients with bipolar I disorder. Divalproex Maintenance Study Group. *Arch Gen Psychiatry* 2000; **57**: 490–2

20   Rasgon NL, Altshuler LL, Gudeman D *et al*. Medication status and polycystic ovary syndrome in women with bipolar disorder: a preliminary report. *J Clin Psychiatry* 2000; **61**: 173–8

21   Ichim L, Berk M, Brook S. Lamotrigine compared with lithium in mania: a double-blind randomised controlled trial. *Ann of Clin Psychiatry* 2000; **12**: 5–10

22   Calabrese JR, Bowden CL, Sachs GS, Ascher JA, Monaghan E, Rudd GD. A double-blind placebo-controlled study of lamotrigine monotherapy in out-patients with bipolar I depression. Lamictal 602 study group. *J Clin Psychiatry* 1999; **60**: 79–88

23   Frye M, Ketter T, Kimbrell T *et al*. A placebo-controlled evaluation of lamotrigine and gabapentin monotherapy in refractory mood disorders. *J Clin Psychopharmacol* 2000; **20**: 607–14

24   Calabrese JR, Suppes T, Bowden CL *et al*. A double-blind placebo-controlled prophylaxis study of lamotrigine in rapid-cycling bipolar disorder. *J Clin Psychiatry* 2001; **61**: 841–50

25   Besag FM, Ng GY, Pool F. Successful re-introduction of lamotrigine after initial rash. *Seizure* 2000; **9**: 282–6

26   Dubovsky SL, Buzan RD. Novel alternatives and supplements to lithium and anticonvulsants for bipolar affective disorder. *J Clin Psychiatry* 1997; **58**: 224–42

27   Dichter MA, Brodie MJ. New antiepileptic drugs. *N Engl J Med* 1996; **334**: 1583–90

28   Erfurth AK, Grunze CH, Normann C, Walden J. An open label study of gabapentin in the treatment of acute mania. *J Psychiatr Res* 1998; **32**: 261–4

29   Knoll JSK, Suppes T. Clinical experience using gabapentin adjunctively in patients with a history of mania or hypomania. *J Affect Disord* 1998; **49**: 229–33

30   Ghaemi SN, Katzow JJ, Desai SP, Goodwin FK. Gabapentin treatment of mood disorders: a preliminary study. *J Clin Psychiatry* 1998; **59**: 426–9

31   Pande A, Crockatt J, Janney C, Werth J, Tsaroucha G, Group at GBDS. Combination treatment in bipolar disorder. *Bipolar Disord* 2000; **2**: 249–55

32   McElroy SL, Suppes T, Keck PE *et al*. Open-label adjunctive topiramate in the treatment of bipolar disorders. *Biol Psychiatry* 2000; **47**: 1025–33

33   Marcotte D. Use of topiramate, a new anti-epileptic as a mood stabilizer. *J Affect Disord* 1998; **50**: 245–51

34   Normann C, Langosch J, Schaerer LO, Grunze H, Walden J. Treatment of acute mania with

topiramate. *Am J Psychiatry* 1999; **156**: 2014

35   Erfurth A, Kuhn G. Topiramate monotherapy in the maintenance treatment of bipolar I disorder: effects on mood, weight and serum lipids. *Neuropsychobiology* 2000; **42 (Suppl 1)**: 50–1

36   Schaffer LC, Schaffer CB. Tiagabine and the treatment of refractory bipolar disorder. *Am J Psychiatry* 1999; **156**: 2014–5

37   Kaufman KR. Adjunctive tiagabine treatment of psychiatric disorders: three cases. *Ann Clin Psychiatry* 1998; **10**: 181–4

38   Grunze H, Erfurth A, Marcuse A, Amann B, Normann C, Walden J. Tiagabine appears not to be efficacious in the treatment of acute mania. *J Clin Psychiatry* 1999; **60**: 759–62

39   Post RM, Weiss SRB, Chuang D-M. Mechanisms of action of anticonvulsants in affective disorders: comparison with lithium. *J Clin Psychopharmacol* 1992; **12**: 23S–35S

40   Bowden CL, Janicak PG, Orsulak P *et al*. Relation of serum valproate concentration to response in mania. *Am J Psychiatry* 1996; **153**: 765–70

41   Calabrese JR, Woyshville MJ, Kimmel SE, Rapport DJ. Predictors of valproate response in bipolar rapid cycling. *J Clin Psychopharmacol* 1993; **13**: 280–3

42   Champel V, Radal M, Moulin-Vallez M, Jonville-Bera AP, Autret-Leca E. Should folic acid be given to women treated with valproic acid and/or carbamazepine? Folic acid and pregnancy in epilepsy. *Rev Neurol* 1999; **155**: 220–4

43   Reiff-Eldridge R, Heffner CR, Ephross SA, Tennis PS, White AD, Andrews EB. Monitoring pregnancy outcomes after prenatal drug exposure through prospective pregnancy registries. A pharmaceutical company commitment. *Am J Obstet Gynecol* 2000; **182**: 159–63

44   Macritchie KA, Hunt N. Does rebound mania occur on stopping carbamazepine? *J Psychopharmacol* 2000; **14**: 266–8

45   Jamison KR. Suicide and bipolar disorder. *J Clin Psychiatry* 2000; **61**: 47–51

46   Simpson A, Jamison KR. The risk of suicide in patients with bipolar disorders. *J Clin Psychiatry* 1999; **60**: 53–6

47   Compton MT, Nemeroff CB. The treatment of bipolar depression. *J Clin Psychiatry* 2000; **61 (Suppl 9)**: 57–67

48   Bottlender R, Rudolf D, Strauss A, Möller H, Mood-stabilisers reduce the risk of developing antidepressant-induced maniform states in acute treatment of bipolar I depressed patients. *J Affect Disord* 2001; **63**: 79–83

49   Peet M. Induction of mania with selective serotonin re-uptake inhibitors and tricyclic antidepressants. *Br J Psychiatry* 1994; **164**: 549–50

50   Young AH, Macritchie KA, Calabrese JR. Treatment of bipolar affective disorder. New drug treatments are emerging, but more clinical evidence is required. *BMJ* 2000; **321**: 1302–3

51   Fink M. Convulsive therapy: a review of the first 55 years. *J Affect Disord* 2001; **63**: 1–15

52   Mukherjee S, Sackeim HA, Schnur DB. Electroconvulsive therapy of acute manic episodes: a review of 50 years' experience. *Am J Psychiatry* 1994; **151**: 169–76

53   Langsley D, Enterline J, Hickerson G. A comparison of chlorpromazine and ECT in treatment of schizophrenic and manic patients. *Arch Neurol Psychiatry* 1959; **81**: 384–91

54   Small JG, Klapper MH, Milstein V, Marhenke JD, Small IF. Comparison of therapeutic modalities for mania. *Psychopharmacol Bull* 1996; **32**: 623–7

55   Montgomery SA, Schatzberg AF, Guelfi JD *et al*. Pharmacotherapy of depression and mixed states in bipolar disorder. *J Affect Disord* 2000; **59**: S39–56

56   Erfurth A, Michael N, Mostert C, Arolt V. Euphoric mania and rapid transcranial magnetic stimulation. *Am J Psychiatry* 2000; **157**: 835–6

57   Grisaru N, Chudakov B, Yaroslavsky Y, Belmaker RH. Transcranial magnetic stimulation in mania: a controlled study. *Am J Psychiatry* 1998; **155**: 1608–10

58   Nedjat S, Folkerts HW. Induction of a reversible state of hypomania by rapid-rate transcranial magnetic stimulation over the left prefrontal lobe. *J Electroconvulsivether* 1999; **15**: 166–8

59   Garcia-Toro M. Acute manic symptomatology during repetitive transcranial magnetic stimulation in a patient with bipolar depression [letter]. *Br J Psychiatry* 1999; **175**: 491

60   Frye M, Denicoff K, Bryan A *et al*. Association between lower serum free T4 and greater mood instability and depression in lithium-maintained bipolar patients. *Am J Psychiatry* 1999; **156**: 1909–14

61 Bauer MS, Whybrow PC. Rapid cycling bipolar affective disorder. II. Treatment of refractory rapid cycling with high-dose levothyroxine: a preliminary study. *Arch Gen Psychiatry* 1990; **47**: 435–40

62 Stancer HC, Persad E. Treatment of intractable rapid-cycling manic-depressive disorder with levothyroxine. Clinical observations. *Arch Gen Psychiatry* 1982; **39**: 311–2

63 Perry A, Tarrier N, Morriss R, McCarthy E, Limb K. Randomised controlled trial of the efficacy of teaching patients with bipolar disorder to identify early symptoms of relapse and obtain treatment. *BMJ* 1999; **318**: 149–53

64 Scott J, Stanton B, Garland A, Ferrier IN. Cognitive vulnerability in patients with bipolar disorder. *Psychol Med* 2000; **30**: 467–72

65 Zaretsky AE, Segal ZV, Gemar M. Cognitive therapy for bipolar depression: a pilot study. *Can J Psychiatry* 1999; **44**: 491–4

Treatment delivery and guidelines in primary care

Robert Peveler and **Tony Kendrick**

Community Clinical Sciences Division, University of Southampton, Southampton, UK

Because depressive illness is so prevalent, the majority of patients are managed in primary care, without recourse to specialist services. Primary care management is seen to fall short of the standards set in secondary care, but unfortunately there is as yet relatively little evidence from primary care to guide management in this distinctive patient population. Guidelines have been introduced as a means of quality management, and their value in improving care has been assessed in trials. To date, the benefits of the implementation of guidelines have been marginal at best. By contrast, strategies which improve the access of patients to specialist services do seem to be beneficial. There is also evidence that such strategies may be associated with 'cost-offset'. Choice of antidepressant medication for maximum cost benefit should also be informed by an evidence base, which is beginning to be accumulated. Further research on this topic in the primary care context is still needed.

Depressive illness is a major public health problem, affecting 5–10% of the population annually, and associated with significant social and occupational disability. Because of its high prevalence, it is mostly managed in primary care, with only a minority of cases referred for specialist assessment and management[1]. Until recently, however, few general practitioners (GPs) in the UK or other countries have received training or specialist experience in the detection and management of depression and other common mental disorders. It is, therefore, not surprising that evidence has accumulated that depressive illness often goes unrecognized in primary care, and even when it is recognized it is often sub-optimally managed[2].

The evidence that treatments for depression are effective has almost all been gathered from secondary care, where the majority of large randomized treatment trials have been carried out. Such trials have inevitably recruited patients who have more severe or enduring depression than those usually encountered in primary care, raising doubts about the generalizability of their findings to primary care. However, until evidence is available directly from primary care trials, concern persists about the failure to deliver treatment consistently with current best evidence.

Correspondence to:
Prof R Peveler, University
Department of Psychiatry,
Royal South Hants
Hospital, Brintons
Terrace, Southampton
SO14 0YG, UK

The nature of practice in primary care brings particular difficulties, as well as opportunities. GPs do have the advantage of continuity of care, but usually work under considerable time pressure, with an average consultation time of only 8 min, and have to deal with the full range of physical and psychological aspects of medical care. The current diagnostic criteria for offering treatment were also developed in specialist practice and, like any criteria developed in secondary care, will have a lower positive predictive value in primary care, due to the relatively lower prevalence of the disorder[3]. This means there is a greater risk of 'false positives'. Because of concern about the consequences of labelling people as depressed unnecessarily, primary care practitioners tend to set a higher threshold for diagnosis[4].

Even when GPs do decide to offer treatment, they find that many people think antidepressants are addictive, do not like taking higher doses, and tend to want to stop treatment as soon as they start to feel better[5,6]. Such attitudes are, of course, far less common in patients who have already accepted referral to secondary care. The remainder of this chapter relies heavily on research comparing primary care practice with standards derived from specialist secondary care settings. The body of research evidence available directly from primary care is relatively much smaller, although now growing more rapidly.

Under-recognition of depression

It has been reported that depressive symptoms are not recognized in around 50% of attending patients with depressive disorders (ascertained by research diagnostic interview) in UK general practice[7-9]. Similar findings have been reported in the US, with detection rates found to be lower in patients in pre-paid health plans than for those in fee-for-service plans[10]. It is important to note though that many of these patients are actually consulting with physical symptoms, and furthermore, whilst depression may not be detected on a single visit, a proportion of the cases missed on that visit may be detected subsequently[11].

The actual proportion of treatable depression that is missed overall is, therefore, hard to estimate accurately, but most of the 'missed cases' are probably close to the threshold for diagnosis, and GPs probably recognize the large majority of patients with more severe depression[4]. For example, more than half of the undetected patients in one study had mild depression (low Hamilton rating scale scores and better social functioning), whereas only 7.5% of the missed patients were severely depressed[12]. It should be noted, in addition, that depression may also be recognised but not recorded[13], perhaps because of the stigma attached to the diagnosis, or its implications for possible increases in insurance premiums or difficulties obtaining or maintaining employment.

The clinical significance of non-recognition has also been questioned, with some experts suggesting this has been overstated[14,15.] Such findings are difficult to interpret, however, if recognition is not always followed by optimal management. Problems are also created by the tendency of the literature to regard depressive illness as a categorical diagnosis, without regard to the continuous distribution of severity and chronicity of depression observed in population studies[16]. The clinical utility of the diagnostic categories used by specialists requires further evaluation in primary care.

Quality of treatment

Antidepressant medication, brief focused psychological treatments and social interventions all have evidence to support their use in secondary care patients. In primary care, medication tends to be the mainstay of treatment, but there is evidence that it is often given in doses below those shown to be effective, and for periods shorter than those which have been shown to be necessary to prevent relapse and recurrence[17]. Non-drug treatments are also under-used, usually because they are difficult to access from primary care as a result of under-provision.

Most authorities believe that a categorical diagnosis of 'major depression' (DSM-IV)[18] represents the threshold at which antidepressant drug treatment is more effective than placebo. It is important to note, however, that the only direct evidence for this in UK primary care comes from a *post hoc* analysis of sub-groups with major and minor depression in one relatively small trial of amitriptyline[19], and may need to be revised in the light of further evidence. Further suggestive evidence supporting the use of this threshold comes from two studies, one of collaborative management[20] and one of compliance therapy[21] in which outcome was improved only in major depressive disorder subgroups.

Another 'structural' difficulty in primary care is that arrangements for routine follow-up, audit and monitoring of treated patients are not well established. Quality control of care is, therefore, difficult to establish even if adequate treatment has been commenced. Disease registers and special chronic disease clinics may represent a partial solution to this problem, but may be constrained by re-imbursement systems[22].

The proliferation of guidelines

In the light of the apparent shortcomings of primary care management, two principal approaches to improving the care of depressed patients in general practice have evolved. One is to improve care delivered by the primary care team, and the other is to improve access to specialist management. Initial efforts to improve care were largely focused on education of GPs in the disease area[23]. However, in the past decade, clinical guidelines have come to the fore as a potential vehicle to increase the impact of education and to support quality improvement initiatives. In 1992, the *Defeat Depression* campaign was launched, heavily based upon the first UK national guideline[2]. Similar initiatives and guideline development have taken place in other countries, including the US[24,25].

Ideally, a clinical guideline should take the form of a systematically developed set of statements designed to help practitioners and patients make decisions about appropriate health care for specific circumstances and should be based upon current best research evidence[26]. Initial attempts to produce guidelines often had significant weaknesses, and there are now clear guidelines for guideline development[27], accompanied by methods of assessing their quality. In short, guidelines have to be simple, specific and user-friendly with a focus on key decisions if they are to be used in routine practice; they must demonstrate how they are derived from research evidence in a way that is relevant to decisions about individual patients; and the evidence and recommendations must be presented in a concise accessible format.

A systematic review[28] concluded that guidelines were most likely to be adopted if local clinicians were involved in their development and had a sense of ownership; if they were disseminated through a specific educational programme; and were implemented with patient-specific reminders available during actual consultations. Attempts to introduce guidelines need to take account of best methods of dissemination, benefits and barriers to adoption, the extent of perception of need for change (*i.e.* recognition of unsatisfactory quality of existing care), the relative priority of the clinical topic, and the usefulness and ease of use of the guideline.

Unfortunately, guidelines may come to have purposes beyond simply enhancing clinical care, often being used as management tools by purchasers and providers of care to contain costs, and having inescapable legal and ethical consequences. This inevitably has had an impact upon their reception by health professionals, and may impede the purposes for which they were originally developed. Thus the development of a high quality guideline does not necessarily ensure its adoption in practice and automatically lead to improvement in quality of care. The costs of producing a guideline, though high, may be dwarfed by the costs of implementation and dissemination.

In the UK, GPs have been described as suffering from a 'tidal wave' of guidelines, with over 2000 guidelines or protocols for different clinical areas identified[27]. A useful review has assessed the quality of depression guidelines produced in Britain between 1991 and 1996[29]. Forty-five guidelines were identified over this period, and a critical appraisal instrument was used to assess the quality of all nine nationally produced guidelines, and a sample of the 36 local guidelines. Most of the guidelines were heavily based upon the earliest UK national guideline[2], adapted to reflect local priorities and circumstances. However, the known gaps in research evidence were clearly apparent in the review process. There was also considerable variation in the style in which information was presented to the clinician, ranging from in-depth discussion of latest research to simple lists of bullet points. The authors comment that debating the strengths and weaknesses of developing and using guidelines is a sterile exercise in the current climate, when the tidal wave shows no sign of abating.

Existing guidelines

The first national guideline on the recognition and management launched in the UK[2] was developed by a consensus conference, and drew explicitly upon available research evidence. Dissemination was via the regional organizations of the Royal College of General Practitioners, supported by a network of regional education fellows, and audio-visual materials including video, slides and booklets.

In 1993, the British Association for Psychopharmacology (BAP) produced their own guideline, with particular emphasis upon choice of drug treatment[30]. This guideline has subsequently been updated following a further consensus meeting in 1998, with the revised version being published in 2000[31]. Also published in 1993, the Department of Health in England commissioned an *Effective Health Care Bulletin* on depression, from the Centre for Health Economics at the University of York[32]. This guideline was notable for its emphasis upon use of cheaper and older medications as first-line treatments. The North of England evidence-based guideline development project produced a further British guideline in 1999[33]. Probably the most detailed current guideline is the American Agency for Health Care Policy and Research guideline (1993)[25].

The range and scope of all the guidelines is broadly similar, considering the epidemiology of depression, the diagnosis of depressive illness, and factors affecting recognition. Guidance for clinical assessment, assessment of suicide risk and initial management usually follows, and the guidelines then discuss longer-term management and prevention of recurrence, with variation in the degree of detail about choice of medication, how long to continue it, and how to stop it. Other issues covered (more variably) include dealing with diagnostic uncertainty and treatment failure, the presence of physical illness, physical complications and side-effects of treatment, other psychiatric co-morbidity including psychotic symptoms, and guidance on when to refer for specialist management. The current version of the BAP guideline[31] probably represents the best and most up-to-date guideline. Its recommendations are clearly summarised in helpful boxes within the text, and the explicit use of evidence is commendable.

Once guidelines have been developed and implementation has begun, it is necessary to address the thorny question of whether they are having any impact upon quality of care, and ultimately on patient outcome. There was preliminary evidence from the Gotland study that education of GPs led to improved patient outcome in terms of reduced sickness absence, hospital referrals, and an apparent fall in the suicide rate on the island, mirrored by a rise in the prescribing of antidepressants[23]. This evidence was based upon a before-and-after comparison rather than a controlled study, however, and the benefits seemed to wane quickly once the intervention was withdrawn[34]. Many evaluations of guidelines have concentrated upon improving the process of care[35,36] making the assumption that improved care must lead to better outcomes. Such an assumption may be unwarranted, however, and there is an obligation on researchers to tackle also the difficult task of seeking benefits in terms of outcome.

A study of guideline implementation: the Hampshire Depression Project

The only study in the UK to date which has attempted to evaluate the implementation of a guideline in terms of both quality of care and patient outcome was the *Hampshire Depression Project*[37], a pragmatic randomized controlled clinical trial of the implementation of a clinical guideline modelled upon that of Paykel and Priest[2]. It was based upon three assumptions: (i) that cases of depression can be reliably identified; (ii) that effective treatments can be generally applied; and (iii) that it is possible to modify the behaviour of health professionals through supported education. The main hypotheses tested were that a group of GPs who had received education built upon a clinical guideline would demonstrate improved recognition of depressive cases, and greater recovery rates in patients treated by their practice teams.

The guideline[38] was presented to the multidisciplinary practice teams via a carefully chosen education team consisting of a GP, a practice nurse and a psychiatric nurse carrying out visits to the intervention practices. Videos, written materials, small group teaching sessions and role play were used, and the educational approach was validated by external educational experts as of the best possible quality likely to be affordable for generalised administration to all practices if it proved to be effective. Great care was taken in training the team to avoid at all costs the perception that the education consisted of 'secondary care telling primary care what to do'. Sixty (out of 232) practices volunteered to take part in the study, and 59 were randomized to receive education immediately, or to wait to receive it in the second year of the study. Consecutive attending patients were screened, and practitioners were asked to indicate if they felt significant depression was present, to enable calculation of the recognition rate. Postal questionnaires at 6 weeks and 6 months were used to estimate recovery rates. The principal outcome variables were compared in the first year between educated and uneducated practices, both immediately after the end of the education sessions, and after a further period of 9 months. Attendance at educational events was good, and feedback from practice teams was strongly positive.

Although the guideline and education were regarded as being of high quality by external peer review, and the education team were perceived to be very helpful, competent and effective by participants, the main finding of the study was that they had no impact on the practitioners' ability to recognize depression, or on patient outcome. Recognized patients of educated practitioners did have better outcomes in the immediate aftermath of the education sessions, but this difference did not persist at follow-up, and was offset by a (non-significant) trend for unrecognized patients in the same practices to have worse outcomes.

There were no significant differences in the proportions of depressed patients prescribed antidepressants, or referred for psychiatric reasons, which might have supported the apparent improvement in short-term outcome. Levels of tricyclic antidepressant (TCA) prescribing were maintained at a significantly higher level in the intervention group, but antidepressant drug costs per patient treated were not significantly lower. Only 15% of those with possible, and 26% of those with probable, major depressive disorder were prescribed an adequate dosage and duration of treatment. Overall, the authors had to conclude that the apparent short-term benefit in patient outcomes in the intervention arm may have been a chance finding, and there were no significant savings in health service costs as a result of this relatively costly intervention.

The failure to observe any positive benefit could obviously have resulted from several factors, including limitations in the guideline itself, the design of the education, the delivery of the education or the design of the evaluation. The guideline was based upon current evidence, which has not changed dramatically since the study was conducted, and so cannot feasibly be improved upon at the present time. The educational approach followed the recommendations of Grimshaw and Russell[28], and so again reflected best practice both at the time of the study and today. Increasing the intensity of education further would have compromised the generalizability of the findings. It is possible that only the most motivated practices decided to take part, and this may have imposed a 'ceiling' effect on potential improvement, but this is unlikely as the performance of the practices was not noticeably better than that reported in previous studies.

The inclusion of prevalent cases introduced a conservative bias for the estimation of outcome, but reflects the reality of the clinical setting, where chronic depression is a large part of the problem. Significantly, around 90% of depressed patients were on non-psychiatric medication, and around 40% were referred to non-psychiatric specialist out-patient clinics, suggesting a high level of physical co-morbidity. The participating GPs might well have thought that if they could solve their patients' physical problems through these responses they would also reduce their psychological symptoms. The doctors' behaviour, therefore, seems to be in line with recent exhortations that we should respect the role of physical health problems in determining psychological disability and not just apply non-specific treatment with antidepressants or referral for psychological treatment[39,40].

An interesting *post hoc* finding of the *Hampshire Depression Project* was that the strongest predictor of both the prevalence of depressive illness and of its persistence was the measure of social deprivation of the area in which each practice was located[41]. This highlights the very important role of social factors in the causation and maintenance of depressive states, particularly for the less severely ill, and casts doubt on the statement in most guidelines that depression responds to medical treatment regardless of the influence of psychosocial factors in its causation. This effect is likely to be far more pronounced in a primary care population than in secondary care, and is an important area for further research. The results re-inforce the view that studies of implementation should not rely solely on the opinion of the participants or measures of process of care, but must include measures of patient outcomes.

Other interventions to improve quality

In contrast to the apparent failure of guideline-based education of practice teams to yield significant improvement in patient outcomes in the UK, studies based upon delivery of intensified treatment to selected populations of patients with major depression in the managed care context of the US have shown benefits. Katon *et al*[20,42] were able to demonstrate that in such a selected patient population intensified care incorporating patient education, shared care between the primary care physician, psychiatrist and psychologist (using a cognitive-behavioural approach), and a relapse prevention plan were associated with improved treatment adherence and patient recovery rates. This improvement in outcome was accompanied by a cost-offset effect such that the additional costs incurred by intensified treatment were compensated for by the improved success rate, resulting in a lower overall cost per case[43]. In a further study, patients who had failed to respond to 6–8 weeks of routine care in general practice were randomly assigned to receive intensified care from the specialist team or further routine care. Even in such relatively persistent cases, benefits from intensified collaborative management were identified.

These studies involved additional resources above and beyond those routinely available in primary care. Wells et al[44] investigated the dissemination of a quality improvement programme in which the additional costs of enhanced depression management were met by the practices themselves. Basing the programme upon the AHCPR guidelines, practice nursing staff were trained to become depression specialists, and to establish a case register of depressed patients within the practice. The nurses carried out regular review of medication. In a second intervention group of practices, enhanced access to cognitive-behavioural treatment was provided. Modest benefits in recovery rates were again demonstrated.

Taking a different approach, Simon et al investigated a telephone case management system operated by nurses[45]. At a relatively low cost (approximately £50 per patient), improvements in the number of patients receiving appropriate medication and in depression outcome were demonstrated. This finding was obtained without selecting only patients with major depression, although the proportion of patients included with milder forms of depression may still have been lower than is the case in UK general practice.

Confirming that such findings are not unique to the US, a further Southampton study demonstrated that minimal extra intervention by a nurse could enhance care. Two sessions with the patient of approximately 20 min focused upon the need for medication and appropriate utilization of medicines led to a significant improvement in adherence, and improved outcome in the subset of patients with major depression who were receiving prescriptions for adequate doses of treatment[21]. This approach is currently being tested further by application to primary care patients selected for the presence of major depression and adequate medication dosage in Ireland (Bradley, personal communication).

Cost-effectiveness of treatment in primary care

It has been suggested that, in spite of their higher unit cost, newer antidepressants may be more cost-effective than older tricyclics, as they may be better tolerated, and therefore, more effective in preventing costly treatment failure[30]. However, this has been the subject of considerable debate[46–48]. Meta-analyses of randomised trials comparing the two groups for their efficacy and discontinuation rates have found no overall difference in efficacy and only small absolute differences (around 3%) in drop-out rates, with more patients in the tricyclic groups citing side-effects as the reason for dropping out[49-52]. The advantage in drop-out rates for selective serotonin re-uptake inhibitors (SSRIs) holds only against the older, more toxic compounds (amitriptyline and imipramine) and not the newer tricyclics (dothiepin, nortriptyline, and clomipramine) or the 'heterocyclics' (mianserin, trazodone, desipramine and maprotiline)[53].

In these clinical trial populations, this advantage does not seem to be clinically important – the number needed to treat with SSRIs to prevent one drop-out is more than 30[53,54]. However, evidence from these trials may not be directly applicable to clinical practice in primary care, as trial populations are often selected for narrowly defined levels of severity of depression and the absence of co-morbid conditions, such as alcohol use, which might make the SSRIs a more attractive option. A study of the ratio of discontinuations to inceptions of treatment in routine general practice found an 11% difference (22% versus 33%) in favour of the SSRIs, and the reported perceptions of the GPs studied suggested that tolerability rather than lack of efficacy explained most of this difference[55]. Similarly Thompson et al[56] were able to show a 15% advantage in compliance for fluoxetine when compared with dothiepin in a primary care population.

As their patents expire, the SSRIs will become cheaper, although not nearly as cheap as the old tricyclics; therefore, this will not end the debate over cost-effectiveness. A cost-effectiveness comparison of imipramine, desipramine, and fluoxetine in a primary care population in Seattle, USA, funded by Lilly Research Laboratories (the makers of fluoxetine), found no significant differences in total healthcare costs over 6 months, with higher antidepressant costs in the fluoxetine group balanced by lower out-patient and in-patient costs[57]. However, it has been pointed out that these findings may not generalise to the UK given the very different patterns of health-care utilisation[58]. We are currently carrying out a study of the relative cost-effectiveness of TCAs, SSRIs, and lofepramine in a more representative sample of UK general practice patients (the AHEAD study).

Implications for future practice and organization of depression management in primary care

As the primary care research agenda has begun to be pursued, a number of messages now seem to be becoming clearer. The first and probably most important discovery is that primary care differs from secondary care in a number of important ways, and it is unwise to extrapolate research evidence beyond the limits of its applicability. The content of guidelines may have to change as new evidence is accumulated, for example about the efficacy of medication in patients with significant social difficulties or milder forms of depression, and about the most effective forms of brief psychological treatment. The threshold at which drug treatment becomes more effective than placebo needs definition as soon as possible, and this information can only be derived from a large pragmatic treatment trial in primary care.

Secondly the extent to which depression should be seen as a chronic disease rather than as an episodic acute illness needs further consideration. The management of chronic diseases is often more effectively organised through the provision of special clinic sessions outside routine surgeries, usually staffed by practice nurses. Such 'mini-clinics' have been shown to improve the outcome of asthma[59] and diabetes[60], and are now widespread in UK general practice, encouraged by the provision of special chronic disease management payments. Special clinic sessions usually feature systematic assessment of symptoms, treatment effects, and side-effects; protocols for modifying management; and pro-active follow-up, with outreach to non-attenders. It is becoming clear that some aspects of the management of depression lend themselves well to this approach.

There is good evidence that, as well as improving adherence to drug treatment[21], practice nurses can be trained to deliver effective structured psychological treatments such as problem-solving in primary care[61]. The US models of intensified case management suggest further research designs for UK teams to adopt, and the development of primary care groups and trusts in England and Wales creates an opportunity to develop sub-specialisation at primary care level, similar to that possible within US-style Health Maintenance Organizations.

Key points for clinical practice

- The prevalence of depressive illness and the nature of mental health service provision dictate that the large majority of patients with depression are managed in primary care

- By comparison with standards derived from secondary care, primary care management often appears to be sub-optimal, but generalising research findings from secondary to primary care settings may not be justified

- Guidelines and education alone are of limited effectiveness in improving primary care management

- Provision of enhanced care supported by additional resource has been shown to be of benefit, involving either placing or developing more specialised workers in primary care

- The benefits of psychological treatments of proven effectiveness are constrained by limited availability in most healthcare systems, while resources are being spent on other treatments of unproven effectiveness, such as non-directive counselling

References

1   Goldberg DP, Huxley P. *Mental Illness in the Community. The Pathway to Psychiatric Care.* London: Tavistock, 1980

2   Paykel ES, Priest RG. Recognition and management of depression in general practice: consensus statement. *BMJ* 1992; **305**: 1198–202

3   McWhinney IR. *An Introduction to Family Medicine.* Oxford: Oxford University Press, 1981

4   Dowrick C. Case or continuum? Analysing general practitioners' ability to detect depression. *Prim Care Psychiatry* 1995; **1**: 255–7

5   Priest RG, Vize C, Roberts A, Roberts M, Tylee A. Lay people's attitude to treatment of depression: results of opinion poll for Defeat Depression Campaign just before its launch. *BMJ* 1996; **313**: 858–9

6   Kendrick T. Why can't GPs follow guidelines on depression? We must question the basis of the guidelines themselves. *BMJ* 2000; **320**: 200–1

7   Marks J, Goldberg DP, Hillier VF. Determinants of the ability of general practitioners to detect psychiatric illness. *Psychol Med* 1979; **9**: 337–53

8   Freeling P, Rao BM, Paykel ES, Sireling LI, Burton RH. Unrecognised depression in general practice. *BMJ* 1985; **290**: 1880–3

9   Dowrick C, Buchan I. Twelve month outcome of depression in general practice: does detection or disclosure make a difference? *BMJ* 1995; **311**: 1274–6

10 Wells KB, Hays RD, Burnam MA *et al.* Detection of depressive disorders for patients receiving prepaid or fee-for-service care: Results from the medical outcomes study. *JAMA* 1989; **262**: 3298–302

11 Freeling P, Tylee A. Depression in general practice. In: Paykel ES. (ed) *Handbook of Affective Disorders.* Edinburgh: Churchill Livingstone, 1992; 651–6

12 Simon GE, von Korff M. Recognition, management, and outcomes of depression in primary care. *Arch Fam Med* 1995; **4**: 98–105

13 Rost KG, Smith GR, Guise B, Matthews D. The deliberate misdiagnosis of major depression in primary care. *Arch Fam Med* 1994; **3**: 333–7

14 Ormel J, Tiemens B. Recognition and treatment of mental illness in primary care. Towards a better understanding of a multifaceted problem. *Gen Hosp Psychiatry* 1995; **17**: 160–4

15 Barrett J. The role of psychiatry in the management of depressive disorders in primary care. In: Michels R, Cooper AM, Guze SB *et al.* (eds) *Psychiatry.* Philadelphia: Lippincott-Raven, 1997

16 Anderson J, Huppert F, Rose G. Normality, deviance and minor psychiatric morbidity in the community. *Psychol Med* 1993; **23**: 475–85

17 Dunn RL, Donoghue JM, Ozminski RJ, Stephenson D, Hylan TR. Longitudinal patterns of antidepressant prescribing in primary care in the UK: comparison with treatment guidelines. *J Psychopharmacol* 1999; **13**: 136–43

18 American Psychiatric Association. *Diagnostic and Statistical Manual of Mental Disorders*, 4th edn. Washington, DC: American Psychiatric Association Press, 1994

19 Paykel ES, Hollyman JA, Freeling P, Sedgwick P. Predictors of therapeutic benefit from amitriptyline in mild depression: a general practice placebo-controlled trial. *J Affect Disord* 1988; **14**: 83–95

20 Katon W, von Korff M, Lin E *et al.* Collaborative management to achieve treatment guidelines. Impact on depression in primary care. *JAMA* 1995; **273**: 1026–31

21 Peveler R, George C, Kinmonth A-L, Campbell M, Thompson C. Effect of antidepressant drug counselling and information leaflets on adherence to drug treatment in primary care: randomised controlled trial. *BMJ* 1999; **319**: 612–5

22 Kendrick T. Depression management clinics in general practice? Some aspects lend themselves to the mini-clinic approach. *BMJ* 2000; **320**: 527–8

23 Rutz W, von Knorring L, Walinder J, Winstedt B. Effect of an educational programme for general practitioners on the pattern of prescription of psychotropic drugs. *Acta Psychiatr Scand* 1990; **82**: 399–403

24 AHCPR Depression Guideline Panel. *Depression in Primary Care: Volume 1. Detection and Diagnosis. Clinical Practice Guideline Number 5*, Rockville, MD: US Department of Health and Human Services, Public Health Service, Agency for Health Care Policy and Research, 1993

25 AHCPR Depression Guideline Panel. *Depression in Primary Care: Volume 2. Treatment of Major Depression. Clinical Practice Guideline Number 5*, Rockville, MD: US Department of Health and Human Services, Public Health Service, Agency for Health Care Policy and Research, 1993

26 Field MJ, Lohr KN. *Guidelines for Clinical Practice: From Development to Use*. Washington DC: National Academy Press, 1992

27 Jackson R, Feder G. Guidelines for clinical guidelines. *BMJ* 1998; **317**: 427–8

28 School of Public Health, University of Leeds and Centre for Health Economics, University of York. *Effective Health Care Bulletin: Implementing Clinical Practice Guidelines 8*. York: Department of Health, 1994

29 Littlejohns P, Cluzeau F, Bale R, Grimshaw G, Feder G, Moran S. The quantity and quality of clinical practice guidelines for the management of depression in primary care in the UK. *Br J Gen Pract* 1999; **49**: 205–10

30 Montgomery SA. Guidelines for treating depressive illness with antidepressants. *J Psychopharmacol* 1993; **7**: 19–23

31 Anderson IM, Nutt DJ, Deakin JFW. Evidence-based guidelines for treating depressive disorders with antidepressants: a revision of the 1993 British Association for Psychopharmacology guidelines. *J Psychopharmacol* 2000; **14**: 3–20

32 School of Public Health, University of Leeds and Centre for Health Economics, University of York. *Effective Health Care Bulletin: The Treatment of Depression in Primary Care, 5*. York, Department of Health, 1993

33 Eccles M, Freemantle N, Mason J. North of England evidence-based guideline development project: summary version of guidelines for the choice of antidepressants for depression in primary care. *Fam Pract* 1999; **16**: 103–11

34 Rutz W, von Knorring L, Walinder J. Long-term effects of an educational program for general practitioners given by the Swedish Committee for the Prevention and Treatment of Depression. *Acta Psychiatr Scand* 1992; **85**: 83–8

35 Feder G, Griffiths C, Highton C, Eldridge S, Spence M, Southgate L. Do clinical guidelines introduced with practice based education improve care of asthmatic and diabetic patients? A randomised controlled trial in general practices in East London. *BMJ* 1995; **311**: 1473–8

36 Hannaford PC, Thompson C, Simpson M. Evaluation of an educational programme to improve the recognition of psychological illness by general practitioners. *Br J Gen Pract* 1996; **46**: 333–7

37 Thompson C, Kinmonth A-L, Stevens L *et al*. A randomised controlled trial of the effects of a clinical practice guideline and practice based education on the detection and outcome of depression in primary care: the Hampshire Depression Project. *Lancet* 2000; **355**: 185–91

38 Stevens L, Kinmonth A-L, Peveler R, Thompson C. The Hampshire Depression Project: development and piloting of clinical practice guidelines and education about depression in primary health care. *Med Educ* 1997; **31**: 375–9

39 Heath I. Commentary: there must be limits to the medicalisation of human distress. *BMJ* 1999; **318**: 439–40

40 Middleton H, Shaw I. Distinguishing mental illness in primary care. We need to separate proper syndromes from generalised distress. *BMJ* 2000; **320**: 1420–1

41 Ostler K, Thompson C, Kinmonth A-L, Peveler RC, Stevens L, Stevens A. Influence of socio-economic deprivation on the prevalence and outcome of depression in primary care. *Br J Psychiatry* 2001; **178**: 12–7

42 Katon W, Robinson P, von Korff M *et al*. A multifaceted intervention to improve treatment of depression in primary care. *Arch Gen Psychiatry* 1996; **53**: 924–32

43 von Korff M, Katon W, Bush T *et al*. Treatment costs, cost-offset and cost-effectiveness of collaborative management of depression. *Psychosom Med* 1998; **60**: 143–9

44 Wells KB, Schoenbaum M, Unutzer J, Lagomasino IT, Rubenstein LV. Impact of disseminating quality improvement programs for depression in managed primary care. *Arch Fam Med* 1999; **8**: 529–36

45 Simon GE, von Korff M, Rutter C, Wagner E. Randomised trial of monitoring, feedback, and management of care by telephone to improve treatment of depression in primary care. *BMJ* 2000; **320**: 550–4

46   Jonsson B, Bebbington PE. What price depression? The cost of depression and the cost-effectiveness of pharmacological treatment. *Br J Psychiatry* 1994; **164**: 665–73

47   Freemantle N, House A, Mason J, Song F, Sheldon T. Economics of treatment of depression. *Br J Psychiatry* 1995; **166**: 397

48   Woods SW, Rizzo JA. Cost-effectiveness of antidepressant treatment reassessed. *Br J Psychiatry* 1997; **170**: 257–63

49   Song F, Freemantle N, Sheldon TA *et al*. Selective serotonin re-uptake inhibitors: meta-analysis of efficacy and acceptability. *BMJ* 1993; **306**: 683–7

50   Montgomery SA, Henry J, McDonald G *et al*. Selective serotonin reuptake inhibitors: meta-analysis of discontinuation rates. *Int Clin Psychopharmacol* 1994; **9**: 47–53

51   Anderson IM, Tomenson BM. Treatment discontinuation with selective serotonin reuptake inhibitors compared with tricyclic antidepressants: a meta-analysis. *BMJ* 1995; **310**: 1433–8

52   Geddes J, Freemantle N, Mason J, Eccles M, Boynton J. *SSRIs versus other Antidepressants for Depressive Disorder*. Cochrane Library Document. Oxford, Cochrane Database of Systematic Reviews, 1999

53   Hotopf M, Hardy R, Lewis G. Discontinuation rates of SSRIs and tricyclic antidepressants: a meta-analysis and investigation of heterogeneity. *Br J Psychiatry* 1997; **170**: 120–7

54   Gilbody S, Sheldon T, Song F, House A. Prescribing antidepressants in general practice. Costs should have been considered. *BMJ* 1997; **314**: 828

55   Martin RM, Hilton SR, Kerry SM, Richards NM. General practitioners' perceptions of the tolerability of antidepressant drugs: a comparison of selective serotonin reuptake inhibitors and tricyclic antidepressants. *BMJ* 1997; **314**: 646–51

56   Thompson C, Peveler RC, Stephenson D, McKendrick J. Compliance with antidepressant medication in the treatment of major depressive disorder in primary care: a randomized comparison of fluoxetine and a tricyclic antidepressant. *Am J Psychiatry* 2000; **157**: 338–43

57   Simon GE, von Korff M, Heiligenstein JH *et al*. Initial antidepressant choice in primary care. Effectiveness and cost of fluoxetine vs tricyclic antidepressants. *JAMA* 1996; **275**: 1897–902

58   Dowrick C. Depression. In: Gabbay M. (ed) *The Evidence-Based Primary Care Handbook*. London: Royal Society of Medicine Press, 1999; 215–22

59   Charlton I, Charlton G, Broomfield J *et al*. An evaluation of a nurse-run asthma clinic in general practice using an attitudes and morbidity questionnaire. *Fam Pract* 1992; **9**: 154–60

60   Parnell SJ, Zalin AM, Clarke C. Care of diabetic patients in hospital clinics and general practice: a study in Dudley. *Br J Gen Pract* 1993; **43**: 65–9

61   Mynors-Wallis LM, Davies I, Gray A, Barbour F, Gath D. A randomised controlled trial and cost analysis of problem-solving treatment for emotional disorders given by community nurses in primary care. *Br J Psychiatry* 1997; **170**: 113–9

Lay attitudes to professional consultations for common mental disorder: a sociological perspective

Roisin Pill*, Lindsay Prior† and Fiona Wood†

*Department of General Practice, University of Wales College of Medicine and †Cardiff School of Social Sciences, Cardiff, UK

How, why, and under what kinds of circumstances lay people consult for symptoms of emotional distress are topics that have commanded various degrees of attention from secondary and primary care professionals. We argue below that many of the responses made by such professionals to these issues carry within them a set of very important assumptions about how members of the lay public view psychiatric symptoms. Whether such assumptions are justified by the evidence is, however, a matter of some debate. In what follows we draw on some recent, sociologically informed research on lay attitudes to emotional distress so as to highlight the debates and to suggest some ways in which they might be resolved.

The professional perspective

Understandably, most of the papers written about depression and its management in the UK are by psychiatrists, although there is a small but growing literature by general practitioner (GP) researchers. The majority of the latter tend to follow the lines laid down by the specialists though, increasingly, the approaches used and interpretation of findings are being queried by some researchers and commentators coming from a primary care background[1,2].

Certain themes found in much of the psychiatric literature on mental illness occur repeatedly in papers about depression in the UK: the seriousness of the condition; the need to ensure that sufferers receive the most effective treatment available; the existence of an unacceptable amount of 'under-treatment'; the importance attached to the role of stigma in contributing to under-treatment; the increasing recognition of the key role that the GP, rather than the specialist, must play in resolving this gap.

Thus we are told that diagnoses of anxiety and depression have a prevalence of about 16% in the UK[3,4]. Moreover, 15–30% of sickness absence can be attributed to these disorders and the associated disability

Correspondence to: Prof. Roisin Pill, Department of General Practice, Llanedeyrn Health Centre, Maelfa, Llanedeyrn, Cardiff CF23 9PN, UK

is comparable to most chronic medical conditions[5,6]. As far as psychiatrists are concerned, there is now good evidence that effective pharmacological and psychological treatments exist for more severe cases of depression and anxiety[7,8]. This is generally accepted among health professionals though some doubt has been expressed about the efficacy of treatment for the mild/moderate cases often seen in primary care[9] or indeed whether it is appropriate to attempt to screen[1] or case-find[2]. While about 90% of people regarded by psychiatrists as having symptoms of depression and anxiety are treated within primary care[10], it has been estimated that possibly as many as 50% of cases go undetected in the GPs surgery[11].

To date, research has concentrated on exploring the perceived failure of GPs to recognise psychiatric disorder with less attention being paid to the reasons why patients may be reluctant to disclose symptoms to their GP. Most psychiatric work on this topic has invoked the concept of 'somatisation'. This is a complex construct, with several different definitions though most require the physical complaint to be ' caused' by the psychiatric disorder. Somatisation defined in this way is relatively uncommon and is found in about 3% of attendees in UK primary care. In contrast, it is relatively common in patients with physical complaints who also have psychiatric disorder and has been estimated as up to 25% of those consulting. It has been suggested that this can be called 'somatic presentation', *i.e.* the patient has a psychiatric disorder (as defined by the specialists) and consults about physical symptoms that may or may not be related to their psychiatric disorder[12].

Most studies have concentrated on the interviewing skills of the doctor[13] and on developing and testing interventions designed to improve detection. There is, indeed, evidence to show that such interventions designed to teach more effective interviewing skills can improve detection rates[14], but it is clear that if patients were readier to discuss emotional problems with their GP this could also dramatically increase the likelihood of recognition. For example, Weich *et al*[12] showed that GPs detected about 20% of the cases of psychiatric morbidity who presented with physical symptoms, 53% of those presenting with both emotional and physical symptoms, and 100% of those who complained of emotional problems. Another recent study[15] has found a strong association between detection by the GP and the psychological style of attribution employed by the patient. In particular, those who 'normalise', *i.e.* find common-sense explanations for their symptoms, are less likely to be detected. These findings suggest that more attention could usefully be paid to exploring people's attitudes to their symptoms and their views about the appropriateness of the services available to them in primary care in order to understand their behaviour in consultations with their GP. In the following section, we examine the work has been undertaken on this topic in the mental health field.

How professionals interpret lay responses

Lay (and professional) attitudes towards mental illness have received greater attention in medical journals in recent years. The context of discussion has usually concerned difficulties surrounding the delivery of effective and timely treatment to those who could benefit. As noted above, 'under-treatment' is seen as the key problem, and lay attitudes are perceived as potential barriers needing to be changed. Thus one of the activities of the 1992 *Defeat Depression Campaign*, supported by both the Royal Colleges of Psychiatrists and General Practitioners, was a survey[16] of public attitudes 'to know which attitudes needed to change and to measure the effectiveness of the campaign in promoting those changes'. The opinions singled out as problematic were the association of stigma with depression, the ambivalence about consulting a family doctor (possibly on account of stigma), and the view that antidepressants were addictive and not particularly effective.

More recently in 1998, the Royal College of Psychiatrists launched another 5–year campaign aimed at the public in general called *Changing Minds; Every Family in the Land*. This was designed to reduce the stigmatisation experienced by people with mental problems and to close the gap between professional and public assessment of treatment by 'de-mythologising' six categories of common mental disorder, including depression[17]. As with many other medical specialities, the perception is that any discrepancy between professional and lay attitudes and beliefs about symptoms, diseases, appropriate behaviour by the sufferer and treatment is generally due to ignorance, prejudice and misunderstanding on the part of the patient. The solution is seen in re-education through the provision of information. Thus, in a recent review article, Jorm summarises his findings as follows[18]:

Many members of the public cannot recognise specific disorders or different types of psychological distress. They differ from mental health experts in their beliefs about the causes of mental disorders and the most effective treatments. Attitudes which hinder recognition and appropriate help-seeking are common. Much of the mental health information most readily available to the public is misleading. However, there is some evidence that mental health literacy (defined as 'knowledge and beliefs about mental disorders which aid their recognition, management and prevention') can be improved.

In relation to the common mental disorders, such as depression, it is very striking how few data there are on the perceptions, beliefs and help-seeking behaviour of people within the UK. Research within Britain has been largely stimulated by concern with the clinical problems that arise in diagnosis and treatment of common mental disorders when professionals and patients come from different cultures – and particularly different ethnic groups[19]. A more recent example can be found in the, as yet, unpublished work of Lloyd and colleagues that has investigated explanatory models of Afro-Caribbean patients in British primary care.

Much of the published work has focused on trying to understand the reasons for not consulting the GP rather than describing beliefs about illness and symptoms. This is perhaps understandable given the fact that only about 5% of those recognised in primary care as emotionally distressed are referred on to mental health services[20] – a figure that has apparently changed little over the years[11].

Existing data on lay views about help-seeking

Given the emphasis on help-seeking, UK studies largely reflect the concerns and assumptions of the health professionals. Thus research has been carried out mainly on service users, and their carers, and/or family members or those defined as in need of psychiatric treatment. This needs to be borne in mind when considering the findings. There appears to be no equivalent in Britain of some of the large-scale surveys of the views of the general public quoted by Jorm[18] for other countries. For example, one German national survey[21] of attitudes towards help-seeking for psychiatric disorder and their determinants found that, for depression, public opinion clearly favoured the lay support system and believed in involving the family physician only if the former resource was exhausted.

The most recent relevant British data have come from the large-scale epidemiological survey, the *OPCS National Survey of Psychiatric Morbidity*. All participants were asked whether they had consulted about an emotional problem within the previous 12 months. Of the 10,000 subjects. 12% had done so, and there appeared to an increased likelihood of so doing among the middle-aged and older people, women and the unemployed.

Using the CIS-R[22] on the OPCS data, Meltzer *et al*[23,24] suggest that roughly 1 in 4 of those people with a neurotic disorder who failed to attend a GP did not think that anyone could help them or that the GP was an appropriate person to deal with their problem. Approximately 1 in 5 of this group appeared to disagree that they had a problem to be dealt with. Similarly, in their analysis as to why these people turned down help that was offered to them, it seems that roughly one-half said that they did not need help and one-quarter that no one could help.

Similar findings were quoted by Cape and McCulloch[25], who carried out post consultation interviews with a sample of primary care patients who had planned to present only somatic symptoms to their GP despite the fact they had high GHQ scores. The most frequently cited reasons that patients gave for not mentioning psychiatric problems to their GPs were: 'Doctors have insufficient time' and 'That there is nothing the doctor can do'.

The relationship between research methods and research findings

In the examples quoted above, the data have come from cross-sectional surveys on patients. Generally, they have employed highly structured questionnaires. While such studies allow data collection from large numbers of people on a variety of indicators thus facilitating the use of sophisticated quantitative approaches, they provide very little opportunity for inquiring about how subjects actually interpret the issues that are placed before them. To gather data on how lay people (rather than professionals) interpret the world and its problems, qualitative methods are required. Such methods enable people to speak in their own terms and to order discussion in their frame of priorities.

A sociological perspective

Research on lay attitudes to mental illness

Having criticised the professional psychiatric literature for the relative lack of attention paid to exploring why individuals in the community are not only apparently so reluctant to seek medical help but also to disclose emotional symptoms/problems to their GP once in the consulting room, it has to be admitted that there is very little in the sociological literature either – at least from the point of view of the general public.

Work on mental illness has been mainly concerned with various aspects of secondary care: for example, such topics as patient experiences and views about services[26], aspects of professional practice including studies of relationships between health professionals in psychiatry[27], and studies of the diagnostic process and its consequences[28]. Work has also been published on what is seen as gender issues in mental illness[29,30]. What sociology **can** offer is a body of research on lay and professional encounters and professional and lay beliefs about health and illness. Such studies offer insights into ways in which topics such as this could be most fruitfully explored.

Sociologists and anthropologists start from the position that each culture (norms, beliefs and behaviour of particular social groups) provides its members with ways of becoming 'ill', of shaping their suffering into a recognisable illness entity, of explaining its cause and of getting some treatment for it[31]. Thus cultures influence the 'language of distress', *i.e* the means by which personal distress is communicated to other people. Both the presentation of illness and others' response to it, are largely determined by sociocultural factors[32].

Over the last 30 years, medical sociologists have traditionally examined and described the social patterning of beliefs about illness in Britain. They have looked at the ways in which these are related to help-seeking behaviour, and examined the crucial role of the medical profession in defining, legitimating and treating illness[33]. For example, they have introduced concepts that distinguish between illness (the subjective experience of symptoms), and disease (the objective pathological entity). They have further distinguished between clinical and lay 'explanatory models', and have analysed the process of help-seeking. This body of work can provide a useful counterpoint to the purely professional view of the world.

For example, it is well-known that only a small proportion of those in the community experiencing either mental or physical symptoms, that a doctor would consider indicative of disease and requiring medical treatment, ever actually present them to their GP. An even smaller percentage of these individuals are then referred on to specialists in secondary care[33]. Mental health problems, including depression, are no exception to this pattern. A number of studies confirm the existence of a clinical iceberg; the organised, legally-sanctioned professional health services treat only the tip of the sum total of ill-health.

Within any modern urbanised society such as Britain, there will also be a large number of therapeutic options potentially available to people. These will range from self-treatment, folk-remedies, advice from family and friends, and increasingly the Internet, over-the-counter pharmaceutical preparations, unofficial and alternative healers, and healers from other non-Western traditions. People make choices about what to do, and who to consult, on the basis of such factors as perceived availability, whether payment has to be made, and the explanatory models (EMs) that they hold, *i.e.* the particular set of beliefs marshalled in order to deal with the current episode of illness. Such EMs are typically rather idiosyncratic and changeable, heavily influenced by both personality and cultural factors, and need to be understood by examining the circumstances in which they are employed[34,35]. The concept of EM has proved a useful tool for looking at the process by which lay people organise and manage episodes of impaired well-being.

Lay views on disclosure of emotional problems in primary care: an illustration

The lack of any previous body of work on this topic was the stimulus for our exploratory study of lay attitudes in Wales. We argued that there was a need to look at the beliefs and attitudes of the general public who may never have come into contact with psychiatry and psychiatrists and who may or may not have presented any symptoms of common mental disorder in primary care. (These, after all, provide the background and the resources from which any one individual constructs his or her explanatory models, seeks to make sense of symptoms, and does or does not take remedial action.)

We wanted to see what beliefs are held in common, the extent to which people feel it is appropriate to disclose emotional distress to a professional, and their assessment of the likelihood of any improvement of their symptoms as a result.

Our purpose here is not to give full details of our findings but, by concentrating on the choices made in the study design, and illustrating the kind of data collected and the way it was analysed, to give the reader some concept of the possibilities of qualitative research, and its potential for increasing understanding of complex processes and developing and testing hypotheses.

An outline of the project

The findings are derived from an all-Wales study of community-based groups stratified by age and sex. Researchers based in University of Wales College of Medicine and Cardiff University asked 20 groups of people (n = 127) to discuss issues relating to reluctance or failure to consult the doctor. Groups were recruited in rural mid Wales, urban West and Southeast Wales, and in the South Wales valleys through a network of general practices associated with the Department of General Practice. Ten of the groups comprised only females and 10 only males. Six groups contained people aged 18–25 years, 6 contained people aged 35–45 years, and 8 contained people aged 55–70 years. Participants were not required to have consulted for emotional symptoms at any point in their lives (though some had done). Focus group techniques were used to generate data, and the data were analysed according to established principles of qualitative social science research.

Choice of method: focus groups

Focus groups[37] were selected as the method for data collection because they are regarded as especially appropriate for the study of attitudes and experiences around specific topics and exploring the participants' priorities, their language and concepts. Kitzinger[38] argues that this method can 'reach the parts that other methods cannot reach, revealing dimensions of understanding that often remain untapped by more conventional data collection techniques'.

The crucial distinction between focus groups (*i.e.* group discussions organised to explore a specific set of issues) and the broader category of group interviews is the explicit use of group interaction as research data. Compared to the two more well-known methods of data collection, questionnaires and one-to-one interviews, focus groups are better for exploring how points of view are constructed and expressed in public settings. Norms and priorities can be highlighted and differences in assumptions thrown into relief by the questions the participants ask of each other, the sources they cite and what explanations appear to sway opinions of other members of the group. Our interest was in understanding the reasoning behind the weight accorded to various factors suggested as influential in the choices people make about consulting, and then about disclosing emotional problems.

The choice of subjects

It was felt that a common background and similar life-cycle experience would facilitate interaction and maximum freedom of expression. Given our intention to compare the views of participants with potentially differing attitudes, behaviours and understandings of emotional problems and their treatment, this decision enabled us to utilise the powerful strategy of comparing and contrasting the perspectives of homogenous groups. Age and sex were already known to be significantly linked with readiness to consult from the OPCS morbidity surveys and we were anxious to tap people from different communities with very different cultural and socio-economic histories to see how far the experience of varied social groups was reflected in the discussion.

Conduct of the focus group

The meetings were conducted by a moderator and were audio-taped (with consent) for later transcription and analysis. The discussion was structured around a number of tasks designed to facilitate discussion. The first, and most important of these, was to respond to short descriptions of the basic demographic characteristics, current situation and symptoms experienced by three individuals. The purpose of these vignettes was to explore respondents' recognition, diagnosis and response to a range of physical and emotional symptoms. Two were adapted from those previously created by the Institute of Psychiatry[39] and have been used in this research project with their kind permission. The example of Miss Jones is of particular interest as it includes a constellation of symptoms and variables that many health professionals would regard as indicative of quite severe depression.

Miss Jones is a 29-year-old single parent with two small children. They live on a fairly run-down estate and rely on benefits. She feels low in energy, has lost weight, is not sleeping properly and feels terrible in the mornings. She also feels that she has no self-confidence and that the future holds nothing for her. At times, if it were not for the children she wonders if it would be worth going on. Her relatives visit her from time-to-time, but they are not prepared to contribute to childcare.

Two main questions were added in relation to each vignette: What is wrong with the person? What (if anything) should they do about it? At this point our particular interest in emotional problems and disclosure had not been made explicit as we wished to explore to what extent the various groups recognised symptom patterns as indicative of common mental disorder. Our agenda was made explicit or confirmed after having obtained the initial spontaneous reactions to the three vignettes.

Analysis

As with surveys, the context in which data are collected inevitably affects the nature of the material collected and we treated the transcripts as 'accounts', recognising that participants would be likely to produce arguments or opinions that they felt would be acceptable to voice in public. Like other qualitative analyses, the key process is the drawing together and comparison of similar themes and examining how these relate to the variation between individuals and between groups. However, with focus groups, the researcher must start from an analysis of groups and seek to strike a balance between the picture provided by the group as a whole and the operation of the individual voices within it. Thus we tried to distinguish between the opinions expressed in spite of, or in opposition to, the group and the consensus constructed by the group.

Once the first few tapes had been transcribed, an initial coding frame was developed by the research team. Disagreements about emergent themes led to further clarification and refinement of the basic categories we were looking for, and helped to ensure reliability. The software programme NUD*IST[40] which is designed specifically to analyse qualitative data was employed at the next stage. This enables the researcher to handle the unstructured data more effectively by managing documents (in an index system), supporting the process of coding (indexing), and asking questions, searching patterns of coding and building and testing theories (via index searches). Since multiple coding of any data segment is possible, more fine-grained coding could be introduced as analysis progressed.

Main findings

Two main reasons why individuals often fail to consult their GP for emotional problems emerged from the focus group discussions. First, our discussants remained unsure as to whether the symptoms of emotional distress constituted legitimate 'illness'. Second, even in those instances where emotional problems were recognised as illness, they remained unconvinced that GPs could deal with the problem in an appropriate manner.

Most people tended to view the symptoms of emotional disorder as 'trivial' and an inevitable part of normal human existence. It was felt that the individual should be able to deal with such symptoms themselves or with the help of their family and friends. Participants did, however, recognise suicidal thoughts as serious, but remained unsure as to how they ought to be dealt with. Emotional symptoms were often discussed by contrasting them with 'real' health problems – which were essentially physical. Physical complaints of all kinds were viewed as appropriate to 'take to the doctor'; emotional complaints were not.

Even in those cases where symptoms of common mental disorders were recognised (such as with depression), consulting the GP was not necessarily seen as the answer. It was assumed that GPs were unable to devote sufficient time to patients with emotional problems. GPs were also seen as being able to offer only palliatives (such as antidepressants), and unable to deal with the 'real causes' of emotional distress. Participants tended to regard medication with suspicion and only those who had suffered from emotional symptoms and had taken prescribed medication spoke up for it.

Discussion

Many of these themes mirror the findings of surveys and other research. For example, the 'normalising' of symptoms was noted in the accounts of women suffering from severe depression[41], three-quarters of whom reported that their families gave little or no support and tended to 'explain away' marked changes in behaviour. Normalising was also observed in patients consulting by Kessler et al[15]. Resistance to the idea of medication is also not peculiar to psychiatric patients. There is now a considerable body of work documenting and explaining lay attitudes[42] and an increasing emphasis on 'concordance', i.e. a partnership between patient and doctor in which each respects the other's point of view, rather than the traditional idea of compliance. It is also interesting to note that, in a recent general population prevalence study examining help-seeking behaviour[43], 86% of the African Caribbean and 90% of white European 'cases' sought no medical help for psychological problems, expressing the view that doctors would not be helpful for such problems. The patterns of belief described for the different ethnic groups were remarkably similar to the Welsh groups.

This overlap and consistency of themes in research conducted at different times and in different ways can be construed as evidence of the validity of our findings. It also suggests that these are important topics though, as we have seen, different interest groups, (such as psychiatrists, GPs and indeed potential patients) are likely to come to different conclusions about the implications for patient management and professional education and training.

Our research indicates that while most people are sensitive about disclosing facts relating to their mental health, sensitivity or stigma could not be said to have been the major reason for an apparent reluctance to declare emotional problems. Instead, two other kinds of barrier emerged. The first concerned an inability or an unwillingness to view what psychiatrists see as the symptoms of minor psychiatric disorder as illness. In short, the symptoms of emotional distress were seen as falling outside lay boundaries of the clinical and treatable. The second barrier to disclosure lay not so much in beliefs and views that members of the public held about minor mental disorder, but rather in assessments or evaluations of the services on offer. Our findings also point to a mismatch between what is on offer as far as GP services for people with common psychiatric disorders are concerned, and what people consider appropriate and worthwhile (even when they classify a problem as psychiatric).

Thus, most people felt that GPs had little time to devote to an analysis of personal problems, and some suspected that GPs might not be too tolerant of a presentation with emotional symptoms. Even if such expectations were confounded, then the GP was seen as having little option other than to prescribe an antidepressant. Unfortunately, the latter were regarded as being potentially addictive, or otherwise harmful, and, in any event, as mere palliatives in place of something that could really get to the root of a person's problems. What members of the various groups would wish for – were they to have an emotional problem – was someone to talk to. 'Counselling', therefore, emerged as the preferred option for the management of minor psychiatric disorder.

Our contribution to the debate is to emphasize that patient view-points about (medical) help-seeking can have a reasoned basis. So the reluctance of people to see their problems as requiring medical intervention has to be distinguished from their capacity to evaluate the services on offer. It is the former that has been the focus of professional psychiatric concern rather than the latter. The lay appraisal of GP services that we have outlined may seem realistic and appropriate to some GPs and worrying to others. What is clear is that the clinicians in both the primary and secondary care settings need to be more aware of their own assumptions and those of colleagues working in very different contexts. Patients are not necessarily irrational in their assessments of what is on offer.

Acknowledgements

The research was funded by a grant from the Wales Research & Development Office for Health and Social Care (WORD).

Our thanks are due to Prof. Glyn Lewis, Department of Psychiatry, University College of Medicine, who was joint applicant with Prof. Pill and Dr Prior on this project and without whose initial questioning this study would not have been started. His support, advice and encouragement throughout have been invaluable. We would also like to thank our colleagues in the Department of General Practice for their support and help and the CAPRICORN Network of Research Practices. The views expressed here are ours and do not necessarily reflect those of the funding body or our colleagues.

References

1   Wright AF. Should general practitioners be testing for depression? *Br J Gen Pract* 1994; **44**: 132–5
2   Heath I. There must be limits to the medicalisation of human distress. *BMJ* 1999; **318**: 436
3   Meltzer H, Gill B, Petticrew M, Hinds K. *OPCS Surveys of Psychiatric Morbidity. Report 1. The Prevalence of Psychiatric Morbidity Among Adults Aged 16–64 Living in Private Households in Great Britain*. London: HMSO, 1995
4   Jenkins R, Lewis G, Bebbington P *et al*. The National Psychiatric Morbidity Surveys of Great Britain: initial findings from the household survey. *Psychol Med* 1997; **27**: 75–90
5   Wells KB, Stewart A, Hays RD *et al*. The functioning and well-being of depressed patients : results from the Medical Outcomes Study. *JAMA* 1989; **262**: 914–9
6   Broadhead WE, Blazer D, George L, Tse C. Depression, disability days and days lost from work. *JAMA* 1990; **264**: 2524–8
7   Anon. The treatment of depression in primary care. *Effect Health Care Bull* 1993; **5**: 1–9
8   Paykel ES, Priest RG. Recognition and management of depression in general practice: consensus statement. *BMJ* 1997; **305**: 1198–202
9   Kendrick A. Prescribing depressants in general practice. *BMJ* 1996; **313**: 829–30
10 Shepherd MS, Cooper B, Brown AC, Kalton G. *Psychiatric Disorders in General Practice*. Oxford: Oxford University Press, 1966
11 Goldberg D, Huxley P. *Common Mental Disorders: A Bio-social Model*. London: Routledge, 1992
12 Weich S, Lewis G, Mann AH, Donmall R. The somatic presentation of psychiatric morbidity in general practice. *Br J Gen Pract* 1995: **45**: 143–7
13 Morris R. Interviewing skills and the detection of psychiatric problems. *Int Rev J Psychiatry* 1992; **4**: 287–92
14 Gask L. Training general practitioners to detect and manage emotional disorders. *Int Rev J Psychiatry* 1992; **4**: 293–300
15 Kessler D, Lloyd K, Lewis G, Periera Gray D. Cross sectional study of symptom attribution and recognition of depression and anxiety in primary care. *BMJ* 1999; **318**: 436–40
16. Priest RG, Vize C, Roberts A, Roberts M, Tylee A. Lay people's attitudes to treatment of depression: results of opinion poll for Defeat Depression Campaign just before its launch. *BMJ* 1996; **313**: 858–9
17 Crisp AH. The stigmatisation of sufferers with mental disorders. *Br J Gen Pract* 1999; **49**: 3–4
18. Jorm AF. Mental health literacy: public knowledge and beliefs about mental disorders. *Br J Psychiatry* 2000; **177**: 306–401
19. Littlewood R, Lipsedge M. Some social and phenomenological characteristics of psychotic immigrants. *Psychol Med* 1981; **11**: 289–302
20 King M. Mental health research in general practice: from head counts to outcomes. *Br J Gen Pract* 1998; **48**: 1295–6
21 Angermeyer MC, Matschinger H, Riedel-Heller SG. Whom to ask for help in case of a mental disorder? Preferences of the lay public. *Soc Psychiatry Psychiatr Epidemiol* 1999; **34**: 202–10

22 Lewis G, Pelosi AJ, Araya R, Dunn G. Measuring psychiatric disorder in the community: a standardised assessment for use by lay interviewers. *Psychol Med* 1992; **22**: 465–86

23 Meltzer H, Gill B, Petticrew M, Hinds K. *OPCS Surveys of Psychiatric Morbidity. Report 2. Physical Complaints, Use of Services and Treatment of Adults with Psychiatric Disorders.* London: HMSO, 1996

24 Meltzer H, Bebbington P, Brugha T, Warrell M, Jenkins R, Lewis G. The reluctance to seek treatment for neurotic disorders. *J Mental Health* 2000; **9**: 319–27

25 Cape J, McCulloch Y. Patient's reasons for not presenting emotional problems in general practice consultations. *Br J Gen Pract* 1999; **49**: 875–9

26 Rogers A, Pilgrim D, Lacey R. *Experiencing Psychiatry: Users' Views of Services.* Basingstoke: Macmillan, 1993

27 Griffiths I. Accomplishing team: teamwork and categorisation in two community mental health teams. *Sociol Rev* 1997; **45**: 59–78

28 Barrett RJ. *The Psychiatric Team and the Social Definition of Schizophrenia: An Anthropological Study of Person and Illness.* Cambridge: Cambridge University Press, 1996

29 Busfield J. *Men, Women and Madness: Understanding Gender and Mental Illness.* Basingstoke: Macmillan, 1996

30 Prior P. *Gender and Mental Health.* Basingstoke: Macmillan, 1999

31 Ohnuki-Tierney E. *Illness and Culture in Contemporary Japan, An Anthropological View.* Cambridge: Cambridge University Press, 1984

32 Helman CG. *Culture, Health and Illness.* Oxford: Butterworth Heinemann, 1992

33 Gerhardt U. *Ideas about illness – an intellectual and political History of Medical Sociology.* London: Macmillan, 1989

34 Armstrong D. *An Outline of Sociology as Applied to Medicine* Bristol: John Wright & Sons, 1980

35 Kleinman A, Eisenberg L, Good B. Culture, illness and care: clinical lessons from anthropological and psychological research *Ann Intern Med* 1978; **88**: 251–8

36 Kleinman A. *Patients and Healers in the Context of Culture.* Berkeley, CA: University of California Press, 1980

37 Barbour R. Kitzinger J. (eds) *The Use of Focus Groups in Health Research.* London: Sage, 1998

38 Kitzinger J. Introducing focus groups. *BMJ* 1995; **311**: 299–302

39 Lloyd KR, Jacob KS, Patel V, Louis ST, Bhugra D, Mann AH. The development of the short explanatory model interview (SEMI) and its use among primary-care attenders with common mental disorders. *Psychol Med* 1998; **28**: 1231–7

40 Anon. Scolari *QSR NUD*IST 4 User Guide*, 2nd edn. London: Sage, 1997

41 Ginsberg SM, Brown GW. No time for depression: a study of help-seeking among mothers of pre-school children. In: Mechanic D. (ed) *Symptoms, Illness Behaviour and Help-Seeking.* New York: Prodist, 1982; 87–114

42 McGavock H, Britten N, Weinman J. *A Review of the Literature on Drug Adherence.* London: Royal Pharmaceutical Society of Great Britain, 1996

43 Shaw CM, Creed F, Tomenson B, Riste L, Cruikshank JK. Prevalence of anxiety and depressive illness and help-seeking behaviour in African Caribbeans and white Europeans: two phase general population survey. *BMJ* 1999; **318**: 302–6

Stigma of depression – a personal view

Lewis Wolpert

Department of Anatomy and Developmental Biology, University College London, London, UK

Depression is a serious illness of which I and other patients should not be ashamed but this is hard to avoid. The stigma of depression is different from that of other mental illnesses and largely due to the negative nature of the illness that makes depressives seem unattractive and unreliable. Self stigmatisation makes patients shameful and secretive and can prevent proper treatment. It may also cause somatisation. A major contributing factor is that depression for those who have not had it is very hard to understand and so can be seen as a sign of weakness. Openness by depressives and education in schools could help.

My first serious depression occurred 6 years ago[1]. I had never before experienced so terrible a set of feelings and was hospitalised because of my suicidal intentions. When I recovered, due to antidepressants and cognitive therapy, I found out that my wife, Jill Neville, had not told anyone that I had been depressed. She said that she was embarrassed about my being depressed and told friends and colleagues that I was exhausted and was suffering from a minor heart condition. She was also very worried that if the truth were known it would have a serious effect on my career. This was my first experience of stigma and I found it upsetting as I believed that I had had a serious illness and it was nothing to be ashamed of. But my position was not that straight-forward.

I was convinced that my depression had a purely biological cause and was induced by the drug flecanide which I was taking to control my atrial fibrillation. I did not think that there was any psychological basis for my depression though my wife thought otherwise. I very much preferred a biological explanation. This is probably because then I was not really responsible for the condition, it was like a physical rather than a mental illness. It was not unlike having a diagnosis of post-traumatic stress disorder, which carries no stigma because the cause is so clearly an external one. But what then was my problem with a psychological basis for the depression? I have had to come to accept that I too stigmatise depression when the basis is psychological and that my public declarations that depression is a serious illness and should carry no stigma are not as honest as I would like them to be.

In trying to understand stigma, it is essential to recognise the effect that depression has on those associated with the depressed individual.

Correspondence to:
Dr Lewis Wolpert,
Department of Anatomy
and Developmental
Biology, University
College London,
Gower Street,
London WC1E 6BT, UK

Depressives are both negative and self involved. For the carer it can often be extremely difficult to understand why their partner should be in such a condition. My wife found it incomprehensible that I should be depressed as we were happily married, I had a fine job at the University, and I had no serious physical illness. Worse still, depressives are almost totally negative in all their attributions and also obsessively self-involved which makes them unattractive company. In an experimental study, subjects were asked to speak on a telephone with a patient who, unknown to them, was depressed. Their reports on their conversation were, not surprisingly, negative.

Other studies confirm that depressed individuals have a negative impact on those with whom they interact, for example, at work. When in a position of power, they tend to exploit their position and in subordinate roles tend to blame others. I recall, now with some guilt, that before my own experience with depression, I had employed on a temporary basis an assistant to work in the laboratory who turned out to be very good at her work but was on the edge of a severe depression. Her effect on the group in the laboratory was so bad that they had great difficulty working, not only with her but even near her, and so I had to let her go. I hope I would now handle it better but it would still not be easy.

There can be no doubt that there is considerable stigma associated with depression. I am repeatedly congratulated for being so brave, even courageous, in talking so openly about my depression. I, in fact, am a 'performer' and there is no bravery, but these comments show how others view depression and that it is highly stigmatised. An example of how stigma can present a particularly difficult problem for sportsmen is provided by the case of a professional footballer, Stan Collymore[2] who played for England. He had a severe depression and his career went into a rapid decline. He says that he can never forgive the Aston Villa manager for the way he reacted to his depression. He told him to pull his socks up and that his idea of depression was that of a woman living on a 20th floor flat with kids. The *Sun* newspaper said that he should be kicked out of football as how could anyone be depressed when he is earning so much money. He bitterly remarks that if you suffer from an illness that millions of others suffer from, but it is a mental illness which leads many to take their own lives, then you are called spineless and weak.

Just as important, perhaps more so, is the self stigmatisation of those with depression as it can have serious effects on how individuals deal with their illness. My experience in talking to others who have had a depression has provided me with numerous accounts of just how much those with depression see it as something to be ashamed of, and so kept secret[3]. One young woman cannot even tell her father who is a psychiatrist and another woman could not confide in her brother or sister who knew nothing of her suicide attempts. While I have no difficulty talking about my depression when I have recovered, when I am in it I must admit I hesitate. One reason is that whoever you tell is embarrassed and does not know quite what to say. There is also a sense of failure in not having handled it. That is why depressives can talk so openly to each other about their experience.

The shame and stigma associated with depression can prevent those with the illness admitting they are ill. It is remarkable how it is sometimes possible to conceal one's depression. It was chilling to hear a mother relate to me how she could talk cheerfully to her son while at the same time composing, in her own mind, the suicide note that she would leave him. There is also the stigma of taking antidepressant medication which is perceived as mind altering and addictive. Stigma may also cause somatic symptoms as it is more acceptable to talk of stomach ache and fatigue than mental problems.

A major difficulty in overcoming stigma, and indeed probably one of the causes, is that it is very hard, perhaps impossible, for those who have not experienced depression to understand what the individual with depression is experiencing. I have colleagues who openly admit that they just cannot understand what I am talking about. As Styron[4] wrote 'the pain of severe depression is quite unimaginable to those who have not suffered it'. The experience is almost impossible to describe and the situation is not helped by the almost total absence of good descriptions of depression in English novels – I know of none. Writers have described their own depression but none in novels; Virginia Woolf, herself a depressive, never does. Perhaps it is just too difficult. It may be that if you can describe your severe depression you have not really had one.

In more general terms, there are many attempts to account for stigmatisation of mental illnesses. Mental illnesses are perceived as different as they express themselves through those very characteristics that make us human – cognitive and affective and behavioural – and thus differ from physical illnesses[5]. Mental illness is thus seen as embodying the core of the person and not just affecting some organ like the heart or lungs. But different mental illnesses each have their own characteristics in relation to stigma. For example, unlike depression, people with schizophrenia or addictions are perceived as being dangerous. But depressives are seen as unpredictable people who, if they really tried, could pull themselves together. I am not persuaded that the stigma in relation to depression has a major evolutionary biological component other than that of avoiding undesirable company[6].

What can be done to reduce the stigma associated with depression? There is no easy answer not least because acutely ill depressives are not attractive company. Perhaps the most important aim would be to publicise just how wide-spread depression is and that it is a serious illness. Most important is that it can be cured. It could help a great deal if those individuals with depression who are well known public figures were to support such a campaign; Collymore is an obvious example. That they do not make their condition public is itself due to stigma which will make their co-operation hard to get.

A neglected area is health education in schools. This is odd as one of the illnesses that children will suffer from when adults is depression and yet they are given no information about its nature. One positive venture is the play for schools by Y Touring, *Cracked*, which not only deals with depression but also has a debate at the end of the play in which the actors remain in character and have a discussion with the audience. In Northern Ireland there is a booklet produced by Aware that explains depression very clearly to children[7]. But the success of such programmes needs careful evaluation.

References

1 Wolpert L. Malignant Sadness The Anatomy of Depression, 2nd edn. London: Faber, 2001
2 Hattenstone S. All played out. Guardian 16 April 2001
3 Byrne P. Stigma of mental illness and ways of diminishing it. Adv Psychiatr Treat 2000; 6: 65–72
4 Styron W. Darkness Visible. London: Picador, 1991
5 Crisp A. The tendency to stigmatise. Br J Psychiatry 2001; 178: 197–9
6 Haghighat R. A unitary theory of stigmatisation. Pursuit of self-interest and routes to destigmatisation. Br J Psychiatry 2001; 178: 207–15
7 Anon. Mood Matters Depression Awareness Program for Schools. Londonderry: Aware

Index

Kendrick T *see* Peveler R

Lader MH, Cowen PJ: Preface, 1–2
Lamotrigine, 179, 181, 183–4, 185–6
Lay attitudes to professional consultations
for common mental disorder: a
sociological perspective: Pill R, Prior L,
Wood F, 207–19
Lay attitudes to professional consultations
for common mental disorder, 207–19
Lewis G, Araya R: Classification, disability
and the public health agenda, 3–15
Life Events, 10
and Difficulties Schedule (LEDS). 11
Lithium, 148, 151, 179–81
Lithium-tricyclic combinations, 151
Lofepramine, 164, 165, 167–8, 175, 202

Maintenance and continuation therapy in
depression, 145–59
Management of depression, and culture, 39
Maprotiline, 164, 165, 170, 202
Mediators of effect, 110
Messenger cascades, regulation of
intracellular, 62–66
Meta-analytical studies on new
antidepressants: Anderson IM, 161–78
Methods for assessing depressive disorders,
5–7
Mianserin, 95, 170, 202
Milnacipran, 88, 149, 166
Mirtazapine, 86, 88, 89, 92, 94, 164, 166,
172–3, 175
Moclobemide, 86–88, 90, 92, 175
Monoamine oxidase inhibitors (MAOIs) as
antidepressants, 86, 94, 145, 147–9, 151
Mood stabilisers
developments in, 151, 179–92
issues relating to prescribing
anticonvulsants, 185–7

National Institute of Mental Health (NIMH)
Treatment of Depression Collaborative
Research Program, 101, 103, 104,
106, 109
Nefazodone, 86, 90, 92, 93, 165, 169, 182
Neostigmine, 95
Neurobiology, depression – emerging
insights from, 61–70
Neurotoxicity with lithium, 180

Newer antidepressants (NA), 166, 167
elderly patients and, 174
Non-directive counselling (NDC), 119–20
Nortriptyline, 53, 87, 202
Number needed to harm (NNH), 162
Number needed to treat (NNT), 162, 163,
169, 173

Odds ratio (OR), 162, 167, 171
Older antidepressants (OA), 164, 165,
166, 167
OPCS National Survey of Psychiatric
Morbidity. 6,12, 210
Outcome research, 103–8
of continuation and maintainence
therapy, 145–7
Overcoming depression course, 141–3

Paroxetine, 87, 90, 91, 92, 169
Patel V: Cultural factors and international
epidemiology, 33–45
Paykel ES: Continuation and maintenance
therapy in depression, 145–59
Peveler R, Kendrick T: Treatment delivery
and guidelines in primary care, 193–206
Phenelzine, 90
Phosphodiesterases (PDEs), 64
Pill R, Prior L, Wood F: Lay attitudes to
professional consultations for common
mental disorder: a sociological perspective,
207–19
Predictors of response, 108–10
Preface: Lader MH, Cowen PJ, 1–2
Primary care guidelines, treatment delivery
and, 193–206
Primary Care Psychiatric Questionnaire
(PPQ), 36
Prior L *see* Pill R
Psycho-education and psychological
treatments, 188
Psychodynamic-interpersonal therapy
(PDIPT), 123–5, 127–9
Psychosocial aspects of depression, recent
developments in understanding the, 17–32
Psychosocial interventions, 52–3
Public health agenda, classification and
disability, 3–15

Randomised control trials (RCTs), 147,
161, 164, 167, 175, 181, 182, 184